HEARTHSIDE COOKING

Hearthside Cooking

*An Introduction to
Virginia Plantation Cuisine
Including Bills of Fare,
Tools and Techniques, and
Original Recipes with Adaptations
for Modern Fireplaces and
Kitchens*

NANCY CARTER CRUMP

EPM Publications, Inc.
McLean, Virginia

To Jim, whose love, enthusiasm, and certainty that this book could be written kept me going in spite of myself, and without whom this book would have never been written.

EPM Publications, Inc., 1003 Turkey Run Road,
McLean, Virginia 22101
Printed in the United States of America
Preface by Alice Ross, Culinary Historians of New York
Cover and book design by Susan Lehmann
Drawings by Emily Whaley
Photography by Emory Waldrop
Cover photographs by *Richmond Times-Dispatch*

Library of Congress Cataloging-in-Publication Data

Crump, Nancy Carter.
  Hearthside cooking.

  Bibliography: p.
  Includes index.
    1. Cookery, American—Southern style. 2. Cookery—
Virginia—History. 3. Fireplace cookery. I. Title.
TX715.C9553   1986   641.59755   86-19808
ISBN 0-914440-94-2

Contents

Foreword

Shortly after we were married, Nancy invited me to observe a hearthside cooking demonstration which she presented at Shirley Plantation on the James River near Richmond. Eager to please my new wife, I went. The kitchen at Shirley is in a large brick outbuilding. I was stunned by the size of the hearth, which is enormous, and overwhelmed by the cranes, pots, and kettles in and on the fire. Nancy and her daughter, Jacqueline, both dressed in colonial garb, were busily making noodles, a chicken fricassee, stews, and vegetable dishes. As a typical middle-American urban male, I was amazed. How in the world could anyone cook like that? Or rather, it might be done, but surely it would be very difficult, and the resulting food would probably be inedible.

I was wrong on both counts. It is not that difficult to do it and the product is superb. Believe it or not, hearthside recipes are delicious. There is a world of difference between the heavy, bland, and stodgy meals of the later 19th century, and the delicious recipes, rich in herbs and spices, of the 18th- and 19th-century Virginia plantations.

If you would like to replicate my experience, and do it in your own fireplace, or on your own woodstove, or even try the recipes in your modern kitchen, read on.

Jim Emory

WEIGHTS AND MEASURES.

Tested and Arranged by Miss Leslie.

WHEAT FLOUR . . one pound of 16 ounces . is one quart.
Indian meal . . . . one pound 2 ounces . . is one quart.
Butter, when soft . . one pound 1 ounce . . is one quart
Loaf sugar, broken up, one pound . . . . . is one quart.
White sugar, powdered, one pound 1 ounce . . is one quart
Best brown sugar, . . one pound 2 ounces . . is one quart.
Eggs . . . . . . ten eggs . . . . weigh one pound.

LIQUID MEASURE.

Four large table-spoonfuls . . . . are . . . . half a jill.
Eight large table-spoonfuls . . . are . . . . one jill.
Two jills . . . . are . . . half a pint.
A common-sized tumbler . . . . holds . . . half a pint.
A common-sized wine-glass . . . holds about . half a jill.
Two pints . . . . are . . . . one quart.
Four quarts . . . . are . . . . one gallon.
About twenty-five drops of any thin liquid will fill a common-sized tea-spoon.
Four table-spoonfuls will generally fill a common-sized wine-glass.
Four wine-glasses will fill a half pint tumbler, or a large coffee-cup.
A quart black bottle holds in reality about a pint and a half, sometimes not so much.
A table-spoonful of salt is about one ounce.

DRY MEASURE.

Half a gallon . . . . is . . . . a quarter of a peck
One gallon . . . . is . . . . half a peck.
Two gallons . . . . . . are . . one peck.
Four gallons . . . . . . are . . half a bushel.
Eight gallons . . . . . . are . . one bushel.

Throughout this book, the pound is avoirdupois weight—sixteen ounces.

(25)

Many 19th-century cookbooks contained tables of weights and measurements such as this one provided in Eliza Leslie's New Cookery Book *of 1857.*

Preface

There simply isn't a better way to experience the past than through food. Get the smoke of the fire into your hair and feel the pull on your muscles as you move the heavy pots. Try the strange-sounding ingredients and unfamiliar combinations of an 18th-century dish and the food will reward you with its delection, tradition, sociability, and downright fun.

Nancy Carter Crump has explored this for some years. Armed with professional expertise in modern and hearth cookery, she has nosed her way through old cookbooks and archival collections, digging out old cooking manuscripts and recipes for the true and representative dishes of her ancestral home.

Part of her challenge lay in recreating these dishes on the hearth. Investigating firewoods and antique pots, her obvious first step, was perhaps the easiest. The food historian working for authenticity is also faced with tracking down the original ingredients mentioned in old cooking manuscripts—hartshorn, for example, or its modern gelatine equivalent. And then the most important, educated instincts come into play: the interpretation of 18th- and 19th-century recipes. The researcher will find scores of versions of the same dishes—tansies and forcemeats and fricassees, walnut ketchups, great cakes and queens cakes—and sense must be made of them. From recipe to recipe, they are never quite the same, just as in today's cookbooks a chocolate mousse may have variations. Ms. Crump needed to know, from hours of testing on the hearth and in modern kitchens, just which was the essential quality of each dish, and whether her recipe writer was more a good cook than a careless plagiarist. Another hurdle was the common practice of writing recipes incompletely (saving space?), leaving standard ingredients or instructions to the cooks who were expected to know what to fill in.

Once Ms. Crump had decoded the recipes and transformed them into tempting and edible creations, she was faced with the choice of which to include in her own book. The leap to modern measurements and familiar utensils brought the tastes and textures of old Virginia plantations within reach of any modern cook who can follow a standard recipe.

But of still more importance, the total process of finding the recipes, testing, selecting, and standardizing their form has been a vital process of definition. Mrs. Crump has, in these efforts, limited and described a regional cuisine. Her unique contribution stands on the large numbers of cooks she has cited, and the union of printed cookbook recipes with unpublished family recipe collections.

At the same time, she has breathed the life of her people into her pages. This cookbook is at least as important for their thoughts and words. Ms. Crump has used their writings almost like decorative illustrations throughout, keeping before the reader the concomitant details of their time and place. Their commentary makes the recipes all the more a document of social history, bringing plantation mistresses to life in their real jobs, hard-working women behind their gracious and leisured manner.

Ms. Crump's achievement is of immense value in the still-new food historiography of the past few decades. She is part of a growing progression of social scientists, beginning with the French Annales school of social history in the 1930s, who use food records and material culture to reconstruct the experience of daily living. She follows the local Virginia food historians Helen Bullock and Jane Carson of Colonial Williamsburg, and the more recent culinary historian Karen Hess. Her pioneering efforts to define the cuisine take authority from her extraordinary and complementing strengths as both historian and cook.

Seen in the perspective of the historian, the recipes are

clearly upper-class, English in origin, and adapted to New World conditions. As Ms. Crump knows all too well, plantation recipes reflect wealth and privilege. And yet because the recipes were often taken from unpublished and handwritten personal records, they can be trusted as working recipes more than printed fashion-guide cookbooks of the day. Southern research cannot avoid the issue of slave kitchen labor and cooking expertise; Ms. Crump may have opened new data on the influence of African culture in recipes such as hoecake, okra, peanuts, and black-eyed peas.

As this is an historical work, a word or two on its background shaping are not amiss. Like others in this new phenomenon of historical cookbooks, it has sprung from the conjoining of several movements. Recent interest in local studies has sent historians to the dusty archives of historical societies and museums, and old recipe collections are coming to light. Our recent bicentennial celebrations, for example, demanded and produced such research. At the same time, the women's movement has legitimized "women's work" and reevaluated the life-supporting work at the hearth. Living museums have expanded their fireside interpretations. And the descendants of America's waves of immigrants have begun a turnaround search for roots which includes, of course, traditional family cooking styles. The publishing world has responded with a rash of regional and ethnic cookbooks.

And so, full cycle, we are back to the kitchen. There are boundless possibilities for the use of these recipes. The most obvious is in the training of museum docents for hearth demonstrations. No less important is the work's potential for the recording of material and social culture, and for comparisons of regional similarities and differences. Hardly the least, it offers modern American cooks the chance to produce honest and delicious food of the somewhat-familiar past, to catch a shadow and a taste thereby.

Alice Ross
Co-founder, Culinary Historians of New York

Soup was an integral part of the great meals eaten by our forefathers and soup recipes, Ms. Crump says, were very precise.

"There is danger that the composition of many an excellent dish may become forgotten lore."[1]

The Pleasures of Hearthside Cooking

Hearthside cooking is not for the faint-hearted. And if you dislike getting your hands dirty, forget it. If, however, you have a sense of adventure and are looking for an innovative way to entertain friends while preparing an elegant meal, then hearthside cooking may be for you. If you are a museum interpreter interested in using the old kitchen at your historic site as a means of recreating early foodways, this book can be of help, for open-hearth cooking brings the past alive in an exciting way.

I have experienced the richness hearthside cooking can bring to historic sites. I have seen the positive reaction from visitors who, through the sights and fragrances they witness during cooking demonstrations, can relate to their forebears in a new and unique way. And in my own home I have prepared open-hearth meals that have been greeted with enthusiasm by family and friends.

My interest in cooking the foods of the past began with childhood summers on a family farm in the Northern Neck of Virginia, where the joys of good food prepared in old-fashioned ways left an indelible memory; with a catering business that specialized in historical parties; with a love of history and research, a fascination with the past, and a desire to teach it in a way that would bridge the gap between "them and us." All this led ultimately to employment as an educational programmer for Colonial Williamsburg. Because of my background, I was immediately involved with open-hearth cooking, then in its infancy at that historic site. Those cooking programs led to the realization that all my interests could be brought into play. Two very different, very intense experiences completed my commitment to the interpretation of foodways and dining customs of the past.

Christmas at Williamsburg centers around recreating the season as it might have been celebrated in Colonial Virginia. My department was involved with a Williamsburg family's holiday hearthside activities.

My fantasy life took over and I left the 20th century behind as I put on 18th-century garb. Lacing up my rust-colored bodice, I was beside myself with excitement. I had risen at 5 A.M., in good pre-industrial fashion, to start the fire and begin other preparations for the sumptuous meal to follow later that day.

By early afternoon, when visitors began to arrive, a stew was simmering in a large iron pot hung on the fireplace's massive crane, while sassafras tea steeped nearby in a bright copper kettle. Trussed on a spit in front of the flames, rabbits were roasting, their juices sizzling into the dripping pan beneath. A huge sea trout, seasoned with herbs and wrapped securely in fresh cabbage leaves, would soon be put in a bed of ashes where it would bake, protected by the natural insulation of the cabbage leaves. Sliced apples, redolent of butter and spices, simmered in a spider placed on live coals we had shoveled into the hearth. Freshly baked bread on a nearby table was surrounded by baskets of bright orange carrots, shiny yellow onions, new red potatoes, dried green beans, and a variety of fresh and dried herbs. We were wrapping a pudding in cloth to be boiled in a pot over the fire, and an already baked pound cake cooled on a shelf, its delicate aroma blending with the other delightful fragrances. The menu was not only authentic and appealing, but it had been designed to show a wide variety of early cooking utensils in action.

Cheerful music and the excited chatter of visitors filled the air. They crowded into the kitchen, curious about the ongoing meal, asking questions that gave us ample opportunity to explain and interpret. Transfixed by the scene, our 20th-century visitors did not want to leave!

That was a day of firsts for me, from putting on a Colonial costume to the realization of my eighteen-year dream of interpreting for the public at Colonial Williamsburg. I have cooked many a hearthside meal since that day. Each time is magic, each provides a kinship with the past that can only happen when one experiences the past firsthand. But that holiday in old Williamsburg holds a special spot in my heart.

My next revelation came a few weeks later, when the worst snowstorm in 100 years engulfed eastern Virginia, knocking out electrical and telephone wires for thirty-six hours. In my all-electric home we were faced with starvation, or with hamburgers at the local fast food place, powered by its own generator.

As I sat woefully in my family room, the cheery fire burning away on the hearth came into sudden, sharp focus. "Why not?" I thought. "If I can cook on the fire at Colonial Williamsburg, I can cook on the fire at home." And so I did.

With only my old cast-iron skillet, a tin coffee pot for boiling water, and plenty of well-seasoned firewood, I fed my children for the next thirty-six hours. The menus were simple: eggs and bacon, French toast, sautéed meats and vegetables. It was all delicious. I must confess to a certain smugness as we snuggled close to our fire, sipping hot chocolate. We had defied the elements, and my epiphany was complete.

This book is a response to those friends and colleagues who for years have urged me to impart my culinary enthusiasms to paper. Its purpose is two-fold: to initiate fireplace owners into the joys and mysteries of cooking on their own hearths, and to show them that, with a modest outlay, they can discover a whole new way of entertaining and preparing a unique cuisine. My second objective is to provide small house museums with authentic recipes and some guidelines for using them in their old kitchens.

The recipes themselves, taken from a variety of primary 18th- and 19th-century sources both published and unpublished, were searched out in archives, libraries, and private collections throughout Virginia and North Carolina. Opening old, handwritten books of receipts (the early word for recipe) was a step back in time for me as well as a chance to get to know the unusual women who had compiled them and shared their knowledge. The leaves of yellowed, crumbling manuscripts, often scorched from fire or marked by the ravages of time, revealed that those women had an awareness of proper culinary techniques equal to any modern chef's.

My research netted literally hundreds of delicious-sounding receipts and, ultimately, I was faced with the dilemma of deciding which ones to use. The receipts finally chosen as representative of the foods being consumed in early Virginia were based on descriptions and other records left by the Virginia gentry and their guests.

Recipes written in the past were far different from those we record today. Ingredients were generally given in avoirdupois weight [see chart on page 8 from *Miss Leslie's New Cookery Book*], and a set of scales was an essential part of old kitchens. It was not until the end of the 19th century that U.S. cup measurements were arbitrarily standardized by Fannie Farmer. Working with older receipts thus requires a sense of adventure as well as a firm understanding of culinary methods. Consider this example, taken from Mary Randolph's *The Virginia House-Wife*, first published in 1824:

Batter Bread

Take six spoonsful of flour and three of corn meal, with a little salt; sift them and make a thin batter with flour, eggs, and a sufficient quantity of rich milk; bake it in little tin moulds in a quick oven.[2]*

What were six "spoonsful"? How much was "a little salt"? Determining the answers to these and other questions was challenging and sometimes baffling, but the original sources provided valuable clues. Mary Randolph, for instance, informed her readers that "a quart of flour should weigh just one pound and a quarter."[3] Weighing with my 20th-century scales, I found that one quart of the soft, stone-ground flour found in Virginia and North Carolina is still approximately the same amount given by Mrs. Randolph.

---

*Source notes are grouped following recipe section at end of book.

Many 19th-century cookbooks contained tables of weights and measurements such as the one provided by Miss Leslie. Using them as a guide, I weighed ingredients on my kitchen scales as cooks had done in the early days. These were then converted to standard cup measurements in order to modernize the old receipts.

Estimating ingredients that were less specific, such as "all the crumb of a stale penny-loaf," had to be largely guesswork on my part. Experience, research, tracing the receipts as they evolved from the 18th century to modern times, and, finally, informed judgment all helped.

The old receipts revealed astonishing sophistication about seasoning with herbs and spices. Until the last of the 19th century, when convenience had taken over and cookery as an art was lost, cookbooks suggested an array of herbs and spices to give food a zest that has only been rediscovered in recent times (see M. H. D. Tebbs' receipt for Savory Patties as an example). Chervil, fennel, coriander, shallots, comfrey, and pennyroyal were among the herbs in common use.

The term "herbs" had a broader meaning than we give it today, including greens and flowers that were used for food or medicine, or in some way for their scent or flavor. In his 1699 book *Aceteria,* which was devoted to salads, John Evelyn recommended many ingredients because of their helpful propensities. Fennel, he wrote, "expels Wind, sharpens the sight, and recreates the Brain."[4] Sage was a favorite, having so many wonderful properties that "the assiduous use of it is said to render Man Immortal."[5] Evelyn was only one of many herbalists and gardeners of the day who looked to herbs for many uses.

Because of convenience, the modern recipes given in the book call for dried herbs, unless otherwise stated within the recipe. However, I heartily recommend growing your own. Even in small apartments, potherbs are possible. Once you are accustomed to growing your own, you will wonder how you ever managed without them. If converting from dried to fresh herbs, use three times the amount specified. For example, one teaspoon dried herbs equals three teaspoons (one tablespoon) fresh.

The following chapter provides technical guidelines on everything from fire preparation and fire safety to techniques to necessary equipment. Possible sources for that equipment and hard-to-find food products are given in the Sources section at the back of this book.

The third chapter contains factual data on the development of Virginia cuisine and dining customs. Fourteen bills of fare based on early sources are in the fourth chapter. The original receipts plus their updated versions follow, with conversions for the hearth as well as the modern kitchen.

As you may have surmised, I love to cook on the fire. It can be messy, time consuming, and a challenge. But the excitement of explaining hearthside cooking to those who visit the sites where I cook, the joy I experience in sharing it with friends in my home, and the connection it gives me with those who lived in an earlier time make it all immeasurably worthwhile.

"You must put your saucepan on a clear quick fire."[1]

Fires, Tools, and Techniques

Today we see a fireplace as a charming optional feature for a home. In yesterday's world a fireplace was essential to living and the very center of family life. It supplied heat, was a major source of light, and provided the means by which all food was prepared. This importance is recorded in the journal of Philip Fithian, who tutored at one of Virginia's largest 18th-century plantations, Nomini Hall. Fithian described life at the magnificent Westmoreland County home where winters were harsh. "Mr. Carter has a Cart & three pair of Oxen which every Day bring in four Loads of Wood, Sundays excepted," Fithian wrote, "& yet these very severe Days we have none to spare; And indeed I do not wonder, for in the *Great House, School* House, Kitchen &c. there are twenty Eight steady fires! & most of these are Very Large!"[2]

Twentieth-century firebuilding is relatively easy, merely a matter of crumpling newspaper, laying on wood, then striking a match. Before the convenience of phosphorous matches, coals were carefully banked at night to ensure a ready fire for the next day's meal. A "cold fire" meant a frustrating struggle with flint and tinder in hope of striking sparks to restart the fire.

Our present-day screened fireplaces, coupled with normal precautions, diminish fire hazards. In the past, however, the fear of fire prompted constant vigilance. In January 1774 Fithian noted in his journal that on returning to his room in the schoolhouse after dinner, he found "a Coal of Fire had by accident (as the Hearth is very narrow) fall'n on the floor, it took fire, and when I entered it was burning rapidly . . . & most certainly in a short time would have been inextinguishable." He thanked "a kind Providence" for preventing the total loss of schoolhouse, furnishings, and clothes.[3] The incident was not uncommon in the days of large fireplaces with steadily burning fires and no protective screening. Hearth injuries were second only to childbearing as the leading cause of death in women.[4]

Today, certain simple safeguards can make the difference between a pleasurable, rewarding experience and possible tragedy.

Keep on hand a bucket of water and a woolen blanket that could smother flames. Protect flooring and carpeting with a hearth rug. Have a fire extinguisher at hand. Never use or wear synthetic fabrics near a fire; they ignite and melt quickly, causing severe burns. Natural, woven fabrics such as wool, linen, or ticking are best. If you are in costume, wear layered clothing. Long skirts should be tucked up and out of the way when you are working at the fire. Check the lower hem of your skirts occasionally; they may begin to smolder if you have unknowingly dragged them across live coals. Your hair should be covered and shoes should be worn.

Guard against accidents by thinking out the steps ahead. In moving hot coals, for instance, be sure the area where you are stepping is clear and that no steaming cooking utensils are in the way. Remember that heavy iron pots filled with simmering liquid or food are not easy to handle. Extreme care must be taken in removing them from the crane or lifting them from the coals. Know where they will be placed before you even begin to move them. If you are working with others, give warning, and be sure they are aware of your actions at the fireplace. Frying foods and roasting meats require care to avoid burns from spattering fat. Staying continually alert is your best protection against mishaps.

It is of paramount importance that chimneys be checked and cleaned professionally at least once a year. Soot and grease accumulate much quicker in a fireplace that is used for cooking, thus creating a potentially dangerous situation.

Hiring a qualified chimney sweep is money well spent.

Everyone has his own theory for "correct" firebuilding. My own method, the one that works best for me, is relatively simple. First, do not start with a clean fireplace. A bed of ashes provides insulation and helps to maintain heat. I crumple several sheets of newspaper on top of the existing ashes, then lay the wood on the newspaper in a grid pattern. Start with soft kindling wood such as pine. On top of the kindling, lay a mixture of hardwood and softwood in slightly larger pieces. Follow with another layer of hardwood. At that point, strike a match to the newspaper at the rear of the fireplace. This allows the fire to start slowly and warm the chimney. After your fire is well established, add large pieces of wood to keep the flames burning steadily. Hardwoods for this purpose include oak and hickory. Cedar has a tendency to "pop," creating a possible fire hazard, and therefore is not recommended. Fruit woods, such as apple and cherry, provide a tantalizing aroma and impart a delicious flavor to roasting meats.

The fire should be started well before actual cooking begins. Those unacquainted with hearthside cooking tend to think it is all done directly over a fire. Though flames *are* necessary for roasting and cooking on a crane, the quantity of coals is more important. It will be at least two hours before a large amount of coals is ready to be raked or shoveled into individual mounds on the hearth, creating cooking areas something like the burners on a 20th-century stove. Most cooking—baking, frying, simmering—is done over glowing embers. The need for a steady supply of embers necessitates a continuously burning fire.

Equipping a fireplace for cooking, whether at home or at an historic site, is becoming easier as interest in early crafts intensifies. While original kitchen tools are rarely seen now except in established museums, artisans are reproducing early ironwork, pottery, woodenware, and tinware that can be purchased at reasonable prices. With a few basic implements, a fireplace can be made ready for cooking. The following are essential for open-hearth food preparation:

1. A swinging crane

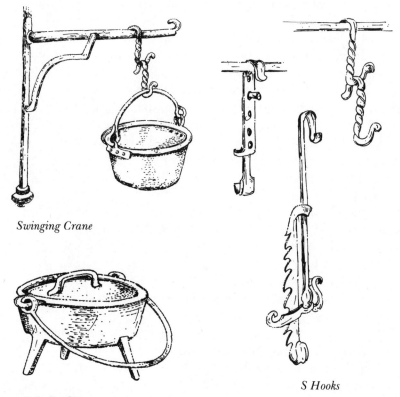

Swinging Crane

Bake Kettle

S Hooks

2. Pothangers—S-hooks, trammel, ratchets
3. Dutch ovens—a minimum of two
4. Long-handled tools including spoons, ladle, meat fork, and spatula
5. Trivets
6. An iron pot
7. Poker, tongs, and shovel

The *swinging crane,* a hinged device bolted into the side of a fireplace, was welcomed by early cooks as a major development in kitchen furnishings. It replaced the lugpole, a fixed device suspended across the upper portion of the fireplace and fitted into the brick itself. The crane was designed for convenience as well as safety. Using the fixed lugpole necessitated stepping on the hearth and leaning into the fireplace to suspend or remove the heavy iron pots filled with food or water. At best, this was dangerous. The swinging crane brought new flexibility and safety since it could be swung out and away from the fire for use.

Pots were suspended from the crane by a variety of hangers. The simplest is the *S-hook,* which can be linked with others to raise or lower a pot over the flames and thus regulate the amount of heat for cooking. Other pot hangers include the *trammel,* basically a flat hanger with a hook-and-eye arrangement, and the more elaborate *ratchet,* a saw-toothed piece of iron with a hook at its lower end to suspend the pot and another hook at the top to secure it on the crane. Heat can be adjusted by changing the placement of the trammel's hook-and-eye, or by pushing the hook into a new position on the "toothed" portion of the ratchet. For modern fireplaces, a few S-hooks are necessary; the trammel and the ratchet are too long and cumbersome for home use, but they are important for the large fireplaces found at historic sites.

A *Dutch oven* is probably the single most important item for hearthside cooking. Favored for generations, it can be used to bake breads and desserts, to stew meats and vegetables, and to brown many foods, including meringues. Standing on three short legs and available in several different sizes, the Dutch oven is placed on a bed of coals and its contents are covered with a tight-fitting lid. Additional coals are then shoveled on top, to be replenished as needed. Generally, cooking times equal those given in modern recipes, although checking at twenty- to thirty-minute intervals is recommended. As one becomes familiar with hearthside cooking, the Dutch oven's versatility is more and more appreciated. With this most important piece of equipment, anything done in a modern oven can be duplicated on the hearth. Dutch ovens can be purchased in at least three different sizes and because of their usefulness, at least two of the largest sizes (approximately 1½ gallons) are advised.

A variety of *long-handled tools* are needed for stirring, mixing, turning, basting, skimming, and ladling. Made of iron or wood, they include *spatulas, meat forks, spoons, strainers,* and *ladles.*

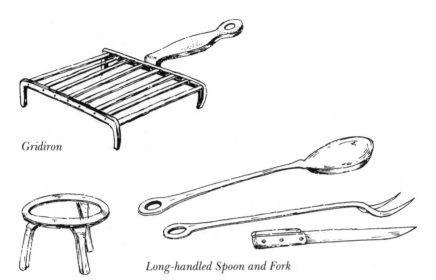

Gridiron

Trivet

Long-handled Spoon and Fork

Trivets are necessary in fireplace cooking to hold pots and kettles for cooking over the coals, and for keeping already prepared foods warm. Trivets can be found in different sizes, heights, and designs.

An *iron pot*, hung on the crane, is indispensable for soups, stews, and boiled puddings. Usually equipped with legs, the pot is also useful for simmering directly over the coals.

The equipment used for today's fireplaces—*tongs, poker,* and *shovel*—are also needed, as in times past, to manipulate the wood and coals used for cooking.

The above items can be supplemented by an endless array of additional utensils, especially those for roasting. If you have a large fireplace you may want to consider the following:

For roasting meats and fowl, a pair of *andirons* or firedogs, fitted with hooks to hold an iron *spit,* are ideal. Food to be cooked is skewered on the spit and then suspended between the firedogs. The simplest of these spits has a handle at one end that is turned by the cook or an assistant to assure even roasting. Fireplaces in the kitchens of wealthier families had mechanical turning devices called *jacks.* Different types were available, regulated by the fire's draft or by weighted chains. They were attached to the spit

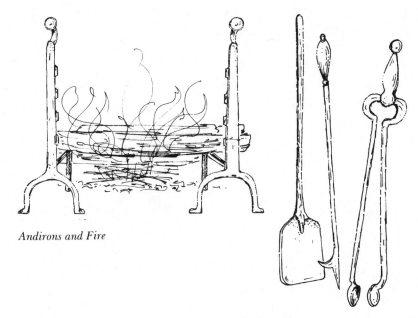

Andirons and Fire

Shovel, Poker and Tongs

Reflector Oven

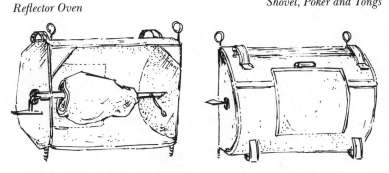

and turned it automatically, thus freeing the cook for other food preparation.

Another means of roasting is the *reflector oven,* also known as a tin kitchen. Shaped like a cylinder cut in half, and set on short legs, the reflector oven is equipped with a spit. The cut side faces the fire and the heat reflected at the back of the cylinder creates an ideal means of roasting birds and smaller cuts of meat. A little hinged door in the rounded side of the oven gives the cook easy access to the food being roasted. It allows for testing the heat, basting, and, finally, determining whether the food is done without having to move the oven from its position in front of the fire. This ingenious late 18th-century American invention is an important auxiliary or substitute for roasting with andirons and spit. Although antique and reproduction reflector ovens are available, one can also be made following the instructions given in the October 1976 issue of *Early American Life*. (See bibliography.)

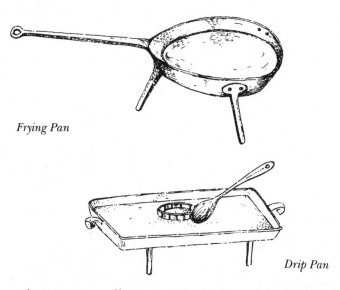

Frying Pan

Drip Pan

A necessary adjunct to roasting is a *dripping pan*, generally made of iron. It is placed underneath the roasting meat to catch its delicious juices or "drippings," which are then used for basting and later sent to table as an accompanying gravy, either by itself or combined with other ingredients.

A long-handled *frying pan* is another helpful utensil for open-hearth cooking. Set on a trivet or made with three legs to stand over the coals, the frying pan, or spider as it came to be called during the 19th century, is helpful for frying or sautéing many foods.

Frying pans and other cooking pots made from a variety of metals were available to the plantation cook. Copper with its even heat-conducting properties, cast iron that provides a steady heat especially good for baking, and forged iron for sautéing foods were used to make frying pans. Pots were constructed from iron, bronze, copper, bell-metal, and brass. Cast-iron pans and pots can be used for all fireplace cooking techniques, but using a variety of metals adds authenticity. It must be stressed, however, that copper, brass, and bronze are poisonous materials. *Warning: On no account use these latter three metals for preparing food unless they are tin- or porcelain-lined.*

The ingenuity of early craftsmen is apparent in the many different designs for a *gridiron,* used for broiling meats. Basically, it has parallel iron bars in rectangular or circular shapes, with short legs to hold it above the coals. Some rotated on a base for ease in turning. Often the bars were grooved to hold the meat drippings.

A *griddle* for baking over the fire is another useful kitchen utensil used to bake a variety of muffins, buns, and pancakes. Its handle is secured to the crane by a pothanger.

Also needed for baking are *pie* and *cake tins* and *tart* and *biscuit pans,* which can be found in many sizes and shapes.

A *hoe* for baking hoecakes in front of the fire, a long-handled *toaster,* a *wafer iron,* and a *salamander* for browning foods are interesting, authentic additions to fireplace cooking.

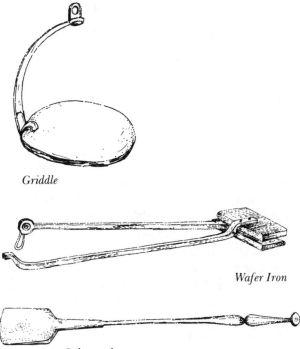

Griddle

Wafer Iron

Salamander

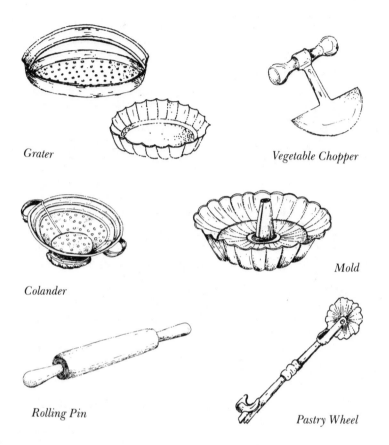

Grater

Vegetable Chopper

Colander

Mold

Rolling Pin

Pastry Wheel

Other early kitchen tools that are nice to have are still found in well-equipped modern kitchens: molds for jellies and creams, colanders, sieves, rolling pins, food choppers, graters, and pastry wheels. For authenticity, a mortar and pestle, scales, dry and wet measures, sugar nippers, a wooden lemon squeezer, a churn, and a coffee roaster could be added. The inventory of early cooking items is profuse.

Proper care of iron utensils is essential, whether antique or reproduction. With patience and a little elbow grease, old, rusted iron can be restored for use. Begin by washing the utensil in hot soapy water, scrubbing gently to dislodge loose particles of rust. Rinse and dry thoroughly, then carefully remove the rust with a fine-grade steel wool. Follow with another hot soap-and-water scrub. Then put the cleaned item into a warm (250°) oven for about half an hour. Remove carefully—it will be hot—and allow it to cool. (This process may have to be repeated if the rust is very heavy.) Then coat the utensil with a thin layer of vegetable shortening or lard. Avoid using cooking oil as it leaves a sticky residue that is hard to remove. Return the coated utensil to the oven and allow it to season for about an hour and a half. When completely cold, wipe thoroughly with toweling. New iron cookware is seasoned in much the same way, except that there is no need, obviously, for rust removal. Unless your pots are heavily encrusted with food after cooking, simply rinse them well with very hot water, wipe, and then allow to dry thoroughly in front of the fire or at a low oven temperature. Cleaned and properly maintained, ironware is virtually indestructible.

Interpreters who work with open-hearth cooking programs at historic sites as well as those who cook in their home fireplace will create a heightened historical ambiance by maintaining as much historical accuracy as possible. Some modern conveniences are necessary, of course, but they should be kept out of sight when interpreting early foodways for the public.

A first consideration is fire safety measures. In addition to proper clothing and a handy water bucket, keep an old chest in the kitchen for blankets or rugs and a fire extinguisher. Should a fire break out, they will be easily accessible, yet unseen by visitors. A long woolen cape, hung on a knob beside a doorway, can be used to smother a fire, yet provides an authentic touch.

Local fire department personnel are usually eager to discuss fire-prevention methods and generally are fascinated with open-hearth cooking. A session for museum interpreters with fire officials is valuable to learn the proper use of fire extinguishers and other means of protection.

To further enhance the historical atmosphere, use appropriate containers for food and equipment—baskets, barrels, wooden chests and shelves, storage jugs, and jars of earthenware or stoneware. When food is being prepared, also use traditional bowls and measuring devices, as well as knives with wooden handles and wooden spoons. Use a mortar and pestle and a grater for chopping herbs and spices, as well as for grinding corn or wheat for breads. If you are fortunate enough to have a working bake oven, a long-handled peel is nice for handling baked goods.

Consider the time period of your historic site in planning kitchen objects and interpretation. Methods for preserving foods, for instance, changed through the years, as did the appearance of numerous utensils. Fireplace cooking itself was outmoded in most places by 1850. All this must be taken into account as the interpretation is developed.

Some curators oppose the use of antique kitchen utensils because of possible damage. Objects made of breakable material or fragile with age should be kept for display only, but ironware, properly cared for, can be used. Since good reproductions are also available, the final decision must rest with the curatorial and administrative staff.

In planning a Colonial meal, keep in mind that the choice of foods in those earlier days was dictated by the season and the weather. Sample bills of fare are given in the fourth chapter of this book, plus sources for developing others. Authentic menus will further enhance historical accuracy, ambiance, and pleasure for you and your visitors.

Traditional Virginia Cuisine

Plenty and abundance are words continually used by early English explorers to describe the array of foods and other natural resources that filled the forests, fields, and waters of primal Virginia. "Paradice itself seem'd to be there,"[2] wrote Robert Beverley, one of Virginia's first historians, recalling the enthusiastic reports composed by Captain Arthur Barlowe, who commanded the second of two vessels Sir Walter Raleigh sent to explore the southeastern coastline of America in 1584. Captain Barlowe's eloquent narrative[3] gives us a memorable picture of the unspoiled, readily available provender to be found in the New World, which included "Deere, Conies, Hares, and Fowle," and the "best fishe in the world." He marveled at the diversity of fruits and vegetables and decided that "in all the world the like aboundance is not to be founde."

Although this rapturous account was intended at least in part to stimulate colonization, other descriptions left by the English settlers echo his portrayal of Virginia's bounty. They were surprised to find an unsophisticated but remarkably well-organized Indian civilization. These Virginia Indians, members of the Algonkian tribe, were primarily an agricultural society. At first they welcomed the white men with awe and a willingness to share what seemed to be the limitless generosity of nature. Their methods of farming, hunting, fishing, preparing, and preserving their foods were carefully scrutinized and recorded by the Englishmen.

Although many foods from the Americas had already reached Europe and England through Spanish explorers, corn and different types of beans and squash were new to the white men. In addition, familiar foods grew in profusion. The greater variety to be found in North America amazed the Englishmen, who had been instructed to bring home "the fruites of the countries . . . the Curnelles of peres, and apples, and the stones of such stone fruittes as you shalle finde there. Also the seedes of all strange herbes and flowres. . . ."[4] Sponsors of the expeditions realized from the start that the exotic provender from the New World meant solid money in their pockets, "for such . . . comming from another part of the world and so farre off, wil delite the fancie of manie. . . ."[5]

Thomas Hariot, a brilliant young mathematician who traveled to Virginia with the first explorers, published his *Briefe and True Report of the New found Land in Virginia* in 1588.[6] He noted in detail the Indians' diet and their methods of preparing many of the foods they consumed. "Their meat is Mayze [corn] . . . deers flesche, or of some other beaste, and feish . . ." he wrote. Their "peaze . . . are far better than our English peaze" prepared "either by boyling them all to pieces into a broth; or boiling them whole untill they bee soft and beginne to breake as is used in England. . . . Sometime they mingle of the wheate [corn] with them. . . ." The Indians favored boiling their foods—certainly the easiest procedure—combining together all manner of vegetables, meats, and fish in a huge earthen pot set over an open wood fire, and replenished daily. They also roasted or broiled many of the foods they consumed, all techniques familiar to their white observers.

Hariot admired the Indians. He understood and could speak their language, which perhaps gave him an awareness of the mysterious red men that the majority of his fellow explorers did not possess. He described their eating habits as "sober," believing that the native Americans lived longer "because they doe not oppress nature." Unlike most of his countrymen, Hariot felt that the English would do well to imitate the Indians' moderate habits. "I would to god wee would followe their example," he asserted, "for wee should bee free from many kynes of diseasyes. . . ."

In addition to studying the American Indian lifestyle,

Hariot used this year in Virginia to detail the rich, easily available food supply. Among other things, he saw chestnuts, walnuts, different types of pears and cherries, grapes, strawberries, and mulberries. The nearby waters held scores of fish, including sturgeon, herring, mullet, "and very many other sortes of excellent good fish," as well as crabs, mussels, and oysters in plenty.

The same abundance greeted the settlers who established the first permanent English colony at Jamestown in 1607. Given the provisions available in early Virginia, it is incredible that the new settlers nearly starved. Used to European agricultural methods and convinced of their superiority, the English immigrants at first refused to accept Indian foodways. Without them, however, the colonists in Virginia's Tidewater region would never have survived. The food supplied by Indians kept many of the Englishmen alive during the first months of settlement, and the red men sent by Chief Powhatan taught the newcomers methods of planting corn and other vegetables and also of making fish traps.[7]

Corn was of particular importance, called by William Byrd "the most useful grain in the whole world."[8] Not only did it have a diversity of uses, it provided a year-round staple that could be eaten fresh or dried for later use in baking and cooking. Corn was also easy to grow and became one of the most essential native products not only for the Virginia settlers' survival but as a cash crop exported to England and then to other countries.

As the newcomers took to New World provender, squash, pumpkin soup, and roasted peanuts, as well as succotash and other corn-related foods, were integrated with familiar English fare. Necessity forced the Colonial housewife to use native provisions, but she clung to culinary traditions to which she had been accustomed. Cuisine in the Mother Country at that time was becoming a hearty blend of regional fare spiced with imported goods from European, Eastern, and South American countries. The restoration of Charles II to the English throne in 1660 had stimulated, among other things, a renewed interest in gardening and in planting different fruits and vegetables. Quickly assimilated into English gardens were such things as red beets, artichokes, asparagus, and cauliflower, brought from France and Italy.[9] Culinary herbs used by the French became part of English cookery, influenced also by French sauces, desserts, and other foods. Building on the merits of its own culinary heritage and incorporating the best from other countries, English cookery by the 17th century rivaled that of any other nation.

The women who emigrated to North America carried that heritage with them. Their treasured family receipts and cookbooks provided a link with their homeland. And they brought with them the seeds of fruits, vegetables, herbs, and flowers to recreate as closely as possible the gardens that were so much a part of their daily lives. In the lush Virginia tidewater, "a Kitchin-Garden don't thrive better or faster in any part of the Universe," historian Robert Beverley asserted. "They have all the Culinary Plants that grow in England, and in far greater perfection."[10]

With the arrival of black slaves, beginning scarcely a dozen years after the settling of Jamestown, a third element was added to the incipient English-American-Indian cuisine slowly taking shape in Virginia. Brought to America from numerous tribes located primarily along the Guinea coast, African women were skilled, innovative cooks, proud of the culinary traditions handed down from their forebears. As with good cooks everywhere, these women, interacting within their plantation communities, exchanged ideas and influenced each others' cooking styles.

Many of the foods now considered an integral part of Southern cooking came from Africa during this time. Among them were okra, watermelon, and black-eyed peas, all of which adapted easily to Virginia's rich soil. Certain African cooking methods were incorporated by the colonists, particularly deep-fat frying.[11] Black cooks excelled in blending spices and other seasonings to create the exotic sauces of their culinary heritage. Essential flavorings included ginger, saffron, thyme, sage, sweet basil, parsley, and especially shallot and hot pepper.[12]

Many African cooks came to Southern homes after years of bondage in the Caribbean Islands. There they were influenced by the heady fare that had evolved from the merging of the islands' ethnic cuisines. These influences included the cookery of the native Carib and Arawak Indians and that of European settlers from Spain, France, England, and Holland. Thus over a period of many years, foodways from different worlds—the old and the new, the black and the Creole—were brought together in Virginia to form a basis for the colony's sophisticated cuisine.

Gradually, settlers from other countries added their own touches. In 1699 French Huguenots, fleeing religious persecution in their own country, began to settle on the James River above Richmond. While French culinary practices had long been familiar to English cooks, the Huguenots quickly assimilated into Virginia society and further influenced the colony's developing cuisine. In addition, immigrants began to come from Holland, Switzerland, and parts of Germany. Virginia colonists, already aware of Germanic cooking traditions such as the Dutch oven, sausages, doughnuts, and other foods, now absorbed more of the Germanic culinary techniques.

Before the middle of the eighteen century, the fusion of these various culinary strains and the easy availability of local foods and seasonings, combined with the ability of wealthy Virginia planters to import the best from other nations, resulted in a sumptuous cuisine. That it was uniquely Virginian and unquestionably delicious has been attested to by visitors traveling in North America up through the second quarter of the 19th century.

The Virginia colonists, secluded on their great river plantations, welcomed any and all to their doors. They vied with one another to present the best, flaunting their wealth with lavish displays of food and hospitality. It was a point of honor for the Virginia aristocracy to have only the finest, and for this they continued to look to England, importing elegant furnishings, linens, and silver, as well as exotic foodstuffs such as spices, nuts, citrus fruits, raisins, sugar, tea, and coffee. "Things that the Country don't produce, they have constant supplies of 'em from England," wrote Robert Beverley."[13] "The gentry pretend to have their Victuals drest, and serv'd up as Nicely, as at the best Tables in London."

Virginians welcomed any excuse for a party. There were balls and barbecues, picnics and housewarmings. Weddings, christenings, even funerals could be counted on as an occasion for socializing. Late in the 17th century at the funeral of Elizabeth Eppes of Henrico County, it was noted that "5 gal wine, 2 of brandy, a stew & 3 sheep were consumed."[14] In his diary for 1726–1727, Robert Carter commented that "Wee had burnt Madera wine, a frosted cake"[15] at the funeral of a friend. It was felt that if guests were kind enough to be there, the hospitable thing to do was to provide refreshments.

Copious amounts of food were presented at Virginia tables. Dinner, served between two and three o'clock in the afternoon, was composed of two courses. The first began with a soup ladeled out ceremoniously from a tureen by the hostess. After the soup was eaten and the bowls removed, another dish would be set in front of the hostess, usually a platter of fish. All other food in that first course was already on the table. It could have included curry, ham, pork cutlets, Sauce Robert, chicken patties, salmon and smelts, oyster patties, veal blanquets, and a "Harrico."[16] Second courses were just as heavy, adding desserts such as stewed fruit and almond cheesecakes plus a variety of made dishes, which were composed of several ingredients, forerunners of today's casseroles. At the conclusion of the second course, the cloth and dishes were cleared and fruit and nuts were presented along with sweet wines.

This profusion of food continued well into the 19th century. Henry Barnard, visiting at Shirley plantation, described a dinner he enjoyed there in 1833. "Mrs. C is at one end of the table with a large dish of rich soup, and Mr. C at the other, with a saddle of fine mutton; scattered around the table . . . ham, beef, turkey, duck, eggs with greens, etc.—vegetables, potatoes, beets, hominy. . . . After that . . . the dessert, consisting of fine plum pudding, tarts, etc. After this come ice cream, West India preserves, peaches preserved in brandy, etc. When you have eaten this, off goes the second table cloth, and then upon the bare mahogany table are set the figs, raisins and almonds . . . two or three bottles of wine, madeira, port and a sweet wine for the ladies. He [Mr. Carter] fills his glass and pushes them on. . . ."[17]

Planning and managing this splendid entertaining was the plantation mistress, trained from girlhood to supervise a huge manor house with its surrounding support buildings and a large staff of servants. Although delegated to a secondary position within the family, plantation wives were the mainsprings that kept the plantations running. Their responsibilities were enormous, their knowledge formidable.

Part of that knowledge was an awareness of proper food and entertaining. Again, these Virginia-born women copied their English counterparts, looking to old traditions in planning extravagant bills of fare.

The actual preparation of the meals was carried out by black servants, usually women, cooking in kitchens separate from the main house. They too possessed far more knowledge than we with our shiny kitchens equipped with food processors and microwaves may realize. Cooking at open fires in huge fireplaces, and directed by their plantation mistresses, the black servants turned out mouth-watering fare that would rival any we know today. Both cook and mistress knew what wood was necessary, what type of fire was needed for a certain dish.

The cook's job was a backbreaking effort. Up before dawn to establish the fire that had been banked the previous night, she faced hours of preparation before the big meal of the day—a midafternoon dinner—could be served. She performed chores we would never imagine. "Stick your pig just above the breast-bone, run your knife to the heart, when it is dead put it in cold water for a few minutes," began one recipe in an old cookery book.[18]

To make a cake, the cook was required to pulverize sugar (it came in loaves or cones), grind the spices, free the flour from possible bugs, beat egg yolks with rods (the modern egg beater was a late 19th-century invention) until "they get so thick as to be of the consistency of boiled custard,"[19] and so on.

The mistress of the house directed the operation. She planned the menus, discussed them with the cook, then doled out the necessary supplies, most of which were kept under lock and key. Aristocratic women usually had a specialty or two they prepared themselves—preserving peaches or making special desserts, perhaps. But the harder tasks such as grinding, chopping, or pounding were handled by the cook, working in a hot, smoky kitchen with open windows. One 19th-century cookbook instructs, "in summer try to churn early in the morning, as fewer flies are swarming then."[20]

To discuss the development of American cuisine requires mentioning Thomas Jefferson, our premiere epicure. His interest in food of every description is well documented, his contributions to American foodways unsurpassed. It was he who gave America the vanilla bean and macaroni products, for instance. He looked for agricultural improvements that would help the young nation's economy, inventing the moldboard plow that aided farming throughout the Western world. He advocated crop rotation to rejuvenate the soil, and he grew the first figs, dates, almonds, and pistachio nuts in the New World.[21] Continually experimenting with new strains of vegetables and fruits, Jefferson exchanged gardening ideas with like-minded men throughout America and Europe.

One of his major contributions, was importing upland rice seed to South Carolina. Traveling in the Italian Piedmont, where local rice was the most valuable commodity, Jefferson slipped some seed into his pockets and, to assure himself that it would get through, bribed a mule driver to bring some out as well. This was a crime punishable by death and the second time Jefferson had risked his life for his country. The first was when he signed the Declaration of Independence.

Jefferson's interest in French cuisine intensified during the years he spent there. However, he never tired of the Virginia food he loved so well. He grew "Indian corn" in his Paris garden, which he served to his French friends, and regularly ordered a variety of foods to be sent from home. Back in Virginia, he employed French or French-trained chefs, and his table became an elegant blend of French and American cuisines. Not all of Jefferson's countrymen were pleased with his interests, however. He "came home from

France so Frenchified," snarled Patrick Henry, "that he abjured his native victuals. . . ."[22]

The "princely hospitality of the gentle-born families"[23] remained untouched until the outbreak of the Civil War. The devastation it caused, along with late 19th-century innovations, brought a whole new way of life. "Gone are the heaped up logs of hickory and the roaring flames, which once widened that family circle till the chairs of the whispering lovers touched the chamber walls; even the coals under the 'trivet' are dead, the coffee untasted, and the single cake of corn-bread on the table is forgotten. . . ."[24]

While plantation life in the old style is gone forever, we can replicate the pleasures of its foods on our own hearths and in our modern kitchens. The bills of fare and recipes that follow are modern adaptations of this extraordinary plantation cuisine.

Shirley Plantation, home of Mr. and Mrs. C. Hill Carter, Jr., in Charles City, VA, has been held by the Hill-Carter families since 1660.

The original recipe for Early Virginia Chicken Pye as it appeared in The Tucker Family Cookbook.

"The dinner was very good—a small roasted pig, boiled leg of lamb, beef, peas, lettuce, cucumbers, artichokes, etc., puddings, tarts, etc. We were desired to call for what drink we chose."

Amariah Frost, on a dinner with Mr. and Mrs. George Washington
Diary of June 1797[1]

Bills of Fare

The fourteen bills of fare presented in this chapter—one for each month, plus a birthday feast and a breakfast—illustrate the great variety and the large number of dishes served at the tables of wealthy Virginians in Colonial days. These bills of fare are based on original sources and reflect the foods available at specific times of year. Choices were dictated by the season as well as the weather. Springs or icehouses were the only means of keeping food cold. Many meats, vegetables, and fruits were dried or pickled to ensure a wintertime supply.

"January is a dead season," wrote Martha Bradley in 1770. "In the Course of this Month there is less Variety than in any other; the Cook therefore is with the upmost Care to make the best of what Nature affords. . . ."[2]

Many early cookbooks, such as those by Hannah Glasse, contain "Bills of Fare" for each month of the year. Other original sources include letters and diaries that mention favorite foods or special meals. Thomas Jefferson's *Garden Book* is another invaluable reference in planning what foods to prepare at a particular time.

Numbers in parentheses following each bill of fare dish indicate the page in this book where the recipe is to be found.

JANUARY

"Eat a little 12th Cake. . . ."
Robert Carter Diary, January 6, 1725/26[3]
Corrotoman, Lancaster County, Va.

*". . . I eat for my dinn^r Peas, a wing of a Chicken ½
doz. fryd Oysters. . . ."*
Robert Carter Diary, January 14, 1725/26

BILL OF FARE

Vermicelli Soup (p. 114)
Martha Washington's Chicken Fricassee
(p. 150)
or
Mary Bolling Banister's Oyster Ragoo
(p. 162)
Mrs. Glasse's Stewed Spinach and Eggs
(p. 210)
Mashed Turnips (p. 213)
Salad with Available Greens
Choice of Bread
Twelfth Night Cake (Kate Powell Carter's
Black Cake) (p. 220)
or
Hannah Glasse's Seed Cake (p. 228)
Araminta G. Paul's Blanc Mange (p. 274)
Choice of Beverage

FEBRUARY

John Page at Rosewell, Gloucester County, Virginia, to St. George Tucker, February 28, 1777[5]

BILL OF FARE

Mary Randolph's Dried Pea Soup (p. 108)
Rappahannock River Roasted Oysters
(p. 161)
or
Eliza Leslie's Roast Venison (p. 168)
Mrs. Cringan's Sweet Potatoes Baked with
Wine (p. 204)
To Dress Salsify (p. 206)
Salad with Available Greens
Hoecake (p. 70)
Pears Stewed with Ginger Root (p. 286)
Shrewsberry Cakes (p. 239)
Hopkins Family Cocoanut Pound Cake
(p. 222)
Choice of Beverage

> **Black Cake**
>
> Prepare 2 pounds of currants by washing picking &c
> and setting them in the sun, or by the fire to dry, then stone
> 2 pounds of raisins, rub them in flour to prevent their
> sticking, pound 2 nutmegs and a table spoon full of
> cinnamon and mace mixed, cut up a pound of citron
> in strips, sift a pound of sugar in one pan and a pound
> of flour in another, stir a pound of butter with the sugar
> to a cream, beat 24 eggs light, then stir them alternately
> into the butter and sugar with the flour then add the
> fruit spice and 2 wine glasses of wine or one of french brandy
> beat the whole well together, put it into a moderate oven
> and bake 4 hours, some persons who wish the cake very
> black carefully brown not burn the flour they make it
> in an oven, some use brown sugar instead of white, and
> some add a teacup of molasses — —

*Kate Powell Carter's Black Cake is a choice for the January Bill of Fare. Mrs.
Alexander Cameron's Fig Pudding appears on the April Bill of Fare.*

> on a plate in back of stove to let the
> heat pass through & dry the rice.
> Turn in a shallow dish & serve at once.
>
> **Fig Pudding   Mrs Alex. Cameron**
> ½ lb. stale bread crumbs. ½ lb. figs put through meat
> chopper. 2 eggs. 6 oz. brown sugar, 2 oz. flour
> ¼ lb. suet, a little milk, about half a cup.
> flavor with nutmeg. Boil 2 hours &
> serve with or without sauce.
>
> **Chocolate cream pudding.   Mrs Rorer**
> 2 oz. chocolate in a double boiler, when melted add a
> pint of hot milk, ½ cup sugar, vanilla & season.
> Moisten 2 tablespoons corn starch, add to the rest &
> cook until smooth & thick. Stir in beaten yolks of

MARCH

"*a fine morn. I was very much Grip[d] last night had eat some shift Bacon Turnip Tops plentifully a wing of a Chicken some Clary Pancak[e] some mutton drank sev[l] glass[e]s madera wine 1 glass Claret was in great pain. . . .*"

Robert Carter Diary, March 28, 1726[6]

BILL OF FARE

Hannah Glasse's Santea Soup (p. 112)
Baked Madeira Ham (p. 144)
or
Mary Randolph's Croquets (p. 149)
Mrs. Moncure's Spinach (p. 207)
Miss Leslie's Stewed Carrots (p. 187)
Salad with Available Greens
Choice of Bread
Tucker Family Quire of Paper Pancakes
(p. 263)
Northern Neck Orange Pudding (p. 270)
French Almond Cake (p. 218)
Choice of Beverage

APRIL

"We had an elegant dinner; Beef & Greens; roast-Pig; fine boil'd Rock-Fish, Pudding, Cheese &c—Drink: good Porter-Beer, Cyder, Rum, & Brandy Toddy."

Philip Fithian Journal, April 3, 1774[7]
Nomini Hall, Westmoreland County, Va.

BILL OF FARE

Mrs. Randolph's Asparagus Soup (p. 94)
Polly Banister's Beef Collops (p. 122)
or
Miss Leslie's Stewed Fish (p. 160)
Cauliflower and Broccoli (p. 188)
Stewed Beets (p. 184)
Salad with Available Greens
Choice of Bread
Mrs. Alexander Cameron's Fig Pudding
(p. 257)
Mrs. Taliaferro's Charlotte Russe (p. 268)
Choice of Beverage

MAY

"I ate mutton and sallet for supper. . . ."
William Byrd Diary, May 5, 1709[8]
Westover, Charles City County, Va.

"I eat green pease & ripe strawberries."
John Harrower Journal, May 20, 1776[9]

BILL OF FARE

Hannah Glasse's Onion Soup (p. 104)
Fried Lamb (p. 148)
or
Battersea Beef Olives (p. 124)
Mrs. Randolph's Peas with Mint (p. 201)
Boiled New Potatoes (p. 202)
Salad with Available Greens
Choice of Bread
Glazed Strawberries (p. 287)
Paul Family Pound Cake (p. 226)
Kate Powell Carter's Rice Pudding (p. 260)
Choice of Beverage

JUNE

". . . I am going to Dinner, after which we have a desert of fine Rasberry's & cream. . . ."
Anne Blair to "Dicky," June 14, 1769[10]

*"For dinner smoack'd bacon or what we cal pork ham
. . . either warm or cold. When warm we have greens
with it, and when cold we have sparrow grass. We have
also either warm roast pigs, Lambs, Ducks, or chickens,
green pease. . . ."*
John Harrower Journal, June 14, 1774[11]

BILL OF FARE

E. Smith's Green Peas Soop (p. 110)
Mr. Blackford's Glazed Ham (p. 146)
or
Mrs. Randolph's Veal Cutlets (p. 136)
A Ragoo of Asparagus (p. 180)
Eliza Leslie's Lettuce Peas (p. 200)
Mrs. Randolph's Squash (p. 209)
Salad with Available Greens
Choice of Bread
Charles Carter's Rasberry Cream (p. 276)
Indian Pound Cake (p. 224)
An Ordinary Bread Pudding (p. 256)
Choice of Beverage

JULY

"We dined to day on the Fish call'd the Sheeps-Head, with Crabs—Twice every Week we have fine Fish, & every Day good Fruit for Dinner, caudled Apples, Hurtle-Berries with milk &c."

Philip Fithian Journal, July 6, 1774[12]

BILL OF FARE

Maryland Crab Soup (p. 101)
Yorktown Baked Sheep's-head (p. 158)
or
M. H. D. Tebbs' Savoury Patties (p. 134)
Oatlands Corn Pudding (p. 191)
Mrs. Randolph's Artichokes (p. 181)
Salad with Available Greens
Choice of Bread
Mrs. Cringan's Stewed Apples (p. 284)
Jumbles (p. 236)
Mrs. Humphrey's Whortleberry Pudding
with Fairy Butter (p. 261)
Choice of Beverage

Crab Soup.

Put on one quart of water; to this add 1½ lbs of tomatoes, (more will make the soup richer), to this add about six cloves, some onion, salt, and pepper, let boil for about half hour; then put in six crabs picked, and a tablespoonful of butter. Slice two hard boiled eggs, squeeze and slice a lemon in the tureen, and pour the soup over the lemon & eggs.

Maryland Crab Soup was a July favorite. Corn fritters were served in August when the corn ripened.

flour, puet milk, salt & pepper.
Put the eggs through the meat chopper
Rub flour, butter & seasoning together & scald in the milk. Put egg yolks through a Sieve & whites through a meat grinder. Arrange Slices of toast on a hot dish, mix the whites in the Sauce pour over the toast & dust the yolks over the top.

Corn fritters

Grate 6 ears of corn, mix yolks of 2 eggs, ½ cup milk, ½ cup flour, salt & pepper. Beat the whites stiff & fold in last. Drop spoonfuls in hot fat & fry brown on both sides.

AUGUST

"for my Din' I eat Veal boild & roasted Eat some Cab-bag also some apples & Ros[e] wat[er] drank wine & water a Glass of Cyd' at night. . . ."
Robert Carter Diary, August 31, 1727[13]

" . . . Yesterday we were at M' Baylors, & made myself sick with Ice-Creams, Water Melons, Plumbs, &c. . . ."
Ann Blair to Eliza Whiting, August 16, 1799[14]

BILL OF FARE

Frances Tucker Coalter's Ochra Soup (p. 102)
Southall Family Cabbage Pudding with Veal Forcemeat (p. 132)
or
Mrs. Tucker's Rump of Beef to Stew (p. 126)
Indian Corn (p. 193)
or
Shirley Plantation Corn Fritters (p. 189)
French Beans the Dutch Way (p. 185)
Salad with Available Greens
Choice of Bread
Ice-creams or Sherbets (pp. 278–283)
Summer Fruit
Queen Cake (p. 240)
Choice of Beverage

SEPTEMBER

"I eat a broiled Pigeon that was highly seasoned wth Peper eat some Bermudas Potatoes & Some Apple Py & drank ab^t a pint of Cyd^r in all. . . ."
Robert Carter Diary, September 1, 1723[15]

"I drank hock this day before dinn^r Eat hominy drank cyd^r eat a little mutton a few mouthfulls of chicken Pye. . . ."
Robert Carter Diary, September 4, 1727[16]

BILL OF FARE

Shirley Plantation Mushroom Soup (p. 100)
Early Virginia Chicken Pye (p. 154)
or
Fried Fish (p. 157)
To Ragou French Beans (p. 182)
Virginia Stewed Tomatoes and Corn (p. 212)
Roasted Bermuda Onions (p. 197)
Salad with Available Greens
Choice of Bread
Mr. Carter's Apple Tart (p. 250)
Gooseberry Fool (p. 275)
Choice of Beverage

OCTOBER

"I dined on fryed Chicken, Ham, with good Porter."
Philip Fithian Journal, October 20, 1774[17]

"I eat green Pease at dinner."
John Harrower Journal, October 27, 1774[18]

BILL OF FARE

Loudoun County Oyster Soup (p. 106)
Mary Randolph's Fried Chicken (p. 152)
or
Mr. Blackford's Pork Cutlets (p. 138)
Field Peas (p. 199)
Mrs. Cringan's Cymlins (p. 208)
Salad with Available Greens
Choice of Bread
Baked Pears (p. 285)
Mrs. Robert E. Lee's Gingerbread (p. 234)
Southall Family Sweet Potato Pie (p. 254)
Choice of Beverage

NOVEMBER

"I ate roast goose."
William Byrd Diary, November 21, 1710[19]

*". . . Sent to Mrs. Wormley 20 l[bs.] Chocolate
Nutts. . . ."*
Robert Carter Diary, November 18, 1727[20]

BILL OF FARE

Mary Stuart Smith's Beef Soup (p. 96)
To Roast A Goose (p. 164)
or
Blackford Family Fricaseed Rabbits (p. 166)
Mrs. Robert E. Lee's Mushrooms au Beurre
(p. 194)
Scolloped Tomatos (p. 211)
Salad with Available Greens
Choice of Bread
Mrs. Tebbs' Chocolate Nuts (p. 233)
Randolph Pumpkin Pie (p. 253)
Miss Leslie's Finest Blanc Mange (p. 272)
Choice of Beverage

DECEMBER

"mama made 6 mince pies & 7 custards, 12 tarts, 1 chicking pye, and 4 pudings for the ball."
Sally Fairfax Diary, December 26, 1771[21]

"A Merry Christmas to you my Dear Grand-Mother. . . . I doubt not but that Cousin Judy is now chief, cook, and bottlewasher preparing minces pies and cheesecakes as well as ot[he]r nic nacs for Christmas. . . . Good health & a Merry Christmas to the household. . . ."
Mira Rosanna Barraud [age 12] in Norfolk to Mrs. Anne Barraud, December 22, 1832[22]

BILL OF FARE

Mrs. Randolph's Chicken Soup (p. 98)
Roast Pork (p. 140)
or
Mrs. Peyton Randolph's Wild Duck (p. 171)
Roasted Sweet Potatoes (p. 205)
Hannah Glasse's Parsnips (p. 198)
Mrs. Banister's Way to Make a Ragoo of Onions (p. 196)
or
Salad with Available Greens
Choice of Bread
Mrs. W. H. F. Lee's Mincemeat Pie (p. 252)
Mrs. Tebbs' Trifle (p. 269)
Centre Hill Plum Pudding (p. 258)
Mrs. Bouvier's Custard (p. 267)
Little Cakes (pp. 234–241)
Choice of Beverage

GEORGE WASHINGTON'S BIRTHDAY PARTY

"D[inner] George Washington. Leg [of] boil[ed] pork . . . goose, roast beef, round cold boil[ed] beef, mutton chops, hommony, cabbage, potatoes, pickles, fried tripe, onions, etc. Tablecloth wiped, mince pies, tarts, cheese; cloth of[f], port, madeira, two kinds [of] nuts, apples, raisins. Three servants."

Joshua Brooks Journal, February 4, 1799[23]

BILL OF FARE

Mrs. Tebbs' Beef Soup with Bouilli (p. 89)
Mary Bolling Banister's to Force the Inside
of a Sirloin of Beef (p. 128)
or
Miss Leslie's Steak and Oysters (p. 123)
Roasted Potatoes (p. 203)
Carrots Dressed the Dutch Way (p. 185)
Mary Randolph's Cabbage A-La-Creme
(p. 186)
Salad with Available Greens
Choice of Bread
Elizabeth Eppes' Washington Cake (p. 230)
Mrs. Cringan's Cheese Cake (p. 262)
Eliza Smith's Very Fine Syllabub (p. 84)
Choice of Beverage

COLONIAL BREAKFAST

*". . . was provided for our breakefast a great bole of In-
dian pease and beanes boyled together, and as much
bread as might have sufficid a dosen hungry men, about
an houer after boyled fresh fish, and not long after that
roasted Oysters, Creuises, and Crabbes."*

Ralph Hamor on breakfast with Chief Powhatan, May
1615[24]

*". . . at breakfast . . . the varieties of hot breads of the
finest kind exceeded any thing I had met with . . . all
hot and all as perfect in the cooking as the material;
and all this as accompaniment to the fish, flesh, and
fowl, and the usual liquid beverage of the breakfast
table."*

William Dunlap on "the living at Weyanoke and Westover," Winter 1822[25]

BILL OF FARE

Friar's Omelet (p. 174)
or
Elizabeth Nicholson's Omelette (p. 172)
Country Ham with Gravy (p. 143)
or
Prosser Tabb's Sausage (p. 147)
Mrs. Glasse's Chicken Hash (p. 156)
Pain Perdu (p. 76)
or
Doughnuts—A Yankee Cake (p. 66)
Mrs. Gray's Light Biscuits (p. 64)
Corn Bread (p. 65)
Fruit in Season
Choice of Beverage

Bernard Carter, the cat at Shirley Plantation, awaits his turn for a taste.

Recipes

Breads

The hot breads presented as part of the elaborate meals served at Virginia plantations delighted 18th- and 19th-century guests, who often left descriptions of the foods they had enjoyed. Cornmeal breads predominated, "for with this," wrote Hugh Jones in 1724, "is made good Bread. . . ."[1] White cornmeal was most often used in the South, considered "the first essential of this fundamental article of Southern diet." Excellent wheat breads were also commented upon, "made of the best wheat flour in the world."[2]

As part of the sumptuous ritual of good food provided in plenty by wealthy Virginians, an array of well-made breads was essential. The variety, brought to the table to be slathered with fresh butter and eaten still warm from the oven, astonished all who sampled them.

Even more astonishing today is the realization of how formidable was the task of bread making. There were no handy grocery stores to pick up a loaf on the way home, no packets of dried yeast. Preparing and baking bread was a time-consuming, arduous process, from making yeast to knowing when the oven was ready to receive the risen loaves.

Commercial yeast was not available until 1868, and recipes for yeast occupy a large part of the bread-making sections in early cookbooks. Cooks kept a starter on hand, made with ingredients that included hops, potatoes, sugar, flour, and water. Combined with more flour to make a "sponge," the dough was set to rise hours ahead of when it was to be eaten. Mary Stuart Smith's instructions are typical: "Make up the sponge before breakfast, if you want light bread for tea [the evening meal]. . . . In summer, for breakfast bread, make the sponge after dinner—that is to say, three or four o'clock P.M."[3]

Kneading was (and is) a major part of the process, and its importance was emphasized. Mrs. Smith, for instance, stressed that "the *best* bread-makers whom I know knead for at least an hour, and with all their might. . . ."[4] Eliza Leslie noted that "the goodness of bread depends much on the kneading."[5] While Miss Leslie's statement holds true today, the lengthy times formerly required for kneading are no longer necessary. The commercial yeast now available has shortened that process considerably. See individual recipes for specific directions.

The actual baking was done in Dutch ovens or brick ovens usually built into the huge kitchen fireplace. A thorough knowledge of the process was vital. A fire was started in the brick ovens about two hours prior to putting in the loaves. The instructions were specific on everything from the size and type of wood needed to the proper oven temperature necessary to bake. "If you can hold your hand within the mouth of the oven as long as you can distinctly count twenty, the heat is about right."[6]

For Dutch oven baking it was necessary to preheat the iron utensil before putting in the prepared bread dough. Once filled and covered, the oven could be suspended from the crane and hung over the fire, or set on coals to bake in a corner of the hearth. Baking in a Dutch oven was more typical of the lower classes than of plantation society, whose kitchens were equipped with built-in bake ovens.

Soft breads such as muffins and pancakes could be baked on a griddle hung on the crane. Simplest of all was the ancient technique, known to Indians, whites, and blacks alike, whereby flat breads were baked "before the Fire . . . or on a warm Hearth, covering the Loaf first with Leaves, then with warm Ashes, and afterwards with Coals over all."[7]

Whatever the baking method, providing delectable breads was essential. As Elizabeth Lea put it, "There is nothing in any department of cooking that gives more satisfaction to a young housekeeper than to have accomplished what is called a good baking."[8]

Basic directions for Dutch oven baking are given below.

1. The Dutch oven must be heated prior to putting in the bread dough. Set the oven and the top in front of the fire about 15 minutes before baking to heat it through.
2. Put a rack, trivet, or small stones in the bottom of the Dutch oven to hold the prepared dough above it.
3. After putting in the bread, cover it and set the Dutch oven on the hearth over hot coals. Cover the top of the oven with additional coals, which should be replenished frequently.
4. The baking process should be slow but steady, with more coals on top of the oven than at the bottom. Unlike modern oven baking, specific cooking times cannot be given. Check the bread every 30 minutes or so, at least until you are more familiar with the process. It may take as long as an hour and a half to bake the bread.
5. As the bread cooks, turn the oven occasionally to assure even baking.
6. After the bread is baked, set the top of the Dutch oven aside and let the bread remain in the warm oven another 15 minutes before removing it. Then set the cooked bread on a rack to thoroughly cool, covering it with a clean cloth.
7. *Most important of all,* observe all safety measures given in Chapter 2.

Mrs. Gray's Light Biscuits

1 quart of sour milk, teas-spoon of saleratus to be beaten well together then worked into as much flour as will make it tolerably stiff.—a small lump of lard.

Gray Family Papers

Makes 10 2½″ biscuits

2 cups sifted flour
¾ teaspoon salt
1 teaspoon soda

¼ cup lard
⅔ to ¾ cup buttermilk

Hearth:
1. Sift flour with salt and soda.
2. By hand work in lard until mixture is crumbly.
3. Add enough buttermilk to make a soft dough, lightly mixing together into a ball.
4. Turn dough out onto a lightly floured board. Knead briefly just enough to incorporate ingredients.
5. Gently roll out dough to ½″ thickness. Cut out with biscuit cutter and place biscuits in ungreased pan.
6. Carefully place pan on trivet or rocks in preheated Dutch oven. Bake, following general directions for Dutch oven baking, for 10 to 15 minutes or until golden brown. Best served warm.

Modern:
1. Follow hearth directions 1 through 5.
2. Preheat oven to 450°. Bake biscuits 12 to 15 minutes or until a light, golden brown.

Mary Randolph's Corn Meal Bread

Rub a piece of butter the size of an egg into a pint of corn meal, make a batter with two eggs and some new milk, add a spoonful of yeast, set it by the fire an hour to rise, butter little pans and bake it.

Mary Randolph

Serves 6 to 8

2 tablespoons butter, melted
2 cups milk
2 cups white cornmeal

2 teaspoons dried yeast
1 teaspoon salt
2 eggs

Hearth:
1. Heat butter and milk until milk is warm and butter begins to melt. Set aside to cool to lukewarm.
2. Combine cornmeal, yeast, and salt in bowl. Stir in milk and butter.
3. Beat eggs lightly and stir into rest of ingredients. Blend well but do not overmix.
4. Pour into well-greased baking pan and set aside to rise 1 hour.
5. Carefully place filled pan on trivet or rocks in preheated Dutch oven. Bake, following general instructions for Dutch oven baking, for about 25 minutes, or until knife inserted in center comes out clean and bread is a rich golden brown.

Modern:
1. Follow hearth directions 1 through 4, using 8″ × 8″ square pan.
2. Preheat oven to 450°. Bake cornbread 20 to 25 minutes or until done.

Dough Nuts—A Yankee Cake

Dry half a pound of good brown sugar, pound it and mix it with two pounds of flour and sift it; add two spoonsful of yeast, and as much new milk as will make it like bread; when well risen, knead in half a pound of butter, make in cakes the size of a half dollar, and fry them a light brown in boiling lard.

Mary Randolph

Makes 3 to 4 dozen

¾ cups milk
½ cup butter
½ cup firmly packed brown
  sugar
2 teaspoons dried yeast
¼ cup lukewarm water

3¼ cups flour
½ teaspoon salt (if desired)
Lard for frying
Granulated sugar (if desired)

Hearth:

1. In a saucepan set on trivet over warm coals, heat milk and butter until milk is warm and butter begins to melt. Remove from heat and stir in brown sugar. Set aside to cool slightly.

2. Dissolve yeast in lukewarm water. Stir into slightly cooled milk mixture.

3. Sift flour and salt into large bowl. Gradually add milk mixture, beating until well blended and smooth. Dough will be somewhat soft. Cover and set aside to rise until doubled in bulk, about 1½ hours.

4. Punch down dough. Turn out onto lightly floured surface and knead briefly. Shape dough into a ball, cover, and let "rest" 10 minutes.

5. Break off pieces of dough the size of a walnut and flatten with hand to ½" thickness, or roll out dough ½" thick and cut with small doughnut cutter. Cover with towel and let rise again until double in bulk, about 45 minutes.

6. Heat enough lard in frying pan set over hot coals to fill pan about half full.

7. Using a long-handled spoon or sieve, carefully slip risen doughnuts into bubbling lard. Use extreme care in cooking

doughnuts, for fire or burns can be a real hazard in deep-fat frying. Observe all safety rules. Fry on both sides until lightly browned and puffy, then remove and drain. Serve warm, sprinkled with granulated sugar if desired.

Modern:
1. Follow direction 1, heating milk and butter over moderately low heat.
2. Follow hearth directions 2 through 7, frying doughnuts in hot oil or lard over moderately high heat. Drain on paper towels, sprinkle with sugar, and serve warm.

Sarah Gray's French Rolls

Sift a quart of flour, add a little salt, a spoonful of yeast, 2 eggs well beaten, & 1/2 a pint of milk,—knead it & set it to rise; next morning work in an ounce of butter, make the dough into small rolls, & bake them. The top crust should not be hard.

Gray Family Papers (taken from Mary Randolph)

Makes about 20 rolls

2 teaspoons dried yeast	4 cups sifted flour
1/4 cup lukewarm water	2 teaspoons salt
3/4 cup milk	2 eggs
2 tablespoons softened butter	Melted butter

Hearth:

1. Dissolve yeast in lukewarm water and set aside to proof.
2. Combine milk and 2 tablespoons softened butter in saucepan. Heat over coals until milk is warm and butter begins to melt. Remove from heat.
3. Sift flour with salt into large bowl. Gradually add milk and butter, blending thoroughly.
4. Blend in eggs, one at a time, beating well after each addition.
5. Blend in yeast and mix thoroughly.
6. Turn dough onto floured surface. Knead until dough is smooth and elastic, about 10 minutes. Shape dough into ball and put into buttered bowl. Turn dough to coat with butter. Cover with cloth and set in a warm place to rise until doubled in bulk, 1½ to 2 hours.
7. Punch dough down. Break off pieces about the size of a large egg and shape into rolls. Put in greased French roll pan or in round pans. Cover and let rise again until doubled, about 1 hour.
8. Bake in preheated Dutch oven set on hot coals 15 to 20 minutes or until golden brown.
9. Remove rolls from pan and set on rack to cool. Brush rolls with melted butter while still warm.

Modern:

1. Follow hearth directions 1 and 2, heating milk and butter over low heat.
2. Follow hearth directions 3 through 7.
3. Preheat oven to 400°. Bake rolls 15 to 20 minutes or until golden brown. Complete, following hearth direction 9.

Note: These French rolls are better served warm.

Commercial yeast was not available until 1868. These instructions for making yeast are from Anna R. Peck's Memorandum Book *in the private collection of Mrs. W. R. Ward, Bladensfield, Richmond County, VA.*

Common Hoe Cake (or Ashcake)

Take an earthen or tin pan, and half fill it with coarse indian meal, which had best be sifted in. Add a little salt. Have ready a kettle of boiling water. Pour into the indian meal sufficient hot water (a little at a time,) to make a stiff dough, stirring it with a spoon as you proceed. It must be thoroughly mixed, and stirred hard. If you want the cakes for breakfast, mix this dough over night; cover the pan, and set it in a cool place till morning. If kept warm, it may turn sour. Early next morning, as soon as the fire is burning well, set the griddle over it, and take out the dough, a handful at a time. Flatten and shape it by patting it with your hands, till you form it into cakes about the size of a common saucer, and half an inch thick. When the griddle is quite hot, lay on it as many cakes as it will hold, and bake them brown. When the upper side is done, slip a broad knife beneath and turn them over. They must be baked brown on both sides. Eat them warm, with buttermilk, sweet milk, butter, molasses, or whatever is most convenient. If you intend these cakes for dinner or supper, mix them as early in the day as you can, and (covering the pan) let them stand in a cool place till wanted for baking. In cold weather you may save trouble by mixing over night enough to last the next day for breakfast, dinner, and supper; baking them as they are wanted for each meal. Or they may be all baked in the morning, and eaten cold; but they are then not so palatable as when warm. They will be less liable to stick, if before each baking the griddle is dredged with wheat flour, or greased with a bit of fat pork stuck on a fork. You may cover it all over with one large cake, instead of several small ones.

This cake is so called, because in some parts of America it was customary to bake it on the iron of a hoe, stood up before the fire. It is better known by that name than by any other.

Eliza Leslie

Makes 4 to 6 hoecakes

1 cup white cornmeal
½ teaspoon salt
Boiling water

Hearth:
1. Mix cornmeal and salt in a bowl. Gradually stir in enough boiling water to make a stiff dough. Mix thoroughly.
2. Cover and set dough in a *cool* place for several hours.

3. Bake hoecakes by one of the following methods:

a. Heat a griddle hung on crane over flames. Grease lightly with melted lard. Shape dough by hand into flat cakes ½″ thick and about as round as a small saucer. Lay as many cakes as will fit on hot griddle and bake turning, until browned on both sides. Brush griddle with melted lard between each baking.

b. Form into cakes as above. Sweep ashes from hearth in front of fire and spread out the cakes. Let them dry a few minutes, then cover with hot ashes and bake about 15 minutes or until firm. Brush off ashes, using a little water to clean them before serving. Hoecakes may be wrapped in cabbage leaves before covering with ashes, if desired.

c. Put the prepared cakes on a heated hoe or heavy board propped up in front of the fire. Brown on one side, then turn and brown on the other.

Modern:
1. Follow hearth directions 1 and 2.
2. Heat griddle over moderate heat and brush lightly with oil or melted lard.
3. Cook hoecakes on both sides until browned.

Note: Hoecakes are best eaten hot.

Mrs. Gray's Muffins

To be made ten o'clock at night for breakfast, or 12 in the day for tea Sift a quart of flour, work in it a piece of butter large as a hen egg—a teaspoonful of salt, & a large tablespoonful of lard beat 2 eggs, have a quart of milk ready & pour a little in the eggs, then add flour & milk alternately until all the flour is in, beat all well, for five or ten minutes then stir in gently a short gill of yeast. Some cream or all cream is still better than milk. If you want waffles, stir in gently a half pint of cream, at day light.

Gray Family Papers

Makes 10 to 12 muffins

2 teaspoons yeast	2 tablespoons butter, softened
2 tablespoons lukewarm water	1 tablespoon lard
2 cups sifted flour	1 egg, slightly beaten
½ teaspoon salt	1 cup half and half

Hearth:

1. Dissolve yeast in water and set aside to proof.
2. Sift flour and salt together into a large bowl. Work in butter and lard.
3. Combine egg with half and half. Gradually blend into dry mixture, blending well. Add yeast and, using wooden spoon, beat batter about 5 minutes to aerate.
4. Cover and let rise in warm place 1½ to 2 hours. With a wooden spoon, push down batter.
5. These muffins can be prepared in two ways:

   a. To bake on a hanging griddle over flames, first heat the griddle, then grease it lightly with lard or butter. Grease muffin rings (can be found in kitchen specialty shops) and put on griddle. Ladle muffin batter into rings, filling half full. Cover with cloth and let rise about 20 minutes, away from fire. When muffins have risen sufficiently return griddle to crane and cook muffins slowly, 8 to 10 minutes on each side, until done. Remove from rings and keep warm by fire until ready to serve.

   b. Muffins may also be baked in a Dutch oven. Fill greased muffin tins half full, cover with cloth, and allow to rise about 20 minutes. Carefully set pans on rack on trivet in preheated Dutch oven. Set Dutch oven over hot coals and bake muffins about 25 minutes until golden brown. Remove from pan and keep warm by fire until ready to serve.

Modern:
1. Follow hearth directions 1 through 4.
2. These muffins may be baked on a stove-top griddle. Heat griddle on low temperature and brush lightly with oil, butter, or lard. Grease muffin rings, place on griddle, and fill about half full with muffin batter. Cover with cloth and let rise about 20 minutes. Return to stove top and cook muffins slowly on moderate to moderately low heat, 8 to 10 minutes per side. Keep warm while baking others.
3. To bake in oven, preheat to 375°. Fill greased muffin tins half full. Cover with cloth and allow to rise about 30 minutes. Bake about 25 minutes or until muffins are golden brown. Remove from pan and keep warm until ready to serve.

Note: Best served warm.

Mrs. M. E. Hite's Sally Lunn

Sift 1½ lbs. of flour, make a hole in the middle and put 2 oz. of butter warmed in a pint of milk, teaspoonful of salt, 3 eggs, beat light and 2 tablespoons of yeast, mix it well, and put into a tin pan that has been greased with butter. Make it in the morning after breakfast, put the butter in and beat it well about 1½ hours before baking it, in summer, and 2 hours in winter, if sour add a little soda.

Jean Brent French Collection (taken from Eliza Leslie)

Fills 1 9″ tube pan

2 teaspoons dried yeast	3½ cups sifted flour
¼ cup lukewarm water	1 teaspoon salt
1 cup milk	2 eggs
¼ cup butter, softened	

Hearth:

1. Dissolve yeast in lukewarm water and set aside to proof.
2. Heat milk and butter until warm. Combine with dissolved yeast.
3. Sift 1½ cups of the flour with salt into a large bowl. Gradually add liquid, beating until smooth.
4. Beat eggs until light. Stir into batter until thoroughly blended.
5. Gradually add remaining flour, beating until smooth. Cover bowl and let batter rise in warm place until doubled in bulk, about 1½ to 2 hours.
6. Stir batter down. Pour into well-greased tube or bundt pan. Cover and let batter rise again until doubled, about 1 hour.
7. Carefully place pan on trivet or rocks in preheated Dutch oven. Following general directions for Dutch oven baking, bake 30 to 40 minutes or until bread tests done. Remove from Dutch oven and turn out on rack to cool.

Modern:

1. Follow hearth directions 1 through 6.
2. Preheat oven to 350°. Bake Sally Lunn for 30 to 40 minutes or until bread tests done. Remove from oven and turn out on rack to cool.

Mother's Spoon Bread

3 cups milk
3 eggs

1 teaspoon salt
lump of butter
cup (1) meal

Pour two cups of the milk over meal and let come to a boil stirring constantly. It will thicken as it begins to boil. Add remaining milk and other ingredients. Bake in hot oven.
  (2 large eggs or 3 small ones)

Carter-Walker Collection

Serves 4 to 6

3 cups milk, divided
1 cup white cornmeal
1 teaspoon salt

2 tablespoons butter
2 eggs

Hearth:
1. Pour 2 cups of the milk over cornmeal in pan.
2. Set pan on a trivet over hot coals and stir mixture constantly until it boils and thickens.
3. Remove pan from coals and stir in remaining milk, salt, and butter.
4. Beat eggs until light and frothy. Thoroughly blend into cornmeal mixture.
5. Pour mixture into greased pan and carefully place on trivet or rocks in preheated Dutch oven. Following general instructions for Dutch oven baking, bake for 25 to 30 minutes or until knife inserted in center comes out clean. Serve immediately.

Modern:
1. Preheat oven to 450°.
2. Follow hearth directions 1 through 5, bringing combined milk and cornmeal to a boil over moderately high heat. Stir constantly.
3. Bake in greased ovenproof dish 25 to 35 minutes or until knife inserted in center comes out clean. Serve immediately.

Pain Perdu*

Three yolks of eggs beat light, with half a cup of brown sugar, add half a cup of cream; cut your bread in slices, soak it in the above, and fry it in butter. On serving, sprinkle each piece with cinnamon and sugar.

Mrs. M. B. Moncure

Serves 4

2 eggs, well beaten
⅓ cup brown sugar
Dash salt
½ cup cream
8 pieces French bread, thickly sliced
1 tablespoon lard
3 tablespoons butter

Topping:
¼ teaspoon nutmeg
1½ teaspoons cinnamon
6 tablespoons granulated sugar

Hearth:

1. Combine eggs with sugar, salt, and cream, beating well.
2. Soak French bread in egg-cream mixture until thoroughly saturated.
3. Melt lard and butter in a frying pan set over hot coals. Add soaked French bread, two slices at a time, and fry on both sides until lightly browned and cooked through. Remove from pan and keep warm while remainder of French bread is cooked. Use more lard and butter if needed.
4. Mix together topping ingredients and sprinkle over hot Pain Perdu. Serve immediately.

Modern:

1. 1 tablespoon cooking oil can be substituted for the lard.
2. Follow hearth directions 1 through 4, cooking French bread over medium heat.

---

*From the French, literally "lost bread," pain perdu was a popular Anglo-Norman dish. Ingredients and procedures were modified over time, making it very much like our modern French toast.

Beverages

Beverages ranging from simple fruit juices to elaborate punches were consumed in early Virginia. Cider and beer were commonplace, as were chocolate, coffee, and tea. The latter was especially fashionable throughout most of the Colonial period. Tea leaves, an expensive commodity imported from China, were kept under lock and key in elaborate chests proudly displayed in the parlors of wealthy Virginia families. The costliness of the tea itself, the specially made chests, elegant tea tables covered with fine cloths, and imported china tea sets were symbols of an affluent society. Virginia hostesses welcomed an opportunity to "take a dish of tea" with the social ceremony it provided. Indeed, the hated tea tax levied by the English government in 1773 inspired an anonymous lament that appeared in the *Virginia Gazette:* "Farewell the Tea Board, with its gaudy Equipage," wrote "A Lady." ". . . No more shall I dish out the once lov'd Liquor."[1]

The elaborate dinners, parties, balls, and other social events so dearly loved by hospitable Virginians were lively affairs at which wine and spirits flowed freely. Gentlemen of the day were heavy drinkers who needed no excuse to raise their glasses. Their diaries and letters provide amusing descriptions of convivial gatherings where toasts were drunk and men made merry. Champagne, claret, Madeira, white and red wines, and many mixed drinks such as punch and toddy were all highly regarded potions.

But then, as now, simple pleasures were often the best. Marietta Minnegerode Andrews, describing her Loudoun

County girlhood in the late 19th century, felt that buttermilk "was a highly prized beverage . . ." sought out by sportsmen when they returned from the hunt to "toss off goblet after goblet of it, thick, icy-cold, lumpy with bits of butter, and served in the great silver trophies."[2]

Old cookbooks contain recipes for many homemade beverages now merely thought of as quaint reminders of the past. Raspberry vinegar, cherry shrub, and the thickened, restorative caudles, possets, and syllabubs could be concocted, as well as wines and cordials, bottled and stored away to age. A representative sampling of these recipes follows.

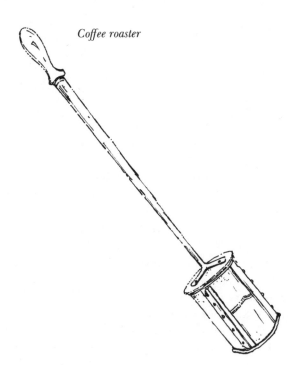

Coffee roaster

Gray Family Blackberry Cordial

To 2 quarts of juice add one pound of loaf sugar ½ ounce nutmeg, ounce cinnamon ¼ ounce cloves ¼ ounce alspice pulverized boil all together for a short time & when cold add a pint of brandy

Virginia Gearhart Gray Collection

Makes 10 to 11 cups

8 cups fresh blackberry juice	½ teaspoon allspice
2 teaspoons nutmeg	2 cups sugar
½ teaspoon cloves	2 cups brandy
2 teaspoons cinnamon	

1. Combine blackberry juice with spices and sugar.
2. Bring to a boil, then simmer uncovered for 15 minutes. Cover and set aside to cool.
3. Strain and discard spices. Stir in brandy and bottle for use.
4. Allow to "mellow" at least two weeks before serving.

Barbados Lemon Punch

The Juice of 3 good Lemons—2 small Coffee Cups rum sweetened as for toddy (1 pound brown sugar to each Gallon of spirit, 1 D° of Fr. brandy and white sugar to your taste will make 3 qts Punch—. . . 5 good Limes equal to 3 Lemons

The Tucker Family Cookbook

Makes approx. ½ gallon

1½ cups sugar	4 cups dark rum
2 cups fresh lemon juice	2 cups brandy

1. Stir sugar into lemon juice. When completely dissolved, add rum and brandy. Stir in well. Cover mixture and set aside to blend flavors for several hours.
2. About 1 hour before serving, pour punch over large chunk of ice in punch bowl. Stir occasionally.

Cherry Shrub

Gather ripe morello or red sour *cherries; pick them from the stalk, and put them in an earthen pot, which must be set into an iron pot of water; make the water boil, but take care that none of it gets into the cherries. When the juice is extracted, pour it into a bag made of tolerably thick cloth, which will permit the juice, but not the pulp, of the cherry to pass through. Put a pound of sugar to a pint of juice, and when it becomes perfectly clear, bottle. Put half a gill of spirit into each bottle before you pour in the juice. Cover the corks with rosin. Cherry shrub will keep all summer in a dry, cool place, and is delicious mixed with water.*

Mary Stuart Smith (taken from Mary Randolph)

3 quarts ripe sour red cherries   Brandy as needed
Sugar as needed

Hearth:
1. Rinse and stem cherries. Cut in half, put them in a deep heatproof bowl and set the bowl in an iron pot. Set on a crane. Fill pot with boiling water; do not let any of it get into the cherries throughout the cooking process.
2. Push crane over flames and cook cherries until they are soft and juice flows from them. Replenish boiling water as needed, being careful not to spill any into the cherries.
3. Remove bowl from pot. Pour cherries into cloth-lined colander set over large bowl. Mash to extract as much juice as possible. Discard pulp.
4. Measure juice and to each pint add 2 cups sugar. Stir to dissolve and set aside to cool.
5. To each pint sweetened juice add ¼ cup brandy.
6. Bottle and set away to "season" at least two weeks before using.
7. For one serving of cherry shrub, pour about ¼ cup over ice in a glass. Add water and stir.

Modern:
1. Prepare cherries as in step 1 above.
2. Put cherries in a large heavy pot, cover, and cook over moderately low heat until they are soft and juice flows from them. Stir often to prevent cherries from sticking to pot.
3. Follow steps 3 through 7 to complete.

Egg Nog

1 doz. eggs, 12 even tablespoonful of sugar, 1 qt of rich milk, 1 pt of cream, 1 pt & 1 gil of whiskey, 1 oz brandy and ½ pt of Jamaica Rum. Beat yolks well and add sugar, then pour in the liquor slowly and beat hard all the time. As the liquor cooks the egg then add the milk and cream and then the whites of the egg beaten very stiff.

Mary Shepherd
(Jean B. French)

Makes approx. ½ gallon

6 eggs, separated
1 cup sugar
1 ½ cups bourbon
¼ cup brandy

½ cup dark rum
2 cups milk
2 cups cream
Freshly grated nutmeg

1. Beat egg yolks until very light. Add sugar a little at a time, blending in well.
2. Slowly add bourbon, brandy, and rum, beating well. Liquors "cook" the egg.
3. Pour in milk and cream.
4. Whip egg whites until stiff and fold into eggnog.
5. Pour into punch bowl and sprinkle with nutmeg.

Oatlands Raspberry Vinegar

"For all virtuous souls who relished a drink which cools, but does not inebriate, there was raspberry vinegar—an unfermented decoction of raspberry juice, very delicious when diluted with water in a glass of crushed ice."

Marietta Minnegerode Andrews,
Memoirs of a Poor Relation

Put a gallon of fresh ripe raspberries in a stone or china vessel, and pour on them 2 quarts of vinegar   let it stand 24 hours and strain it through a seive pour the liquid over a gallon of fresh raspberries and let it again stand for 24 hours, Then strain it a second time, allow a pond [sic] of loaf sugar to every pint of juice, break up the sugar and let it melt in the liquor. Then put the whole in a stone jar, cover it and set it in a pot of water, let it remain in for one hour after it commences to boil, being careful to see that the water is kept boiling and does not boil into the jar. Take off the skum and when cold bottle the vinegar for use, Raspberry vinegar mixed with water is a delightful drink in summer, and particularly grateful in sickness—

Kate Powell Carter

Makes about 1 gallon

8 cups fresh raspberries,   Sugar
    divided
1 quart cider vinegar

1. Combine 4 cups raspberries with vinegar in a stone crock. Cover and set aside for 24 hours.
2. Strain mixture, discarding berries. Combine remaining liquid with rest of berries. Cover and set aside for 24 hours.

3. Strain again, discarding berries. Measure liquid, and to every pint add 2 cups sugar. Stir to dissolve.

4. Return mixture to crock. Cover and set in large pot of water. Bring water to a boil and simmer for an hour. Do not let water boil high enough to get into the raspberry mixture. Skim mixture while cooking.

5. At the end of one hour, remove the crock containing the raspberry vinegar. Set aside to cool, then bottle for use. Store in refrigerator, or bottle under sterile conditions to keep unrefrigerated.

Mrs. Eliza Smith's Sack Posset Without Eggs

Take a Quart of Cream or new Milk, and grate three Naples-biskets in it, and let them boil in the Cream; grate some Nutmeg in it, and sweeten it to your Taste; let it stand a little to cool, and then put half a Pint of Sack a little warm in your Bason, and pour your Cream to it, holding it up high in the pouring; let it stand a little and serve it.

Eliza Smith

Makes about 12 ½-cup servings

2 cups cream	½ teaspoon freshly grated
2 cups milk	nutmeg
3 Naples biscuits (Mrs. Tucker's recipe on p. 238), grated or crumbled	½ to ¾ cup sugar
	1 cup sack or cream sherry

1. Combine cream, milk, Naples biscuits, nutmeg, and sugar in a saucepan. Heat, stirring constantly, to scalding. Remove from heat and let mixture cool briefly.

2. Warm sack slightly (do not boil) and pour into punch bowl.

3. Stir cream mixture vigorously and pour into punch bowl.

4. Serve warm.

A Very Fine Syllabub

Take a Quart and half a Pint of Cream, a Pint of Rhenish, half a Pint of Sack, three Lemons, near a Pound of double-refined Sugar; beat and sift the Sugar and put it to your Cream, grate off the yellow Rind of your Lemons and put that in; squeeze the Juice of the three Lemons into your Wine, and put that to your Cream; then beat all together with a Whisk just half an Hour; then take it all up together with a Spoon, an fill your Glasses: It will keep good Nine or ten Days, and is best three or four Days old. These are called The ever-lasting Syllabubs.

Eliza Smith

Makes about 3 quarts

5 cups cream
1 ½ cups sugar, divided
Juice and rind of 3 large
   lemons

2 cups white wine
1 cup sack or cream sherry

1. Combine cream with sugar and lemon rind in a large bowl. Set aside.
2. Combine wine, sack, and lemon juice and very slowly beat into cream mixture. Whip ingredients together until syllabub is light and frothy, about ten minutes.
3. Cover and chill overnight to allow flavors to ripen.

Note: When syllabub, one of early America's favorite drinks, is served, it is sipped through the foamy cream which rises to the top.

Judge Tucker's Mulled Wine

Grate half a Nutmeg into a pint of wine and sweeten to your taste with loaf sugar—set it over the fire and when it boils take it off the fire to cool—Beat the Yolks of 4 Eggs very well—strain them and add to them a little cold wine—then mix them with your hot wine gradually pour it backward and forward several times till it looks fine and light—then set it on the fire and heat it very gradually till it is quite hot and pretty thick and pour it up and down several times Put it in chocolate cups and serve it with long narrow toasts—

The Tucker Family Cookbook

Serves 4 to 6

2½ cups red wine, divided
½ teaspoon freshly grated
   nutmeg
Sugar to taste

4 egg yolks
Strips of toast

1. Combine 2 cups of the wine, nutmeg, and sugar to taste. Bring to a boil, stirring occasionally. Immediately remove from heat.
2. Beat egg yolks until light, then strain them. Stir in the remaining ½ cup wine.
3. Slowly add egg mixture to hot spiced wine, stirring constantly. Pour mixture back and forth several times to blend and lighten.
4. Reheat on low heat until hot and beginning to thicken, stirring constantly. Again pour mixture back and forth.
5. Pour into small cups and serve hot with strips of toast.

Mary Stuart Smith's Lemon Sirup

In the spring, when lemons are cheap, a large family would always find it to their advantage to buy a whole box. Some dozens squeezed, and the juice made into sirup, enables one to have lemonade at a moment's notice for months, and give much needed refreshment to the sick or weary. To two pounds of loaf or crushed sugar put two pints of water and the juice of eight good lemons, boiled for about twenty minutes with the rind of three. After the sugar-water and rind are boiled and skimmed till clear, you then add the juice, not to be strained till the sirup is done; when boiled for about five minutes, take it off the fire, strain and bottle it. This quantity makes two quart-bottles full, bringing the cost to from twenty to thirty cents each.

Mary Stuart Smith

Makes 1 to 1½ gallons

Freshly ground peel of 3 large lemons
4 cups water
4 cups sugar

1 cup fresh lemon juice
Fresh mint sprigs (optional)

1. Combine lemon peel, water, and sugar. Cover and bring to a boil. Reduce heat and simmer about 20 minutes. Set aside to cool.
2. Strain into lemon juice, stir well and bottle for use.
3. For each glass, pour about ½ cup of the syrup (or to taste) over ice. Add cold water and stir well. Garnish with mint sprigs if desired.

Soups

Soup was an integral part of the copious meals consumed by our forefathers. Always included in the first course, the soup was ceremoniously served from a tureen by the hostess to begin the meal.

Cookbook writers in the 18th and 19th centuries were very precise in giving soup-making directions. Hannah Glasse, for instance, admonished her readers to "take great care the pots or sauce-pans and covers be very clean and free from all grease and sand" and to "be sure that all the greens and herbs you put in be cleaned, washed, and picked." She recommended that soups and broths be stewed (simmered) "as softly as possible," set on embers for a length of time so that "both the meat and broths will be delicious."[1] Her recipe for "strong Broth" (page 92) is an elegant stock that is strained on completion and put by for later use.

Perceptive 19th-century cook Eliza Leslie also insisted on straining the stock, since a clear base is more elegant and less "disgusting," while Maria Parloa asserted that "no household . . . should be without a stock-pot"[2] in which accumulated meat and bones could be simmered two or three times a week to produce the all-important basis for making soups, as well as sauces and other made dishes.

We think of store-bought bouillon cubes as a modern convenience, but early recipes are given for "pocket" or "portable" soup, which is essentially the same thing. Beef is boiled for hours in a highly seasoned broth until the mixture is reduced to jelly. Strained, measured into individual cups, then further reduced to a "stiff glue," it is then dried, wrapped individually, and stored for later use. The recipes give directions for reconstituting this portable soup, which could be transported and stored easily. The Virginian William Byrd recommended it in 1728. He provided his own recipe, saying that two or three pieces of the "glue" dissolved in boiling water provided a half pint of good broth, "nourishing, but likewise very wholesome."[3]

In making the soups given on the following pages, homemade stocks are preferred. Use a favorite recipe or try the one on page 92, based on Hannah Glasse's 18th-century receipt.

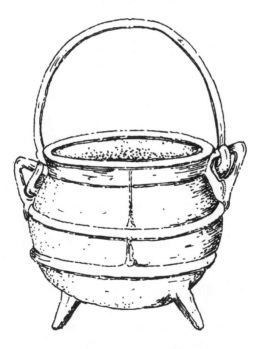

Mrs. Tebbs' [Beef] Soup with Bouilli

Take the nicest part of the thick brisket of beef about eight pounds. put it into a pot, and sprinkle over it one small tablespoonful of pounded black pepper and two of salt three onions the size of a hens egg, cut small—six small carrots scraped and cut up and two small turnips pared and cut into dice—pour on three quarts of water and let it boil steadily and gently always take of the scum carefully as it rises—When it has boiled four hours put in a small bundle of thyme and parsley and pint of celery cut small or a teaspoonful of celery seed pounded and boil one hour longer then take out the beef and cover up the soup and set it near the fire to keep hot—Just before you take it up for dinner brown in this manner— Put a small tablespoonful of brown sugar into an iron skillet—set it on the fire and stir it till it melts and looks very dark pour into it a ladle of soup a little at a time stirring it all the while—strain this browning and mix it well with the soup—take out the bundle of thyme and parsley and serve it up in a tureen with a bit of toasted bread. The Boulli *is prepared in the following manner.*

Take the skin off the beef have the yoke of an egg well beaten dip a feather in it and wash the top of the beef, sprinkle over it the crumbs of stale bread nicely grated put it in a Dutch oven previously heated, put the top on with coals enough to brown without burning the beef—let it stand nearly an hour and prepare your gravy thus—Take sufficient quantity of the soup and the vegetable boiled in it—a tablespoonful of red wine—two of mushroom catsup—thicken with a little bit of butter and little brown flour—make it very hot pour it in your dish and put beef on it.—Garnish it with green pickle cut in thin slices.—

M. H. D. Tebbs Receipt Book

Serves 6-8

Soup

3½ to 4 pounds beef brisket
1 teaspoon pepper
2 teaspoons salt
1 cup coarsely chopped onion
4 small carrots, trimmed, scraped, and sliced ½″ thick
2 small turnips, peeled and diced
8 cups water
2 teaspoons dried thyme
5 tablespoons fresh minced parsley
1 cup diced celery
1 tablespoon brown sugar
Toasted bread, cubed

Bouilli

Cooked beef brisket (see soup recipe)
1 egg yolk, slightly beaten
Stale bread crumbs
1 tablespoon red wine
2 tablespoons mushroom catchup(page 313)
2 tablespoons butter
2 tablespoons brown flour (see page 319)
Sliced sweet pickle

Hearth:

1. Place meat in large pot and sprinkle with pepper and salt. Add chopped onion, carrots, and turnips. Hang pot on crane, pour on water, and cover.

2. Bring to boil over flames, then adjust height of crane so soup can be kept at a gentle simmer throughout cooking time.

3. Simmer 2 hours, then add thyme, parsley, and celery. Cover and continue to simmer another hour or until beef is tender. Remove from heat.

4. Carefully lift beef out of soup and put on clean board or plate. Skin beef. Brush egg yolk over surface of meat. Sprinkle with bread crumbs.

5. Put meat in heated Dutch oven. Cover and place oven on the hearth near fire. Shovel a few hot coals on top and leave for meat to brown while gravy and rest of soup are prepared.

6. To prepare bouilli: Measure 2 cups of the soup into a pan with some of the cooked vegetables. Stir in red wine and mushroom catchup. Mix butter and brown flour together. Add to soup, stirring until butter melts and soup begins to thicken. Cover and keep warm by the fire.

7. In a small frying pan set on a trivet over the hot coals, melt brown sugar, stirring constantly until it is a dark brown. Gradually stir in a little of the hot soup. Remove from heat and return mixture to rest of soup, blending thoroughly. Keep warm.

8. When ready to serve the soup and bouilli, pour soup (first removing fresh herbs) into a tureen. Top with toasted bread cubes.

9. Pour bouilli gravy into deep serving dish. Remove browned beef from Dutch oven and add to gravy in serving dish. Garnish with thinly sliced pickle and serve along with soup.

Modern:

1. Follow hearth directions 1 and 2, bringing soup to boil over high heat. Reduce heat and simmer soup throughout cooking process.

2. Follow hearth directions 3 and 4. Put prepared beef on cookie sheet and broil in oven until browned on top. Keep warm in oven while completing hearth steps 6 and 7. Prepare gravy and browning for soup over moderate heat.

3. Follow hearth directions 8 and 9 to serve.

Note: Mrs. Tebbs identified Mary Randolph, author of *The Virginia House-wife,* as the source for this unusual, delicious soup with beef. Mrs. Randolph presents it as two separate receipts, "To Make Beef Soup" and "Soup with Bouilli" (pages 28–31 of 1824 edition).

Strong Broth for Soup or Gravy (Basic Stock)

Take a shin of beef, a knuckle of veal, and a scrag of mutton, put them in five gallons of water, then let it boil up, skim it clean, and season it with six large onions, four good leeks, four heads of celery, two carrots, two turnips, a bundle of sweet herbs, six cloves, a dozen corns of all-spice and some salt; skim it very clean and let it stew gently for six hours; then strain it off, and put it by for use.

When you want very strong gravy, take a slice of bacon and lay it in a stew-pan; take a pound of beef, cut it thin, lay it on the bacon, slice a good piece of carrot in, an onion sliced, a good crust of bread, a few sweet herbs, a little mace, cloves, nutmeg, whole pepper, and an anchovy; cover it and set it on a slow fire for five or six minutes, and pour in a quart of the above gravy; cover it close, and let it boil softly till half is wasted: this will be a rich, high brown sauce for fish, fowl, or ragoo.

Hannah Glasse

Makes approximately 2 gallons

4 to 6 pounds meaty beef bones
2 to 3 pounds veal knuckles
6 large onions, peeled and quartered
4 leeks, trimmed, thoroughly rinsed, and sliced thickly (may substitute green onions)
1 bunch celery with leaves, rinsed, cored, trimmed, and cut in half
6 large carrots, trimmed and well scrubbed under running water (not necessary to scrape carrots)

2 tablespoons dried marjoram
1 tablespoon dried chervil
Large bunch fresh parsley
10 whole cloves
15 allspice berries
10 peppercorns
2 tablespoons salt
1 teaspoon pepper
6 quarts water

Hearth:

1. Hang a large iron pot on crane and add all ingredients. Cover the pot and bring to a boil, stirring occasionally. Adjust height of the pot so that the stock is maintained at a slow simmer.

2. Simmer stock, covered, 4 to 5 hours, occasionally stirring and skimming away any accumulated scum. Correct seasoning as necessary.

3. Strain thoroughly, reserving liquid. Pour back into pot and return to crane.

4. Allow stock to simmer uncovered another hour or so to reduce and concentrate liquid. Remove from heat and set aside to cool for about an hour.

5. Strain stock thoroughly until soup is clear, using a muslin cloth if necessary. Cover and refrigerate, or freeze for use in several of the recipes that follow.

Modern:

1. Combine all ingredients in large pot, cover, and bring to a boil over high heat.

2. Reduce heat to simmer and cook stock, following hearth directions 3 through 5.

Relatively simple procedures that are easily followed make soup-making a good introduction to open-hearth cooking. The first step, as always, is to establish a steadily burning fire following the directions given in Chapter 2. Then hang the soup pot on a swinging crane, which for safety should be pulled out and away from the flames while adding ingredients or carrying out any other cooking activities.

After the soup has begun to boil, adjust the height of the pot on its hanger so that the soup simmers gently over the flames throughout the cooking process. Remember that soups were much thinner than the heavily thickened mixtures to which we are accustomed today.

Mrs. Randolph's Asparagus Soup

Take four large bunches of asparagus, scrape it nicely, cut off one inch of the tops, and lay them in water, chop the stalks and put them on the fire with a piece of bacon, a a [sic] large onion cut up, and pepper and salt; add two quarts water, boil them till the stalks are quite soft, then pulp them through a sieve, and strain the water to it, which must be put back in the pot; put into it a chicken cut up, with the tops of asparagus which had been laid by, boil it until these last articles are sufficiently done, thicken with flour, butter, and milk, and serve it up.

Mary Randolph

Serves 4 to 6

1 ½ pounds fresh asparagus	3 tablespoons butter
6 cups chicken broth	3 tablespoons flour
⅓ cup diced salt bacon	½ cup cream
½ cup finely chopped onion	Salt to taste
⅛ teaspoon pepper	

Hearth:

1. Wash asparagus. Break off tips and lay aside in ice water while proceeding with rest of recipe.

2. Chop asparagus stalks coarsely and put them in an iron pot hung on crane. Add chicken broth, diced bacon, and chopped onion. Cover and bring to a boil over flames. Adjust height of pot so that soup can simmer gently until asparagus stalks are tender, about 45 minutes.

3. Strain soup, reserving broth. Discard only the bacon. Press the remaining ingredients through a sieve, mashing with a spoon to extract as much pulp as possible.

4. Pour mixture back into pot and add asparagus tips. Return pot to fire and simmer, covered, until tips are barely tender, 5 to 10 minutes.

5. Blend together butter and flour and stir into soup. Simmer gently, stirring until butter has melted and soup thickens slightly.

6. Stir in cream, add salt if needed, and heat slowly until soup is steaming. Do not allow to boil. Pour into tureen and serve immediately.

Modern:
Follow hearth instructions, bringing soup to boil over high heat, then simmering over low heat throughout.

Mary Stuart Smith's Beef Soup

Beef is decidedly the best meat for the substratum of every-day soup, and may be used daily, with slight variations, without wearying a common palate. Get from your butcher a shin-bone, if he has it, or else the coarse neck pieces will answer, that are good for nothing else, and can be purchased cheap. Put it on in a gallon of cold water as early in the morning as you can; set it on the back of the stove, in a covered kettle, where it may simmer slowly till dinner is ready—not boil. In winter add, about an hour before dinner, any vegetables almost that you have at hand and like—dried tomatoes are invaluable for this purpose—potatoes, turnips in moderation, carrots too, to be used also cautiously; dried corn a handful, Lima beans ad libitum, a teacupful of rice, etc. If you like soup thickened, it is done by rubbing up flour carefully with a piece of butter, and adding it just before you want to serve the soup, allowing it, of course, time enough to serve its end. If you want your soup brown, add some browned flour, of which you should always keep a supply by you in the kitchen. Remove the soup from the fire a while before you are ready for it, skim off every particle of grease, and then return it to the fire, so that it may become perfectly hot.

Mary Stuart Smith

Serves 6 to 8

2 to 3 pounds stew beef
8 quarts basic stock (page 92)
2 quarts tomatoes
1 cup peeled, diced potatoes
2 cups scraped, sliced carrots
2 cups corn
3 cups baby lima beans
1 cup diced celery

1 medium turnip, peeled and diced
4 tablespoons mushroom catchup (page 313), or more as needed
2 cloves garlic, minced
1 tablespoon dried marjoram
Pepper to taste
½ cup raw long-grain rice

Hearth:

1. Combine all ingredients except rice in large iron pot. Hang on crane, cover, and bring to a boil. Adjust height of pot so that soup can simmer gently several hours. Stir occasionally.
2. About 45 minutes before ready to serve, correct seasoning. Stir in rice, cover pot, and continue cooking until rice is tender.
3. Pour into tureen and serve.

Modern:

1. Combine all ingredients except rice, cover, and bring to boil over high heat. Reduce heat and allow soup to simmer several hours, stirring occasionally.
2. Follow hearth directions 2 and 3.

Mrs. Randolph's Chicken Soup
To Make Soup of Any Kind of Fowl.

(The only way in which they are eatable.)

Put the fowls in a coop and feed them moderately for a fortnight; kill one and cleanse it, cut off the legs and wings, and separate the breast from the ribs; which, together with the whole back, must be thrown away, being too gross and strong for use. Take the skin and fat from the parts cut off which are also gross. Wash the pieces nicely and put them on the fire with about a pound of bacon, a large onion chopped small, some pepper and salt, a few blades of mace, a handful of parsley cut up very fine, and two quarts of water if it be a common fowl or duck—a turkey will require more water. Boil it gently for three hours, tie up a small bunch of thyme, and let it boil in it half an hour, then take it out. Thicken your soup with a large spoonful of butter rubbed into two of flour, the yelks of two eggs, and half-pint of milk. Be careful not to let it curdle in the soup.

Mary Randolph

Serves 4 to 6

4 cups chicken stock
⅓ cup diced salt bacon
1 cup coarsely chopped onion
¾ teaspoon salt
¼ teaspoon pepper
¼ teaspoon mace
1 teaspoon thyme

3 tablespoons fresh minced
   parsley
2½ to 3 cups diced, cooked
   chicken
1 tablespoon butter
2 tablespoons flour
2 egg yolks
½ cup milk
Additional minced parsley for
   garnish

Hearth:

1. In an iron pot combine stock, bacon, onion, salt, pepper mace, thyme, and parsley. Cover and place pot on crane. Bring to a boil over fire, then adjust height of pot on crane to allow mixture to simmer for about 45 minutes. Remove from heat and strain broth into another pot. Discard bacon, onion, and seasonings.

2. Set pot on a trivet over warm coals. Carefully add chicken and gently simmer for 10 to 15 minutes.

3. Combine butter and flour. Add to soup and stir until butter is melted and soup thickens slightly.

4. Lightly beat egg yolks. Combine with milk in small bowl.

5. Gradually pour about 1 cup of the soup mixture into the egg and milk, stirring constantly to prevent curdling.

6. Pour all back into pot with rest of soup. Stir until soup is steaming hot and slightly thickened. Do not allow soup to boil.

7. Correct seasoning. Pour soup into tureen, garnish with chopped parsley, and serve immediately.

Modern:

1. Follow hearth direction 1, bringing soup to boil on high heat, then simmering for about 45 minutes.

2. After straining broth and discarding bacon, onion, and seasonings, return broth to moderate heat and add chicken. Follow hearth directions 3 through 7 to complete recipe.

Shirley Plantation Mushroom Soup

½ lb. fresh mushrooms, peel & put the caps & stems chopped fine in a saucepan with 2 tablespoons of butter. Cover, heat slowly & simmer 20 minutes. Stir in 2 tablespoons of flour, add slowly 5 cups of hot milk, stir until smooth & thickened, season with salt & cayenne. May be served in cups with very stiff whipped cream on top at the last minute.

Shirley Plantation Collection

Serves 6 to 8

1 pound fresh mushrooms	3 cups milk
6 tablespoons butter	1½ teaspoons salt
5 tablespoons flour	¼ scant teaspoon cayenne
3 cups cream	pepper

Hearth:
1. Rinse, trim, and finely chop mushrooms.
2. While the mushrooms are being prepared, place a pan with butter on a trivet on the hearth, near but not in the fire. Allow butter to melt slowly.
3. Stir in mushrooms. Cover pan and shovel a few coals under the trivet. Allow mushrooms to simmer slowly, stirring occasionally, until done, about 15 to 20 minutes.
4. Stir in flour and continue cooking mushroom mixture, stirring occasionally, until liquid is absorbed and flour is cooked. Replenish coals if necessary, but keep the mixture at a simmer.
5. In the meantime, combine cream and milk in a separate pan and heat over flames to scalding. When mushroom mixture is ready, slowly add hot liquid, salt, and cayenne pepper, stirring constantly. Continue to let soup cook for a few minutes while stirring, until slightly thickened. Do not let soup boil. Correct seasoning and serve immediately.

Modern:
1. Follow hearth direction 1.
2. Slowly melt butter in saucepan over low heat. Stir in mushrooms and cover pan. Allow mushrooms to cook 15 to 20 minutes until done, stirring occasionally.

3. Stir in flour and continue to cook mixture at a gentle simmer. Do not allow liquid to boil.
4. Follow hearth directions 4 through 5.

Maryland Crab Soup

Put on one quart of water, to this add 1½ lbs of tomatoes, (more will make the soup richer), to this add about six cloves, some onion, salt, and pepper, let boil for about half hour; then put in six crabs picked, and a tablespoonful of butter. Slice two hard boiled eggs, squeeze and slice a lemon in the tureen, and pour the soup over the lemon & eggs.

Gray Family Papers

Serves 6 to 8

4 cups water	1½ cups chopped onion
3 pounds fresh tomatoes, peeled and quartered	1 pound fresh lump crabmeat
6 whole cloves	1 tablespoon butter
8 peppercorns	2 hard-boiled eggs
2½ teaspoons salt	Juice of one lemon

Hearth:
1. Bring water and tomatoes to a boil in a large pot hung on a crane.
2. Put cloves and peppercorns in a small muslin or cheese-cloth bag and add to pot along with salt and chopped onion. Cover and adjust height of pot so that soup will simmer about 45 minutes. Stir occasionally.
3. Add crabmeat and butter. Simmer soup an additional 10 to 15 minutes.
4. When ready to serve, shell and slice hard-boiled eggs into soup tureen. Add lemon juice. Pour the soup over the sliced eggs and lemon juice and serve immediately.

Modern:
1. Bring water and tomatoes to boil over high heat. Add seasonings and proceed as in hearth directions 2 through 4, reducing heat to simmer.

Frances Tucker Coalter's Ochra Soup

Set on a Gallon of Water let it boil cut in two double handfuls of tender Ochra—½ hour after put in a handful of Lima Beans—3 Cymlines— and a bit of fresh meat or a fowl, which is better than anything except Beef or Veal—About an hour before you take up your Soup put in 5 large Tomatas cut in pieces or more if you desire when all are well boiled together add Butter rolled in flour, but not to make the soup to thick, and pepper & salt,—Observe to make Soup with ochra in a stone vessle and to stir with a wooden spoon as Metal turns it black—and to put on all soups very early that they may only simmer on the fire.

The Tucker Family Cookbook (taken from Mary Randolph)

Serves 6 to 8

4 cups chicken broth
1 pound okra, washed, trimmed, and sliced into 1" pieces
1 cup chopped onion
1½ cups lima beans
4 cups sliced yellow squash

1¼ teaspoon salt
½ teaspoon pepper
4 cups fresh tomatoes, peeled and quartered
2 tablespoons butter, softened
2 tablespoons flour

Hearth:
1. Pour chicken broth into iron pot. Hang pot on crane. Cover pot and allow broth to come to a boil. Add okra and adjust height of pot so that soup maintains a gentle simmer. Cook for half an hour, covered.

2. Add onion, lima beans, squash, salt, and pepper. Continue to simmer for 1 hour or until beans are very tender. Stir occasionally.
3. Add tomatoes and cook another hour.
4. Blend butter and flour together in a small bowl and add to soup, stirring until butter melts. Allow to simmer a few more minutes until soup is slightly thickened. Correct seasoning. Pour into tureen and serve piping hot.

Modern:
1. In a large saucepan over high heat, bring chicken broth to a boil. Add okra, cover pot, reduce heat, and allow soup to simmer for half an hour.
2. Follow hearth directions 2 through 4.

Note: Mary Randolph gives a similar recipe in *The Virginia House-wife*. Based on her ingredients, I have added onion to those given by Mrs. Coalter.

Hannah Glasse's Onion Soup

Take half a pound of butter, put it in a stew-pan on the fire, let it all melt, and boil it till it has done making any noise; then have ready ten or a dozen middling onions peeled and cut small, throw them into the butter and let them fry a quarter of an hour; then shake in a little flour, and stir them round; shake your pan, and let them do a few minutes longer; then pour in a quart or three pints of boiling water, stir them round; take a piece of upper crust, the stalest bread you have, about as big as the top of a penny-loaf cut small, and throw it in; season with salt to your palate; let it boil ten minutes, stirring it often; then take it off the fire, and have ready the yolks of two eggs beat fine, with half a spoonful of vinegar; mix some of the soup with them, then stir it into your soup and mix it well, and pour it into your dish. This is a delicious dish.

Hannah Glasse

Serves 6 to 8

½ cup butter
7 to 8 cups coarsely chopped
   onions (2½ pounds)
⅓ cup flour
4 cups water
2 cups basic stock (92)

1 slice bread, toasted and diced
1 teaspoon salt
2 egg yolks, slightly beaten
1 tablespoon red wine vinegar

Hearth:

1. Set a frying pan on a trivet over warm coals. Add butter and allow it to melt slowly.
2. Stir in chopped onions. Cover pan and cook slowly, stirring occasionally, for about 15 minutes or until onions are very soft. Replenish hot coals as needed to maintain simmer.
3. Shake on flour, stir in well, and continue to cook mixture slowly, uncovered, for about 45 minutes. Stir often, scraping onions up from bottom of pan to prevent sticking. Onions will gradually turn a dark, golden brown.
4. About 15 minutes before onions are done, combine water and stock in a large pot. Hang on crane and bring to boil over fire.
5. When onions are thoroughly cooked, pull crane out from fire and carefully stir them into soup mixture.
6. Pour about 1 cup of the hot broth into frying pan and with a spoon scrape up any particles remaining. Pour back into pot.
7. Add diced toast and salt. Cover and simmer about 10 minutes.
8. Combine slightly beaten egg yolks with wine vinegar. Remove soup from fire and gradually mix 1 cup into the egg mixture. Stir all back into pot of soup. Blend thoroughly, correct seasoning, and serve.

Modern:

1. Melt butter in a heavy skillet over moderate heat.
2. Follow hearth directions 2 through 8, cooking on moderately low heat.

Loudoun County Oyster Soup

Stew some Slices of Bacon, and Parsley in two pints of Water.—two quarts of oysters—stew them half an hour—thicken it with half a pint of cream—the yolks of two eggs and a quarter of a pound of butter rolled in flour & serve it up

M. H. D. Tebbs Receipt Book

Serves 4 to 6

1 pint oysters with liquor
3 slices bacon
½ cup chopped onion
2 tablespoons flour
2 tablespoons softened butter
½ teaspoon marjoram
½ teaspoon thyme

¼ teaspoon chervil
¾ teaspoon salt
¼ teaspoon pepper
1 ½ cups milk
1 cup cream
2 egg yolks, slightly beaten
1 tablespoon fresh minced
   parsley

Hearth:
1. Put oysters in strainer over bowl and set aside to drain thoroughly.
2. In a heavy saucepan set on a trivet over hot coals, sauté bacon until crisp. Remove from pan, set aside to cool, then crumble and reserve.
3. Pour off all but 1 tablespoon of the bacon drippings. Add chopped onion to remainder of drippings in pan and sauté until onions are translucent.
4. Blend together flour and butter and add to onion. Cook and stir until butter is melted and mixture is well incorporated.
5. Measure oyster liquor and if necessary add enough water to make ½ cup. Stir into mixture in pan along with marjoram, thyme, chervil, salt, and pepper. If necessary, shovel more coals under trivet to maintain slow cooking. Cook while stirring until mixture is well blended and slightly thickened.

6. Gradually add milk and cream, stirring constantly until mixture is steaming and almost boiling. Remove from heat and slowly blend about ¾ cup of the hot liquid into the egg yolks, stirring constantly. Return mixture to pan and reheat until soup is steaming, continuing to stir. Do not allow soup to boil or it will curdle.

7. Stir in oysters and heat through. Correct seasoning.

8. Pour soup into tureen. Garnish with crumbled bacon and minced parsley and serve immediately.

Modern:
Follow hearth directions, preparing soup over moderate heat throughout.

Note: This is a very thin soup, typical of the period. Eliza Leslie recommended seasoning oyster soup with "a bunch of sweet marjoram and other pot-herbs." These seasonings have been added to the original Loudoun County receipt.

Mary Randolph's Dried Pea Soup

Take one quart of split peas, or Lima beans which are better, put them in three quarts of very soft water with three onions chopped up, pepper and salt; boil them two hours; wash them well and pass them through a seive; return the liquid into the pot, thicken it with a large piece of butter and flour, put in some slices of nice salt pork, and a large tea-spoonful of celery-seed pounded; boil it till the pork is done, and serve it up; have some toasted bread cut into dice and fried in butter, which must be put in the tureen before you pour in the soup.

Mary Randolph

Serves 4 to 6

2 cups dried peas	½ teaspoon celery seed,
6 cups water	crushed
2 cups chopped onion	¼ cup diced salt pork
2 teaspoons salt	2 tablespoons butter
¼ teaspoon pepper	2 tablespoons flour

Hearth:

1. Rinse and sort peas. Combine with water, onion, salt, pepper, celery seed, and diced salt pork in large pot hung on crane. Cover pot.

2. When soup mixture has come to a boil, adjust height of pot on crane so that soup simmers. Cook about 2 hours or until peas are very soft.

3. Strain mixture, reserving broth. Discard salt pork and press remainder of ingredients through a sieve into broth, mashing with a spoon to extract as much of the pulp as possible.

4. Return mixture to heat. Combine butter and flour and stir into soup. Simmer gently, stirring until butter has melted and soup thickens. Correct seasoning and serve immediately.

Modern:

1. Follow hearth direction 1, bringing soup mixture to a boil over high heat. Reduce heat and simmer, covered, until peas are very tender, about 2 hours.

2. Follow hearth directions 3 and 4. Peas can be pureed in food processor by blending with part of the reserved broth and then combining with remainder to complete preparation.

Green Peas Soop

Take half a Bushel of the youngest Peas, divide the great from the small; boil the smallest in two Quarts of Water, and the Biggest in one Quart; when they are well boiled, bruise the Biggest, an when the thin is drained from it, boil the Thick in as much cold Water as will cover it; then rub away the Skins, and take a little Spinnage, Mint, Sorrel, Lettuce, and Parsley, and a good Quantity of Marigolds; wash, shred, and boil these in half a Pound of Butter, and drain the small Peas; save the Water, and mingle all together, and a Spoonful of Pepper whole; then melt a quarter of a Pound of Butter, and shake a little Flour into it, and let it boil; put the Liquor to the Butter, and mingle all well together, and let them boil up; so serve it with dry'd Bread.

Eliza Smith

Serves 6 to 8

8 cups freshly shelled green
  peas, divided
6 cups water, divided
1 teaspoon salt
¼ teaspoon pepper
¼ pound spinach
¼ pound sorrel
¼ pound Boston lettuce

1 tablespoon minced fresh
  mint
¼ cup minced fresh parsley
1 to 2 tablespoons shredded
  marigold flowers (optional)
6 tablespoons butter, divided
3 tablespoons flour
Diced toasted bread

Hearth:

1. Put 6 cups of the peas and 2 cups of water in a pot. Cover, hang pot on crane. When mixture has come to a boil, reduce heat by adjusting pot on hanger. Simmer until the peas are very soft, 45 minutes or longer.

2. Drain peas, reserving liquid. Rub peas through a sieve. Discard the skins and combine the pulp with reserved liquid. Cover and set on the hearth near the fire to keep warm.

3. While first batch of peas is cooking, combine remainder with 4 cups of water in another pot. Set this pot on a trivet over hot coals. Cover and allow to simmer gently until peas are just tender, 25 to 30 minutes or less. Stir into pureed peas, cover, and keep warm by the fire.

4. Rinse and drain thoroughly spinach, sorrel, and lettuce. Chop coarsely and combine with mint, parsley, and marigold leaves (if used).

5. Slowly melt 4 tablespoons of the butter in a saucepan set over warm coals. Add chopped vegetables, minced herbs, and marigolds. Cook, stirring constantly, until mixture is just barely limp. Immediately remove from coals and set by the fire to keep warm without further cooking. Do not cover pan.

6. Set pot with pea puree mixture over warm embers. Blend remaining butter with the flour and stir into mixture. Heat and stir until butter melts and soup thickens slightly. Stir in cooked vegetables and herbs. Heat and stir mixture until well blended and bubbly.

7. Remove from heat and pour into tureen. Top with diced toast and serve immediately. Sprinkle on additional marigold leaves if desired.

Modern:
1. Combine 6 cups of the peas and 2 cups of water in a large saucepan over high heat. Cover, bring to a boil, then reduce heat and simmer until peas are very tender, 45 minutes or longer.

2. Follow hearth directions 2 through 7, using moderate to low heat throughout. Do not overcook the vegetables as they lend color and texture to the somewhat bland basic pea soup.

Note: The use of marigolds and other flowers in cooking is an ancient flavoring technique now generally out of use. Their flavor is sharp, so start with 1 tablespoon of the shredded flowers, adding more if desired. Only use marigolds grown without chemicals. Rinse thoroughly before use.

Hannah Glasse's Soup-Santea, or Gravy-Soup

Take six good rashers of lean ham, put it in the bottom of a stew-pan; then put over it three pounds of lean beef, and over the beef three pounds of lean veal, six onions cut in slices, two carrots, and two turnips sliced, two heads of celery, and a bundle of sweet herbs, six cloves, and two blades of mace; put a little water at the bottom, draw it very gently till it sticks, then put in a gallon of boiling water; let it stew for two hours, season with salt, and strain it off; then have ready a carrot cut in small slices of two inches long and about as thick as a goose-quill, a turnip, two heads of leeks, two heads of celery, two heads of endive cut across, two cabbage-lettuces cut across, a very little forrel and chervil; put them in a stew-pan and sweat them for fifteen minutes gently, then put them in your soup, boil it up gently for ten minutes; put it in your tureen with the crust of a French roll.

N.B. You may boil the herbs in two quarts of water for ten minutes (if you like them best so); your soup will be the clearer. . . .

Hannah Glasse

Serves 4 to 6

½ pound country ham
1½ pounds lean beef, cubed
1½ pounds lean veal, cubed
3 cups sliced onion
1 large carrot, scrubbed and quartered (not necessary to scrape carrot)
½ cup peeled, diced turnip
4 stalks celery with leaves, rinsed and quartered
¼ cup fresh thyme
1 teaspoon dried marjoram
1 teaspoon dried chervil
1 teaspoon dried summer savory
¼ cup chopped fresh parsley
3 whole cloves
¼ teaspoon mace

1 cup water
2 quarts boiling water
2 teaspoons salt
1 large carrot, trimmed, and scraped, then cut into matchstick-size pieces
1 cup peeled, diced turnip
1 leek, white part and 2 inches of green part only, trimmed and thinly sliced (or 1 cup thinly sliced green onion)
1 cup thinly sliced celery
1 endive, sliced
2 cups shredded Boston lettuce
½ cup chopped sorrel
½ teaspoon dried chervil
4 to 6 slices toasted French bread

Hearth:

1. In an iron pot, combine ham, beef, veal, onion, quartered carrot, ½ cup turnip, celery with leaves, herbs, and spices. Add 1 cup water. Set pot on crane, bring to a boil over fire, and cook briefly without stirring.

2. Add 2 quarts boiling water. Cover and adjust height of pot on crane to gently simmer soup, about 1½ hours. Add salt and continue simmering soup another ½ hour.

3. Strain soup into colander lined with cloth set over a smaller pot. Reserve broth and discard meat, vegetables, and herbs. Keep broth hot by the fire.

4. Combine carrot "matchsticks," 1 cup turnip, leek, celery, endive, Boston lettuce, sorrel, and chervil in a heavy pan. Cover tightly and set pan on trivet over hot coals. Allow vegetables to "sweat" gently for 15 minutes, stirring occasionally.

5. Add vegetables to hot broth. Return mixture to crane and allow to simmer, uncovered, 10 minutes.

6. Correct seasoning if necessary. Pour into a tureen.

7. To serve, place 1 slice toasted French bread into each individual soup bowl. Ladle soup over.

Modern:

1. Follow hearth directions 1 through 3, bringing soup to boil over high heat, then simmering for 1½ hours.

2. Continue with hearth direction 4. Combined vegetables should be tightly covered and cooked over moderately low heat for 15 minutes. Add to reserved broth and simmer gently, uncovered, 10 minutes.

3. Follow hearth directions 6 and 7 to complete recipe.

Vermicelli Soup

Take three quarts of the broth and one of the gravy mixed together, a quarter of a pound of vermicelli blanched in two quarts of water; put it into the soup, boil it up for ten minutes and season with salt, if it wants any; put it in your tureen, with a crust of a French roll baked.

Hannah Glasse

Serves 4 to 6

4 to 5 cups basic stock (page 92)

3 tablespoons mushroom catchup (page 313)

4 ounces homemade vermicelli (recipe follows)

Toasted French bread slice

Hearth:

1. Combine stock and mushroom catchup. Pour into iron pot and place on crane. Bring to boil, then adjust height of pot so stock can simmer for about 15 minutes. Do not cover.
2. Stir in vermicelli. Cook until barely tender, about 10 minutes. Remove from fire.
3. Place toasted French bread in tureen. Pour in soup and serve.

Modern:

1. Bring stock to a boil over high heat. Reduce to simmer and prepare soup following hearth directions 2 and 3.

Mrs. Randolph's Vermicelli

Beat two or three fresh eggs quite light, make them into a stiff paste with flour, knead it well and roll it out very thin, cut it in narrow strips, give them a twist, and dry them quickly on tin sheets. It is an excellent ingredient in most soups, particularly those that are thin. Noodles are made in the same manner, only instead of strips, they should be cut in tiny squares and dried. They are also good in soups.

Mary Randolph

Makes about 1 pound

3 cups flour	3 eggs
1 teaspoon salt	¼ to ⅓ cup water, as needed

1. Sift flour and salt together in a large bowl.
2. Beat eggs until foamy. Make a well in the center of the flour and pour in eggs.
3. Work into a stiff dough, adding enough water to keep dough firm.
4. Gather into a ball and roll out on a lightly floured surface. Knead dough until smooth and elastic. Cover and allow to "rest" about 10 minutes.
5. Divide in half and roll out dough into very thin sheets. Stretch and pull dough as you roll to make it as thin as possible.
6. Cut dough into narrow strips, ¼" to ½" wide. Either hang to dry or cut strips in half, twist each piece, and dry quickly on tin sheets.
7. When ready to use, bring large pot of salted water to a boil. Throw in noodles and cook until just tender, 10 to 12 minutes. Drain.

Entrées

The seemingly limitless supply of produce found in early Virginia astounded the colonists. Once again their descriptions give us insight into the enormous amount of seafood, flesh, and fowl that was available.

"As for Fish," Robert Beverly wrote ". . . no Country can boast of more Variety, greater Plenty, or of better. . . ."[1]

Captain John Smith, exploring Virginia in 1607, found the waters teeming with fish "lying so thick with their heads above the water [that] as for want of nets . . . we attempted to catch them with a frying pan. . . ."[2]

Shellfish abounded, and oysters were an especially popular staple. "I can testify from experience . . . that these oysters are one of the best and most agreeable foods in the whole world, since one . . . can prepare and serve them in a hundred ways," William Byrd II asserted[3].

The air was filled with a multitude of game birds—wild turkey, pheasant, partridge, geese, ducks. Nicholas Cresswell, visiting Virginia in 1775, amused himself "with shooting wild Geese and Ducks . . . incredible numbers in the River. . . ."[4] Indeed, hunting was an important means of supplying food, for the forests abounded with deer, rabbit, beaver, squirrel, and other animals.

Pigs, brought to Virginia by the earliest settlers, adapted quickly to their new habitat. Roaming freely in the woods, they foraged on mast, "the best fattening which is to be found,"[5] and their succulent meat was "not to be equalled in any part of the world."[6]

Hams and bacon were the pride of Virginia tables. The

method of preparing them became "a fine art in Virginia households, from the feeding of the hogs to the last manipulation. . . ."[7] Proper curing of the hams was important, and many Virginia households had their own "secret" methods. At Bladensfield plantation in the mid-19th century, Evelyn Ward remembered her father's procedure in which "exactly [the] right amount of salt, saltpetre, & molasses was used, the proper length of time to be kept in the salt, & the proper amount of smoking . . .[we] used only oak & hickory chips, & strips of leather, with the blaze smothered down to make a good smoke."[8]

Delicious beef, veal, lamb, and mutton were also to be found, prepared in a number of ways.

One of the many misconceptions about early foods would have us believe that our ancestors ate spoiled meat, disguising the taste and smell with spices, herbs, and sauces. While it may be true that in England the poorer classes consumed produce that was not the best, the gentry had a ready supply of freshly killed or caught meat, fish, and fowl. Salting, pickling, drying, and potting various meats were forms of preserving them for later use in the days before refrigeration. No doubt their flavors were delicious.

In Virginia concern for spoilage, particularly in the extreme summer heat of the Tidewater region, kept cooks busy with the same traditional methods of preservation. But the unlimited bounty of all sorts of food meant meats, seafood, and poultry were available to everyone, even during the winter months when game, fish, and oysters were easily obtained.

The early cookbooks provide guidance on the various ways of cooking meats, seafood, and poultry. Their instructions help in recreating proper hearthside techniques.

ROASTING:

1. Preparation of both the fire and the roasting equipment is important. "Prepare the fire, in time to be burning well, when the meat is put down, [two to three hours ahead of time]. It should have plenty of hot coals, and no part of the fire black, ashy or smoky."[9] Set your meat before "a

clear, steady fire" and maintain a good fire throughout the roasting process.

2. "The spit should always be kept perfectly clean when not in use; and well washed, wiped, and rubbed immediately after using."[10] This holds true if roasting on a spit with fire dogs or with a reflector oven. If using the latter (see illustration), it must also be kept clean and bright, scrubbed well after each use. Keep it well tinned and shiny, as the fire reflecting on the back of the oven is important to roasting.

3. When the meat has been prepared for roasting (see specific recipes), run the spit carefully through the meat. "Take care not to set it at once too close to the fire, but place it rather more than two feet distant, that the meat

Author roasts chicken in a reflector oven.

may heat gradually. If too near the fire at first, the outside will scorch, and leave the inside red and bloody."[11] Some of the old recipes require covering the meat with paper (for example, Roasted Venison on page 168) to prevent it from darkening too quickly.

"At first, baste the meat as soon as it begins to roast [with lard or butter] . . . when its own fat begins to drip, baste it with that, all the while it is cooking. Gradually move it nearer to the fire, turning the spit round frequently, so that the meat may be cooked equally on all sides."[12]

4. Determining a specific timetable for roasting is all but impossible, as much depends on your own taste. Mary Randolph called for shorter cooking times than those later in the century when rare meat was out of fashion.

Some basic guidelines:

a. Goose: 1½ hours

b. Wild duck: 20 minutes

c. Beef and venison: 10 to 12 minutes per pound, depending on taste

d. Pork: 15 minutes per pound

Although only a few recipes for roasting have been included in this book, other cuts of meat and fowl can be used, based on these guidelines. Remember, however, that "the young and tender should be roasted; the strong and full grown animal boiled or stewed."[13]

Recipes that purport to be for roasting in modern ovens cannot begin to duplicate the succulent roasts of the past. In truth, these recipes *bake* rather than roast the meat; the result is often a stringy, unappealing mess. With care, it is possible to replicate roasting in a modern oven using high temperatures. To do so, the oven must be preheated to 500° before putting in the prepared meat. Depending on the heat retention of your oven, either cook the meat at 500° for 15 minutes and then reduce the temperature to 350° for the remainder of the cooking time, or turn down the temperature to 350° immediately after putting the meat into the oven. Again, temperatures are flexible according to your taste. The object is to form a "lovely, light, caramelized crust" contrasting with the "juicy interior."[14] As Mary Randolph wrote, "No meat can be well roasted, except on a spit turned by a jack, and before a steady clear fire—other methods are no better than baking."[15]

Writing in 1885, Mary Stuart Smith summed up the transition:

> All of the old Virginia recipes for cooking meats speak in general of roasting them, where baking must be substituted in modern times. Large, open fireplaces, with tin kitchens and spits, were in universal use in that State until within the last thirty years. As roasting proper is by far the best way of cooking, and is still adhered to where taste has not been forced to yield to economy, we still give many such recipes . . . every *well*-appointed kitchen should have at hand the appliances for roasting meats, but in the large majority of well-to-do families throughout the Union epicurism has given way, in this particular, to convenience.[16]

A simple method of cooking fish comes from Indian traditions.

1. Scale and clean a whole fish, weighing anywhere from 4 to 6 pounds.

2. Season lightly with salt and pepper. Put fresh herbs, such as thyme and marjoram, into the cavity of the fish, along with sliced onion. Brush the outside with melted butter.

3. Rinse enough large cabbage leaves to wrap the fish completely, securing them with butcher's twine.

4. The wrapped fish may be laid directly on hot ashes in the fireplace or first put on a flat cast-iron pan. Cover the fish with a fairly deep layer of hot ashes, then with hot coals. Leave it in the fireplace to roast until done, replenishing the hot ashes as necessary. It will take from 1 to 2 hours to roast, depending on the size of the fish.

5. Carefully brush away the hot ashes and ease the fish out of the fireplace. Cut away the twine and remove the cabbage leaves.

Grilling is another means of fireplace cooking. Set a gridiron (see illustration on page 27) over hot, bright orange coals and broil steaks, chicken, or other meats just as you would over a charcoal grill. Use care with this as in all fireplace procedures, for spattering juices cause burns.

A representative sampling of recipes follow.

Mary Bolling Banister's Beef Collops*

Cut them into thin pieces about two inches long, beat them with the back of a knife very well, grate some nutmeg, flour them a little, lay them in a stew-pan, put in as much water as you think will do for sauce, half an onion cut small, a little piece of lemon-peel cut small, a bundle of sweet herbs, a little pepper and salt, a piece of butter rolled in a little flour. Set them on a slow fire: when they begin to simmer, stir them now and then; when they begin to be hot, ten minutes will do them, but take care they don't boil. Take out the sweet herbs, pour it into the dish, and send it to table.

Mary Bolling Banister

Serves 4 to 6

2½ pounds top round steak	½ teaspoon savory
½ teaspoon nutmeg	¼ teaspoon chervil
¼ cup flour for dusting beef	1 tablespoon parsley
1 to 2 tablespoons lard	¼ teaspoon pepper
½ cup chopped onion	¼ teaspoon salt
1 teaspoon freshly grated	1½ cups water
lemon peel	2 tablespoons softened butter
½ teaspoon marjoram	2 tablespoons flour
½ teaspoon thyme	

Hearth:

1. Trim steak of any fat and bone. Cut into diagonal slices ¼" to ½" long.
2. Combine nutmeg with ¼ cup flour. Dredge steak in flour mixture.
3. Heat lard over hot coals. Brown steak on both sides.
4. Add onion, lemon peel, herbs, pepper, salt. Pour on water. Cover and simmer about 15 minutes.
5. Combine butter and 2 tablespoons flour. Stir into steak mixture until well blended. Cook, uncovered, until tender, 5 to 10 minutes.

Modern:

Follow hearth directions 1 through 5, simmering steak over low heat.

---

*Courtesy of Virginia Historical Society. A "collop" is a thinly-sliced piece of meat.

Beef Steak with Oysters

Take very fine tender sirloin steak, divested of fat and bone; cut them not larger than the palm of your hand; lay them in a stew-pan with some bits of fresh butter rolled in flour. Strain over them sufficient oyster-liquor to cook them well, and to keep them from burning, and to make a gravy so as to stew, but not to boil them. Season them with some blades of mace, some grated nutmeg, and a few whole peppercorns. Let them cook till they are thoroughly done, and not the least red. Then put in some fine large oysters. Set the stew-pan again over the fire till the oysters are plump, which should be in about five or six minutes. If cooked too much, the oysters will toughen and shrink. When done, transfer the whole to a deep dish, mixing the oysters evenly among the meat. Before you take them up, make some sippet or thin toast, in triangular or pointed slices, with the crust cut off   Dip the slices (for a minute) in boiling water: then take them out, and stand them in a circle all round the inside of the dish, the points of the sippets upwards.

Eliza Leslie

Serves 4 to 6

1 pint oysters with liquor	¼ teaspoon mace
3 pounds boneless top sirloin	¼ teaspoon nutmeg
2 tablespoons softened butter	¼ teaspoon pepper
2 tablespoons flour	Toast points for garnish

Hearth:

1. Put oysters in colander, set over bowl, and drain. Reserve liquor.
2. Trim steak of any fat and cut in small, flat slices.
3. Combine butter and flour. Put in frying pan set over hot coals and stir well while butter begins to melt.
4. Add steak and seasonings. Pour in oyster liquor.
5. Simmer steaks, covered, until well done, turning occasionally.
6. Add oysters and cook about 5 minutes or until oysters are plump. Remove from heat.
7. Pour into deep serving platter, garnish with toast points and serve, piping hot.

Modern:

Follow hearth directions 1 through 7, simmering steaks over low heat.

Mary Bowling Banister, 1789–1853, whose home was Battersea near Petersburg, VA.

Battersea Beef Olives*

Take a rump of beef, cut it into steaks half a quarter long, about an inch thick, let them be square; lay on some good force meat [a finely ground meat or poultry used in stuffing or as a garnish, from the French farce, *meaning "to stuff"] made with veal, roll them, tie them once round with a hard knot, dip them in egg, crumbs of bread, and grated nutmeg, and a little pepper and salt. The best way is to roast them, or fry them brown in fresh butter, lay them every one on a bay leaf, and cover them every one with a piece of bacon toasted, have some good gravy, a few truffles and morels, and mushrooms, boil all together, pour into the dish and send it to table.*

Mary Bolling Banister

---

*Courtesy of the Virginia Historical Society

Serves 4 to 6

2½ pounds thinly sliced sirloin steak
Veal forcemeat (page 131)
1 egg
1 cup freshly grated bread crumbs
½ teaspoon nutmeg
¼ teaspoon salt
¼ teaspoon pepper
¼ cup butter
2 to 3 bay leaves
3 cups beef or veal stock
¼ pound cleaned, chopped mushrooms
Bacon for garnish

Hearth:

1. Cut steak into 4″ × 4″ squares. On each square spread about 2 tablespoons forcemeat. Roll up steaks and tie at each end with string.

2. Beat egg until frothy. Combine bread crumbs, nutmeg, salt, and pepper.

3. Dip rolled steaks ("olives") first into egg, then into crumb mixture, coating well.

4. Melt butter in frying pan set over warm coals. Fry olives on all sides until browned, adding more butter if needed.

5. Add bay leaves. Pour in stock and add mushrooms. Set pan over hot coals, cover, and simmer until done, 30 to 40 minutes. Uncover pan during last 10 minutes of cooking.

6. Fry 1 bacon strip for each olive. Curl up while hot, then drain.

7. When olives are ready, put them in a serving dish, cover with gravy, and garnish with bacon curls.

Modern:

1. Follow hearth directions 1 through 3.

2. Melt butter over moderate heat and brown olives on all sides.

3. Follow hearth directions 5 through 7 to complete.

Mrs. Tucker's Rump of Beef to Stew

If you intend to have your dinner from 3 to 4 o'clock, put on your beef at 10, in a pot which must be set (not hung) on the fire—prepare your beef as follows—Take 6 cloves 1 even teaspoon of beaten black pepper—½ the quantity of mace & mix with them (when beaten fine together) 4 even teaspoonfuls of salt—Rub all on the beef, & put it in the pot with 5 quarts of water—make it stew slowly—put in 4 bay leaves & 1 quarter of orange peel—Do not suffer the Beef or gravy to burn—turn it frequently in the pot When you find the gravy is brown & thick, & reduced to a small quantity, take off all the fat that is on it & pour it in 1 & a ½ pints of boiling water—Let it stew till your meat is well browned all over then put in 1 glass of red wine, 1 of white, & 1 of walnut liquor or catsup—turn your beef several times in the gravy & dish it up—again taking off the fat—Add salt if you find necessary & take out the orange peel & bay leaves—Note—A round of beef (not of the largest size) will weigh about 29 lb—of which the bone weighs about 10 lb

The Tucker Family Cookbook

Serves 4 to 6

4 ½ to 5 pounds rump roast
2 teaspoons salt
1 teaspoon pepper
¼ teaspoon ground cloves
½ teaspoon mace
Water

3 bay leaves
1 to 2 tablespoons freshly
   grated orange peel
½ cup red wine
½ cup white wine
¼ cup walnut catchup (page
   314)

Hearth:

1. Rinse off beef and pat dry. Combine salt, pepper, cloves, and mace and rub over surface of beef.

2. Put beef in pot or Dutch oven. Cover with water. Add bay leaves and orange peel.

3. Set pot over hot coals and simmer, uncovered, for 2 to 3 hours or until tender. Occasionally turn beef in pot and stir liquid.

4. When beef is nearly done and liquor is reduced and browned, add 1 cup boiling water, wines, and catchup. Continue cooking beef until very tender, turning occasionally.

5. Remove beef to serving platter. Stir gravy and correct seasoning. Pour in sauce boat and send to table with beef.

Modern:

1. Follow hearth directions 1 through 5, simmering beef over low heat.

Mary Bolling Banister's to Force the Inside of a Sirloin of Beef*

Take a sharp knife and carefully lift up the fat of the inside, take out all the meat close to the bone, chop it small, take a pound of suet and chop fine, about as many crumbs of bread, a little thyme and lemonpeel, a little pepper and salt, half a nutmeg grated, and two shalots chopped fine; mix all together with a glass of red wine, then put it into the same place, cover it with the skin and fat, skewer it down with fine skewers, and cover it with paper. Don't take the paper off till the meat is in the dish. Take a gill of red wine, two shalots shred small; boil them, and pour into the dish, with the gravy which comes out of the meat; it eats well. Spit your meat before you take out the inside.

Mary Bolling Banister (taken from Hannah Glasse)

Serves 6 to 8

6 to 8 pound boneless sirloin
   tip roast
1 pound beef suet
4 cups freshly grated bread
   crumbs
Juice of 1 lemon
1 teaspoon salt
¼ teaspoon pepper
½ teaspoon nutmeg

1 teaspoon thyme
4 shallots, finely chopped
¾ cup red wine

Sauce:
2 finely chopped shallots
¼ cup red wine
Juices from meat

---

*Courtesy of the Virginia Historical Society

Hearth:

1. Trim fat from sirloin tip and put aside. Using a very sharp filet knife, cut a pocket in the side of the beef, reserving meat that is cut out. Grind reserved meat with beef suet.

2. Sauté meat mixture gently over warm coals until lightly browned, about 5 minutes. Drain thoroughly in a colander. Allow to cool to room temperature.

3. In a large bowl, combine bread crumbs with lemon juice, salt, pepper, nutmeg, thyme, and chopped shallots. Add browned beef mixture and ¼ cup of the wine. Mix thoroughly. Stuff mixture into beef pocket, packing tightly. Cover the pocket with thin strips of the reserved fat, skewering on with picks to seal forcemeat in pocket.

4. Skewer meat. Roast in front of fire, following general instructions for roasting meats on pages 118–121. While meat is roasting, baste occasionally with the additional ½ cup wine.

5. To make sauce: While meat is roasting, make sauce by combining chopped shallots with ¼ cup red wine in small saucepan. Set pan over warm coals and simmer briefly until shallots are tender. Set aside. When beef has finished cooking, pour off juices and combine with shallots and wine. Bring to a rapid boil over hot coals and let boil, stirring occasionally, until sauce is slightly reduced, 5 to 10 minutes. Correct seasoning and serve with beef.

Modern:

1. Follow hearth directions 1 through 4, putting meat on rack in roasting pan. Preheat oven to 450°. Using a meat thermometer, bake until meat is of desired doneness, basting occasionally with additional ½ cup red wine and juices from meat.

2. To make sauce, follow hearth direction 5. Simmer over low heat. Combine beef juices with shallots and wine. Bring to a boil over high heat and complete according to hearth directions.

Mary Randolph, 1762–1828, author of The Virginia House-Wife.

Tuckahoe, birthplace of Mary Randolph, in Goochland County, VA.

Mary Randolph's Forcemeat Balls

Take half a pound of veal, and half a pound of suet cut fine and beat in a marble mortar or wooden bowl; add a few sweet herbs shred fine, a little mace pounded fine, a small nutmeg grated, a little lemon peel, some pepper and salt, and the yelks of two eggs; mix them well together, and make them into balls and long pieces, then roll them in flour, and fry them brown. If they are for the use of white sauce, do not fry them, but put them in a sauce pan of hot water, and let them boil a few minutes.

Mary Randolph

Makes 12 to 20

½ pound ground veal
½ teaspoon thyme
¼ teaspoon chervil
¼ teaspoon pepper
¼ teaspoon mace
½ teaspoon freshly grated lemon peel
½ pound pork

½ teaspoon marjoram
1 tablespoon fresh minced parsley
½ teaspoon salt
¼ teaspoon nutmeg
1 egg
Flour
2 to 4 tablespoons lard for frying

Hearth:

1. Combine all ingredients except flour and lard, mixing by hand until well blended.
2. Shape into small balls and ovals, then dust with flour.
3. Heat 2 tablespoons lard in frying pan set over hot coals. Brown the balls well on both sides. Add more lard as needed.
4. Use as garnish for a variety of meat recipes.

Modern:

1. Follow hearth directions 1 through 4, frying forcemeat balls on moderate heat.

Note: This forcemeat mixture is used as the stuffing for Battersea Beef Olives (page 124).

Southall Family Cabbage Pudding with Forcemeat

[Recipe badly torn on left side.]
    . . . of lean meat. Beef, Mutton, ____ [veal?], chop it very fine with a pound [of] suet, a little Parsley, thime, and marjoram, half an onion, chop [all] small together put it to the ____ [meat?] take six eggs, leave out [the] whites put them to your meat ____ such grated bread as will [stif?] fen it, season it with pepper salt and mace according to your taste. mix [it] all together, then take a large Cabbage scoop out the inside and fill it with the force Meat. butter a cloth. tie up the Pudding and let it boil two hours. then take it up and tie it as tight as you can. let it boil two [ho]urs longer. Then serve it with melted Butter for Sauce.

Southall Family Collection

Serves 4 to 6

2 large cabbages	1 teaspoon salt
1½ pounds ground veal	¼ teaspoon pepper
1 cup finely chopped onion	½ teaspoon mace
1 cup diced whole-wheat bread	½ teaspoon cayenne pepper
1½ teaspoons thyme	3 eggs, lightly beaten
1½ teaspoons marjoram	Softened butter
2 tablespoons minced fresh parsley	Fresh parsley sprigs for garnish

Hearth:

1. Make pudding cloths by cutting two squares 18″ to 24″ out of muslin. (After using cloth, wash and dry, then put away to use with other boiled pudding recipes.)
2. Fill a large iron pot with water. Hang on crane and bring to a boil over flames.
3. Remove and discard outer core and tough outer leaves from cabbages. Rinse and then place cabbages in a large pot of rapidly boiling water. Boil 10 minutes, drain, and set aside to cool. Set another pot of water on crane to boil while proceeding with remainder of recipe.
4. Combine veal with onion, bread, seasonings, and eggs as for meatloaf.

5. When cabbages are cool, gently fold back about ⅓ of the outer leaves. With a sharp knife, carefully cut out most of the inner cabbage leaves, leaving the outer leaves attached to the base. Shape veal into two rounds and stuff in center of hollowed-out cabbages. Fold cabbage leaves still attached to core back over veal stuffing, covering it completely so that cabbage looks intact.

6. Wet pudding cloth thoroughly in very hot water, then coat with softened butter. Gather loosely around the stuffed cabbages. Tie securely with string, leaving 1″ to 2″ space for cabbage to expand.

7. When second pot of water reaches a rapid boil, carefully ease in cabbages. Keep at a steady boil for 1 hour, replenishing with additional boiling water if needed. Turn puddings occasionally to assure even cooking.

8. Pull crane out from fire and carefully lift wrapped cabbages out of pot. Drain thoroughly in colander.

9. Unwrap the pudding cloths and place cabbages on serving platter. Garnish liberally with parsley sprigs. Slice and serve at table.

Modern:
Follow hearth directions 1 through 8, boiling cabbages over high heat.

M. H. D. Tebbs' Savoury Patties

Lay puff paste in your tins, take one pound of veal of [sic] one of lean ham—a quarter of a pound of beef Suet—chop it together as small as possible Season it well with Pepper—Salt—& Nutmeg.—put it into a pan with half a pint of veal gravy and two Spoonfuls of thick cream—a little flour and butter. Shake it over the fire two minutes—fill your Patties put paste lids on them & bake them a nice brown in your oven.—

M. H. D. Tebbs (taken from Hannah Glasse)

Serves 6–8

1 pound ground veal
1 pound ground smoked, lean
    ham
¼ pound ground beef
½ teaspoon pepper
½ teaspoon nutmeg
1 tablespoon butter

2 tablespoons flour
1 cup chicken broth
½ cup cream
Salt, if desired
Common Pie Crust, or Lard
    Paste (pages 246–247)

Hearth:
1. Combine veal, ham, and beef, mixing together thoroughly. Season with pepper and nutmeg. Brown in skillet set on hot coals until meat is cooked through, stirring and breaking the meat apart so that it cooks completely. Blend in butter and flour.
2. Stir in broth and bring mixture to a simmer. Stir constantly until mixture has thickened. Blend in cream. Taste and add salt if necessary. Set mixture aside to cool to room temperature.
3. Prepare pie crust. Grease patty pans and line with crust.
4. Fill each shell with cooled meat mixture. Cover with top crust, tucking into sides of pans. Poke a small hole in the center of each top crust.
5. Put a trivet on rack in bottom of warmed Dutch oven. Carefully set filled patty pans on trivet. Cover oven and set on embers. Bake, following general directions on pages 216–217, until top crusts are a light brown, 25 to 30 minutes.

Modern:

1. Follow hearth direction 1, browning meat mixture in frying pan over moderately high heat.
2. Follow hearth direction 2, reducing heat to moderate.
3. Follow hearth direction 3. Preheat oven to 350°. Bake patties on cookie sheets for 30 to 35 minutes or until top crusts are light brown.

Mrs. Randolph's Veal Cutlets from the Fillet or Leg

Cut off the flank and take the bone out, then take slices the size of the fillet and half an inch thick, beat two yelks of eggs light, and have some grated bread mixed with pepper, salt, pounded nutmeg and chopped parsley; beat the slices a little, lay them on a board and wash the upper side with the egg, cover it thick with the bread crumbs, press them on with a knife, and let them stand to dry a little, that they may not fall off in frying, then turn them gently, put egg and crumbs on in the same manner, put them into a pan of boiling lard, and fry them a light brown; have some good gravy ready, season it with a teaspoonful of curry powder, a large one of wine, and one of lemon pickle, thicken it with butter and brown flour, drain every drop of lard from the cutlets, lay them in the gravy, and stew them fifteen or twenty minutes; serve them up garnished with lemon cut in thin slices.

Mary Randolph

Serves 4

¾ to 1 cup finely grated fresh
    bread crumbs
¼ teaspoon pepper
½ teaspoon salt
¼ teaspoon nutmeg
2 tablespoons parsley
2 pounds boneless veal, cut in
    thin slices
2 eggs, lightly beaten
2 tablespoons lard

1 ½ cups chicken stock
1 teaspoon curry powder
¼ cup white wine
1 tablespoon fresh lemon juice
2 tablespoons softened butter
1 tablespoons brown flour
    (page 319)
Thinly sliced lemon

Hearth:

1. Combine bread crumbs, pepper, salt, nutmeg, and parsley in a bowl.
2. Dip veal slices first into egg and then into crumb mixture, coating well on each side. Let veal stand for about 10 minutes.
3. Melt lard in frying pan set on trivet over hot coals.
4. Lightly brown veal slices, turning once. Remove from pan and keep warm. Pour off lard.
5. In same pan, bring stock to a boil. Add curry powder, wine, and lemon juice. Simmer briefly.
6. Combine butter and brown flour. Blend into gravy and stir until mixture thickens.
7. Return veal slices to gravy. Cover and let simmer 15 to 20 minutes. Correct seasoning.
8. Pour into serving platter. Garnish with thinly sliced lemon.

Modern:

1. Follow hearth directions 1 through 3.
2. Heat 2 tablespoons oil in skillet over moderately high heat and lightly brown veal slices, turning once. Remove from pan and keep warm.
3. Follow hearth directions 5 through 8 to complete recipe.

Mr. Blackford's Pork Cutlets

Cut them from the leg and remove the skin; trim and beat them and sprinkle them with pepper and salt. Prepare some beaten egg in a pan and on a flat dish a mixture of bread crumbs, minced onion & sage—Put some lard or drippings into a frying pan over the fire and when it boils put in the cutlets—having dipped every one, first in the egg and then in the seasoning. Fry them 20 or 30 minutes turning them often After you have taken them out of the frying pan, skim the gravy sprinkle on a little flour, give it one boil, and then pour it in the dish round the cutlets.

Eat them with apple sauce.

Blackford Family Cookbook

Serves 4

4 boneless pork cutlets, about ½ pound each
Salt and pepper
2 eggs beaten to a light froth
1 cup freshly grated bread crumbs
1 tablespoon freshly minced onion

½ teaspoon sage
2 to 4 tablespoons lard
1 to 2 tablespoons flour
Parsley for garnish

Hearth:

1. Lightly salt and pepper cutlets. Dip each one into beaten egg, turning to coat well on both sides.
2. Combine bread crumbs, onion, and sage in a shallow bowl. Dip in each egg-coated cutlet, turning to cover with crumb mixture. Set aside, covered, until ready to fry.
3. Melt lard in frying pan set over hot coals. Brown cutlets on both sides, then cover pan and fry them 20 to 30 minutes until cooked through, turning often. Add more lard as needed.
4. Remove cutlets to serving platter and keep warm. Scrape and stir juices remaining in pan. Sprinkle in flour and cook until mixture is thickened. Pour over cutlets, garnish with parsley, and serve hot.
5. Accompany with applesauce (recipe on page 292).

Modern:

1. Follow hearth directions 1 through 3, browning cutlets over moderately high heat.
2. Cover pan and cook cutlets thoroughly, turning often, about 20 to 30 minutes.
3. Complete by following hearth directions 4 and 5.

To Roast Pork

The roasting pieces are the loin, the leg, the saddle, the fillet, the shoulder and the spare-rib, (which last is found between the shoulder or fore-leg,) and the griskin or back-bone. All roast pork should be well seasoned; rubbed with pepper, salt, or powdered sage or marjoram. Score the skin with a sharp knife, making deep lines at regular distances, about an inch apart. Cross these lines with others, so as to form squares or diamonds. Make a stuffing of minced sage or marjoram leaves; breadcrumbs; if liked, a very little minced onion previously boiled; and some powdered mace. Introduce this stuffing profusely wherever it can be inserted, loosening a piece of the skin, and fastening it down again with a small skewer. In a leg or shoulder you can put in a great deal at the knuckle. In a fillet or large end of the leg, stuff the place from whence you have taken the bone. Put the pork down to roast not very close to the fire, but place it nearer when the skin begins to brown. You can soon baste it with its own gravy; and see that it is thoroughly cooked, before removing it from the spit. After taking up the meat, skim the fat from the gravy, and stir in a little flour to thicken it.

The crackling or skin will be much more crisp and tender if you go all over it with sweet oil, or lard, before you put it to the fire.

Always accompany roast pork with apple sauce, served in a deep dish or a sauce-tureen.

Cold roast pork is very good sliced at tea or breakfast.

Eliza Leslie

Serves 6 to 8

6 to 8 pounds pork loin roast
Salt and pepper
Sage or marjoram
1 cup chopped onion
2 cups freshly grated bread
  crumbs
¼ cup minced fresh parsley
½ teaspoon salt

¼ teaspoon pepper
½ teaspoon sage
½ teaspoon marjoram
1 egg, slightly beaten
2 to 3 tablespoons melted
  butter
Melted lard for basting
Mrs. Randolph's Applesauce
  (page 292)

Hearth:

1. Clean pork roast. Season lightly with salt and pepper as well as sage or marjoram. Score surface of roast.

2. Combine onion, bread crumbs, parsley, salt, pepper, sage, and marjoram in a large bowl. Add egg and enough butter to bind the stuffing.

3. Make incisions or small pockets along fat line of roast and stuff lightly. Secure stuffing with small skewers. Brush surface of meat with melted lard.

4. Spit pork and roast, following directions on pages 118–120, until juices run clear, 3 to 4 hours. Baste occasionally with melted lard.

5. Accompany with Mrs. Randolph's Applesauce.

Modern:

1. Follow hearth directions 1 through 3.

2. Preheat oven to 500°. Put prepared pork on rack in roasting pan, fat side up. Place in oven and immediately reduce heat to 350°. Bake, until done, allowing 30–40 minutes per pound. Baste occasionally. Juices will run clear when roast is cooked. To assure thorough cooking, a meat thermometer is suggested.

3. Serve with Mrs. Randolph's Applesauce.

William A. Jones's Recipe for Curing Hams

Cut them out and let them remain over night in a cool place. The next morning rub each piece with a mixture made with

1 teaspoonful of salt petre
1 teaspoonful of red pepper
2 teaspoonsful of black pepper

mix in good black molasses—Rub in well on flesh side then salt well or leave in a box for six weeks, then hang up and smoke well. If the ham is large let the teaspoonful be heaping with salt-petre—if small use less in proportion.

Ward Family Collection

Methods for Preparing Virginia Ham*

COOKING INSTRUCTIONS FOR GENUINE

SMITHFIELD HAM

Soak overnight in cold water before cooking. Wash ham, put in a boiler, skin down, add cold water to cover, let come to boiling point, then simmer, allowing 20 to 25 minutes per pound from time ham begins to simmer. Add hot water as needed to keep ham covered. When done, take ham from boiler and remove skins while warm, dot the back of ham with cloves and sprinkle with brown sugar and cracker crumbs and bake in oven till brown. An alternative method, not requiring a large boiler, follows.

BOILING METHOD

Wash thoroughly and soak ham 12 hours or longer as desired. Wrap in heavy aluminum foil, joining the edges and forming a vessel with the bottom layer. Add 5 cups of water within the foil and place in oven with a tray or shallow pan underneath. Heat oven to 400° and cook for 20 minutes. (Start timing when oven reaches 400°.) Turn off oven for 3

*Courtesy of Smithfield Packing Company, Incorporated.

hours. Reheat to 400° and cook for 20 minutes. Turn off oven and let ham remain for 6 to 8 hours or longer (overnight is satisfactory).

Important: *Do not open oven door until the cook cycle is complete. This includes the last 6 to 8 hours.*

Traditional Fried Ham with Country Gravy*

Serves 4 to 6

8 to 12 ounces cooked Virginia ham (page 142), cut into 2-ounce portions
Pan drippings, plus 1 to 2 tablespoons lard or fresh pork fat if needed

1 tablespoon brown flour (page 319)
¾ to 1 cup water

Hearth:
1. Fry ham slices in frying pan over hot coals. Remove to a serving platter and keep warm by fire.
2. Return frying pan to hot coals. Scrape up browned particles and drippings still in pan, adding lard or rendering pork fat if needed to make about 2 to 4 tablespoons pan drippings.
3. Sprinkle on brown flour, stirring constantly to blend into drippings. Cook and stir briefly.
4. Gradually add water to desired consistency. Stir just until it boils, then remove from heat and pour into sauce boat as accompaniment to fried ham. Serve hot.

Modern:
1. Follow hearth direction 1, frying ham over moderately low heat. Keep ham warm while preparing country gravy.
2. Complete, following hearth directions 2 through 4.

---

*No early recipe given. This is the traditional method for preparing Southern fried ham gravy.

Baked Madeira Ham

This is a dish only seen at dinner parties. No one can believe, for a moment, that hams really cooked in Madeira wine are served up every week at hotels, particularly at those houses where there is no other superfluity, and where most of the great dishes exist only in the bill of fare. A genuine Madeira ham is cooked as follows:—Take a ham of the very finest sort; should be a Westphalia one. Lay it in hot water, and soak it all day and all night, changing the water several times, and every time washing out the pan. Early in the morning of the second day, put the ham into a large pot of cold water, and boil it slowly during four hours, skimming it well. Then take it out, remove the skin entirely, and put the ham into a clean boiler, with sufficient Madeira wine to cover it well. Boil, or rather stew it, an hour longer, keeping the pot covered except when you remove the lid to turn the ham. When well stewed take it up, drain it, and strain the liquor into a porcelain-lined saucepan. Have ready a sufficiency of powdered white sugar. Cover the ham all over with a thick coating of the sugar, and set it into a hot oven to bake for an hour.

Mix some orange or lemon-juice with the liquor adding plenty of sugar and nutmeg. Give it one boil up over the fire, and serve it up in a tureen, as sauce to the ham.

What is left of the ham may be cut next day into small pieces, put into a stew-pan, with the remains of the liquor or sauce poured over it, and stewed for a quarter of an hour or more. Serve it up all together in the same dish. While it is on the fire, add a little butter to the stew.

Eliza Leslie

Serves 6 to 8

6 pounds picnic shoulder ham	½ cup orange juice
3½ cups Madeira wine	½ teaspoon freshly grated
½ cup granulated sugar	nutmeg
	1 tablespoon lemon juice

Hearth:

1. Put ham in iron pot and cover with cold water. Cover and place pot on crane. Bring to boil over fire. Adjust height of pot on crane to allow ham to simmer gently for an hour.

2. Drain ham, discarding liquid. Let ham cool until it can be handled easily. Remove skin, leaving a thin layer of fat.

3. Rinse pot and replace ham in pot. Pour in Madeira wine. Cover pot and place on crane. Bring just to boiling point, then adjust height of pot on crane. Simmer ham about 45 minutes, turning occasionally.

4. Remove pot from crane. Drain ham, reserving wine. Reserving 1 tablespoon of the sugar, cover ham with remainder and put in warmed Dutch oven. Cover and place oven over hot coals.

5. Measure wine. You should have 3 cups remaining. Add ¼ cup orange juice and ¼ teaspoon nutmeg to 1 cup of the wine. Use this mixture to baste ham every 15 minutes. Bake ham 1 hour, covered, replenishing coals as needed.

6. While ham is baking, reduce remaining wine to 1½ cups by boiling rapidly in a pan set over very hot coals. Remove from fire and stir in remaining sugar, orange juice, nutmeg, and the lemon juice. Keep this sauce warm by fire.

7. When ready to serve ham, carefully remove from Dutch oven. Place on platter.

8. Heat sauce just to boiling. Pour into sauce boat and serve with ham.

Modern:

1. Follow hearth directions 1 through 3, bringing ham to a boil over high heat, then covering and reducing heat to simmer ham gently 1 hour. Drain, cover ham with wine, and continue simmering, covered, 45 minutes.

2. Remove from heat. Preheat oven to 350°. Bake ham 1 hour, following hearth directions 4 through 7.

Mr. Blackford's Glazed Ham

With a brush or quill feather go over the whole ham with the beaten yolk of egg. Then cover it thickly with finely powdered cracker made as fine as flour or grated cold bread. Lastly go over it with a thick cream. Brown it on a spit or in a stove-oven. The glazing will be found delicious. (warranted good)

Blackford Family Cookbook

8 to 10 pound baked Virginia ham
2 to 3 egg yolks, or as needed

2 cups freshly grated bread crumbs, or as needed
1 cup cream, or as needed

Hearth:
1. Prepare ham following recipe on page 142.
2. When ham has cooled to room temperature, brush egg yolk over entire upper surface.
3. By hand, press on a thick covering of bread crumbs.
4. Beat cream until it holds a soft shape. Cover bread crumbs with cream.
5. Carefully put ham on trivet in preheated Dutch oven. Cover and set on hot coals. Cover top with hot coals and brown ham, checking every 5 to 10 minutes, until glaze is a golden brown.
6. Serve warm or cold.

Modern:
1. Follow hearth directions 1 through 4.
2. Preheat oven to 450°. Brown prepared ham in baking pan 10 to 20 minutes.
3. Serve warm or cold.

Prosser Tabb's Sausage

6 lbs lean } *cut in cu[bes]*
3½" fat

3 table spoons ground [sage]
6 teaspoons salt
6   "   "   black pepper
¼   "   ·   "   red   "
Mix lean & fat meat together & sp[oon] the sage etc. over. grind twice

Uncle Prosser Tabb

Makes 30 to 40 sausage patties

6 pounds pork butt
1½ pounds fresh pork fat
3 tablespoons sage (or more to
   taste)

6 teaspoons salt (or more to
   taste)
6 teaspoons pepper
¼ teaspoon red pepper

Hearth:
1. Cube pork and pork fat.
2. Add seasonings and mix together well.
3. Grind sausage ingredients together once.
4. Make a small patty and fry over coals. Cool and taste for seasoning. Add more, if necessary; sage should predominate.
5. Form into patties and fry as needed over hot coals.

Modern:
1. Follow hearth directions 1 through 4, frying patties over moderate heat.
2. Patties can be shaped and wrapped, then frozen for later use.

Mary Randolph's Fried Lamb

Separate the leg from the loin, cut off the shank and boil the leg; divide the loin in chops, dredge and fry them a nice brown, lay the leg in the middle of the dish and put the chops around, pour over parsley and butter, and garnish with fried parsley.

The leg cut into steaks and the loin into chops will make a fine fricassee, or cutlets.

Mary Randolph

Serves 4

2 to 4 tablespoons lard
8 lamb chops, ½″ to 2″ thick

Melted butter sauce with
  minced parsley (page 290)
Fried parsley for garnish (page
  318)

Hearth:

1. Melt 2 tablespoons lard in frying pan set over hot coals. Add chops and brown on both sides, adding more lard if needed. Cook chops to desired "doneness," drain, and put on serving platter.
2. Have ready some melted butter sauce and fried parsley. Pour sauce over chops, garnish with fried parsley, and serve.

Modern:

Follow hearth directions, frying chops over moderate heat until done.

Mary Randolph's Croquets

Take cold fowl or fresh meat of any kind, with slices of ham, fat and lean, chop them together very fine, add half as much stale bread grated, salt, pepper, grated nutmeg, a teaspoonful of made mustard, a table spoonful of catsup, and a lump of butter; knead all well together till it resembles sausage meat, make them in cakes, dip in the yelk of an egg beaten, cover them thickly with grated bread, and fry them a light brown.

Mary Randolph

Serves 6 to 8

1½ cups ground raw chicken breast
1½ cups ground country ham
¾ cup freshly grated whole-wheat bread crumbs
¼ teaspoon freshly grated nutmeg
½ teaspoon pepper
½ teaspoon thyme
¼ teaspoon mace

1 rounded teaspoon prepared mustard (page 316)
1 tablespoon mushroom catchup (page 313)
½ cup combined milk and cream (or half-and-half)
3 eggs
Flour as needed
Additional bread crumbs as needed
Lard for frying

Hearth:

1. Thoroughly combine chicken, ham, bread crumbs, nutmeg, pepper, thyme, mace, mustard, mushroom catchup, milk and cream with 1 egg. Shape into croquettes or patties. Brush lightly with flour.
2. Beat remaining 2 eggs until well blended. Dip each croquette into egg and then into bread crumbs, covering well.
3. Melt lard in frying pan set on trivet over hot coals. Fry croquettes until golden brown.
4. Serve with Mrs. Tebbs' Celery Sauce (recipe on page 293) or Mary Randolph's Mushroom Sauce (page 297).

Modern:

Follow hearth directions 1 through 4, frying croquettes over moderately high heat.

Martha Washington's To Make A Frykecy

Take 2 Chicken, or a hare, kill & flaw* them hot. take out theyr intrills & wipe them within, cut them in pieces & break theyr bones with A pestle. Y^{n}* put halfe a pound of butter into y^{e}* frying pan, & fry it till it be browne, y^{n} put in ye Chiken & give it a walme* or two. Y^{n} put in halfe a pinte of faire water well seasoned with pepper, & salt, & a little after put in a handfull of parsley, & time, & an ounion shread all smal. fry all these together till they be enough, & when it is ready to be dished up, put into ye pan ye youlks of 5 or 6 eggs, well beaten & mixed wth A little wine vinegar or juice of leamons. stir thes well together least it Curdle, y^{n} dish it up without any more frying.

Martha Washington

Though Martha Washington's receipt is used here as an early example of chicken fricassee, the one given below has been adapted for modern use from a combination of Colonial recipes.

Serves 6 to 8

½ cup unsalted butter
1 to 2 tablespoons lard
8 large chicken breast halves, or a combination of breasts and thighs
4 to 5 cups chicken stock, or as needed
1 large onion, chopped
1 teaspoon salt
¼ teaspoon pepper

1 teaspoon thyme
1 teaspoon marjoram
1 teaspoon rosemary
¼ teaspoon ground cloves
3 egg yolks, slightly beaten
¼ cup fresh parsley, minced
1 tablespoon lemon juice

---

* Flaw meant to skin.

* In 18th-century script "y" was usually (but not always) equal to modern-day "th." Thus "y^{n}" for "then," y^{e} for "the."

* Walme was to bubble or boil.

Hearth:

1. In a large spider or Dutch oven over hot coals, melt butter and lard. Add chicken and sauté until golden brown. Barely cover with stock; add onion and seasoning.
2. Cover pan and bring stock to simmer. Maintain heat by replenishing coals until chicken is tender, about 45 minutes. Remove chicken to heated platter and place near edge of fire to keep warm.
3. Measure stock; there should be 3 to 3½ cups (see note at end of recipe). Gradually add ½ cup hot stock to egg yolks, stirring constantly to prevent eggs from curdling. Return mixture to rest of stock and toss in parsley. Correct seasoning and allow sauce to simmer briefly, stirring all the while. Blend in lemon juice. Pour sauce over chicken and serve.

Modern:

1. One tablespoon cooking oil may replace lard if desired.
2. Brown chicken over medium high heat and, after adding stock, bring it to a boil, reduce heat, cover pan, and allow to simmer until chicken is fork tender, about 30 to 40 minutes.
3. Recipe can be prepared ahead of time up to this point. When ready to serve, reheat slowly, until sauce bubbles and chicken is heated through. Proceed, following hearth direction 3.

Note: If you end up with only 2 cups of broth, use only 2 yolks. The rule of thumb here is 1 yolk per 1 cup liquid. The liaison of egg yolks, seasoned broth, and lemon juice results in a delicious, elegant sauce.

Mary Randolph's Fried Chickens

Cut them up as for the fricassee, dredge them well with flour, sprinkle them with salt, put them into a good quantity of boiling lard, and fry them a light brown, fry small pieces of mush and a quantity of parsley nicely picked to be served in the dish with the chickens, take half a pint of rich milk, add to it a small bit of butter with pepper, salt, and chopped parsley, stew it a little, and pour it over the chickens, and then garnish with the fried parsley.

Mary Randolph

Serves 4 to 6

3- to 3½-pound frying chicken
Salt
Pepper
Flour
Lard for frying
Sauce:
1 cup milk
1 tablespoon softened butter

½ teaspoon salt
⅛ teaspoon pepper
1 tablespoon fresh minced
  parsley

Garnish:
Fried parsley (page 318)

Hearth:

1. Cut chicken into serving pieces. Sprinkle all over with salt and pepper.
2. Dip chicken pieces in flour, covering on all sides.
3. Heat lard in frying pan over hot coals. Fry chicken in hot lard until lightly browned on both sides. Cover and cook chicken until tender and juices run clear from chicken when pierced with a fork. Be certain to observe all safety precautions while frying.
4. Remove cooked chicken, drain well, and keep warm by fire while preparing sauce.
5. To prepare sauce: Pour off all but 1 tablespoon of lard. Set frying pan back over hot coals. Stir in milk, butter, salt, pepper, and minced parsley. Simmer and stir about 5 minutes until sauce is slightly reduced.
6. Place chicken on serving platter. Pour half of sauce over chicken and garnish with fried parsley. Pour remaining sauce in sauce boat to pass at table.

Modern:
1. Follow hearth directions 1 and 2.
2. Oil may be used in place of lard. Heat oil or lard to moderate temperature and fry chicken on both sides until lightly browned. Cover chicken and cook over moderately low heat until juices from chicken run clear when pierced with a fork. Remove chicken from oil, drain on paper towels, and keep warm while preparing sauce.
3. To prepare sauce: Follow hearth direction 5. Oil may be used in place of lard. Prepare sauce over moderate heat.
4. Complete, following hearth direction 6.

Early Virginia Chicken Pye

Put y *paste in the dish (in the winter make it with full weight of Butter, and in the summer with as much Butter as the flour will take in) Lay in two large or three small Chickens cut up strew between the Layers and at Top a double handful of bits of lean Bacon boiled or raw (if boiled y* pie will require less salt—Lay at Top several large lumps of Butter about ¼ pound strew over a heaped Table spoonful of salt and an even one of fine pepper black, Fill last of all with cold water—Put into a dutch oven first laying in the bottom a little warm ashes and let it bake gradually with the top of very moderate heat and put coals under from time to time when nearly done increase the fire on the top to brown the paste—It will take near two hours baking.*

The Tucker Family Cookbook

Serves 6 to 8

2 pounds chicken, cut up	1¼ teaspoons salt
3½ cups chicken broth	¼ teaspoon pepper
½ cup chopped onion	6 tablespoons softened butter
2 carrots, scraped, trimmed, and quartered	6 tablespoons flour
2 whole cloves	½ teaspoon nutmeg
1 bay leaf	2 egg yolks, slightly beaten
½ teaspoon thyme	¾ cup cream
3 thin slices lemon	2 tablespoons capers
	½ recipe Pie Crust (page 246)

Hearth:

1. Cover chicken with water in iron pot. Set pot on crane, cover, and bring to a boil over flames. Adjust height of pot on crane and simmer chicken until very tender, 45 to 60 minutes. Remove from heat and carefully strain chicken in a collander, reserving broth. Set chicken aside to cool, then bone.

2. In a pot combine broth with onion, carrots, cloves, bay leaf, thyme, lemon slices, salt, and pepper. Bring to a boil over hot coals and cook, covered, until vegetables are barely tender, about 20 minutes. Strain and reserve broth.

3. Pick out and discard cloves, bay leaf, and lemon slices. Reserve remainder of vegetable mixture.

4. In a separate pan set over hot coals, melt butter. Blend in flour and cook, stirring constantly, about 5 minutes. Gradually add reserved broth and nutmeg, stirring until mixture thickens.

5. Combine egg yolks with cream. Gradually add about ½ cup of the hot sauce, stirring constantly. Return mixture to rest of sauce, continuing to stir.

6. Correct seasoning. Add capers, reserved chicken, and reserved vegetable mixture. Heat until mixture bubbles.

7. Pour into buttered heatproof dish and top with pie crust. Cut slit in top of crust.

8. Carefully place filled dish in preheated Dutch oven. Cover and bake over hot coals, following directions on pages 216–217, until crust is golden brown, about 25 to 30 minutes. Remove from heat and serve immediately.

Modern:

1. Follow hearth direction 1. Boil chicken in water over moderate heat until tender, 45 to 60 minutes.

2. Follow hearth directions 2 and 3.

3. Melt butter in saucepan over moderately low heat. Follow hearth directions 4 through 7.

4. Preheat oven to 425°. Bake chicken pie until crust is a golden brown. Serve immediately.

Mrs. Glasse's Chicken Hash

To hash a Fowl. Cut it up as for eating, put it in a tossing pan, with half a pint of gravy, a tea-spoonful of lemon-pickle, a little mushroom cat-chup, a slice of lemon, thicken it with flour and butter; just before you dish it up, put in a spoonful of good cream; lay sippets round your dish, and serve it up.

Hannah Glasse

Serves 4 to 6

2 to 3 cups cooked leftover cubed chicken or turkey
1 cup chicken stock
1 to 2 tablespoons mushroom catchup (page 313)
1 teaspoon lemon catchup (page 312)
1 teaspoon lemon juice (or more to taste)

3 tablespoons softened butter
3 tablespoons flour
1½ cups cream
Salt, if needed

Hearth:
1. Combine chicken, stock, catchups, and lemon juice in frying pan. Set pan over hot coals and simmer mixture 5 to 10 minutes until well blended, stirring occasionally.
2. Combine butter and flour and stir into chicken mixture. Cook and stir until butter melts and mixture thickens.
3. Blend in cream, stir, and cook until mixture is bubbling hot. Taste and add salt if needed.
4. Serve over hot biscuits (page 64) or cornbread squares (page 65).

Modern:
1. Follow hearth directions 1 through 4, simmering chicken mixture over moderate low heat.

Fried Fish

To fry trout. Having cleaned the fish, and cut off the fins, dredge them with flour. Have ready some beaten yolk of egg, and in a separate dish some grated bread crumbs. Dip each fish into the egg, and then strew them with bread crumbs. Put some butter or fresh beef-dripping into a frying-pan, and hold it over the fire till it is boiling hot; then, (having skimmed it,) put in the fish and fry them.

Prepare some melted butter with a spoonful of mushroom-catchup and a spoonful of lemon-pickle stirred into it. Send it to table in a sauce-boat to eat with the fish.

You may fry carp and flounders in the same manner.

Eliza Leslie

Serves 4 to 6

2 to 3 pounds flounder or freshwater trout
Salt
1 to 2 egg yolks, slightly beaten
Freshly grated bread crumbs as needed

Butter and lard for frying
Mrs. Randolph's Melted Butter Sauce (page 290)
1 tablespoon mushroom catchup (page 313)
1 tablespoon lemon pickle (page 312)

Hearth:

1. Scale, clean, and if desired, filet fish. Salt lightly.
2. Dip fish first into egg yolk and then into bread crumbs, coating well on each side.
3. In a frying pan set over hot coals, melt butter and lard (3 parts butter to 1 part lard) until sizzling hot.
4. Carefully add fish (use a spatula or sieve) and fry until done, 3 to 5 minutes on each side. Remove from fire and drain. Put fish on serving platter and keep warm while making sauce.
5. Prepare butter sauce & add mushroom catchup and lemon pickle. Stir well, pour into sauce boat, and send to table as accompaniment to fried fish.

Modern:

Follow hearth directions 1 through 5, frying fish over moderately low heat.

Yorktown Baked Sheep's-head

When ready for cooking, salt and pepper well, gash the sides in three or four places. Cut four onions very fine, to which add one pint bread crumbs, fat meat minced very fine, as it suits better than lard, cayenne pepper, thyme, a little salt, and the yolks of two eggs, all mashed together, with which stuff the fish inside and gashes on the outside. Then sprinkle over the flour and black pepper; put into a large pan with one quart cold water. Bake two hours, slowly. Serve with or without sauce, according to taste.—

Marion Cabell Tyree

Serves 4

2½ pounds firm white fish, such as porgies or croakers*
Salt and pepper
¾ cup minced onion
3 cups freshly grated bread crumbs
⅛ teaspoon cayenne pepper
1 teaspoon thyme
¼ teaspoon salt
1 egg, slightly beaten
2 tablespoons melted butter
Flour
½ cup water
½ cup white wine

Hearth:
1. Clean and scale fish. Remove gills but leave fish whole. Make 3 or 4 gashes on upper side of fish. Sprinkle lightly, inside and out, with salt and pepper. Set aside.
2. Combine onion, bread crumbs, seasonings, egg, and butter. Mix well, then lightly stuff mixture into fish cavity and gashes. Sprinkle on flour.
3. Carefully put fish in greased, preheated Dutch oven. Combine water and wine and pour over fish.
4. Set oven over hot embers. Cover and bake for 20 to 25 minutes, following general directions on page 121, or until fish flakes easily with a fork. Baste fish occasionally with wine-and-water mixture while it is baking.
5. Remove oven from coals. Ease fish onto serving platter and garnish as desired.

---

*Since Sheepshead fish is no longer found in Virginia waters, substitute another firm, white fish as suggested.

6. Sauce to accompany fish may be made by rapidly boiling down liquid remaining in Dutch oven for about 5 minutes. Season to taste, pour into sauce boat, and serve.

Modern:
1. Preheat oven to 400°. Follow hearth directions 1 through 5, baking fish in greased 9″ × 13″ pan. Remove baked fish from pan and keep warm while making sauce.
2. Strain liquid from pan into saucepan. Cook at a rapid boil for about 5 minutes, or until sauce is slightly reduced. Season to taste. Pour into sauce boat and serve as accompaniment to baked fish.

Miss Leslie's Stewed Fish

Take any nice fresh fish of moderate size, and when it is drawn and washed, cut it into three or four pieces, and put them into a stew-pan with amply sufficient hot water to keep them from burning. Season them with a little salt and cayenne. After it has simmered steadily for half an hour, and been skimmed, have ready a quarter of a pound of fresh butter, mixed into a smooth paste with a heaped table-spoonful of flour. Add this to the stew, with a bunch of sweet marjoram chopped fine, and a sprig of chopped parsley. If approved, add a small onion pared and sliced very thin. Cover it closely, and let it stew another half hour. Then sent it to table. This is a family dish. Any fresh fish may be stewed thus.

Eliza Leslie

Serves 4 to 6

3 to 4 pounds firm white fish, scaled and cleaned	2 tablespoons minced fresh onion
¾ cup water	2 tablespoons softened butter
¾ cup white wine	1 tablespoon flour
½ teaspoon salt (or more as needed)	1 teaspoon marjoram
⅛ teaspoon cayenne pepper	1 tablespoon fresh minced parsley

Hearth:

1. Cut fish into chunks. Put into saucepan.
2. Combine water, wine, salt, cayenne pepper, and onion. Pour over fish. Cover and set over hot coals. Simmer 15 minutes.
3. Combine butter and flour. Blend into fish mixture along with herbs. Cover and simmer mixture until fish flakes easily with a fork, 10 to 15 minutes. Serve hot.

Modern:

Follow hearth directions 1 through 3, cooking fish over moderately low heat.

Rappahannock River Roasted Oysters

The old-fashioned way of roasting oysters is to lay them on a hot hearth, and cover them in hot cinders or ashes, (taking them out with tongs when done,) or to put them into a moderate fire. When done, their shells will begin to open. The usual way now is to broil them on large gridirons of strong wire. Serve them up in their shells on large dishes, or on trays, at oyster suppers. At every plate lay an oyster knife and a clean coarse towel, and between every two chairs set a bucket to receive the empty shells. The gentlemen generally save the ladies the trouble of opening the oysters, by performing that office for them.

Have on the table, to eat with the oysters, bread-rolls, biscuits, butter, and glasses with sticks of celery scraped, and divested of the green leaves at the top. Have also ale or porter.

Eliza Leslie

Serves 6 to 8

Roasting unshelled oysters on the open hearth is a simple procedure, another way to explore the pleasures of fireplace cooking. For 6 to 8 people, provide:
½ bushel unshelled oysters
Plenty of melted butter, seasoned with mushroom ketchup (page 313) if desired.

Hearth:
1. Scrub oysters thoroughly under clear water.
2. Lay oysters close to but not in fire and cover them with hot ashes.
3. When oysters are done their shells will begin to open.
4. Using fireplace tongs, carefully pull the oysters from the ashes. Open and serve immediately with melted butter.
5. If preferred, oysters may be broiled on a gridiron set over hot coals.

Mary Bolling Banister's Ragoo of Oysters*

Open twenty large oysters, take them out of their liquor, save the liquor, and dip the oysters in a batter made thus: take two eggs, beat them well, a little lemon-peel grated, a little nutmeg grated, a blade of mace pounded fine, a little parsley chopped fine; beat all together with a little flour, have ready some butter or dripping in a stew-pan; when it boils, dip in your oysters, one by one, into the batter and fry them of a fine brown, then with an egg-slice take them out, and lay them in a dish before the fire. Pour the fat out of the pan, and shake a little flour over the bottom of the pan, then rub a little piece of butter as big as a small walnut, all over with your knife, whilst it is over the fire; then pour in three spoonfulls of the oyster liquor strained, one spoonful of white wine, a gill of gravy; grate a little nutmeg, stir all together, throw in the oysters, give the pan a toss round, and when the sauce is of a good thickness, pour all into the dish and garnish with raspings.

Mary Bolling Banister (taken from Hannah Glasse)

Serves 4 to 6

1 pint fresh oysters with liquor

Batter:
2 eggs, lightly beaten
1 tablespoon freshly grated
   lemon peel
¼ teaspoon nutmeg
¼ teaspoon mace
1 tablespoon fresh, minced
   parsley
½ teaspoon salt
⅛ teaspoon pepper
¼ cup flour
4 to 6 tablespoons lard for
   frying

Sauce
2 tablespoons flour
2 tablespoons butter
¼ to ½ cup oyster liquor
¼ cup white wine
½ cup chicken stock
¼ teaspoon nutmeg
Salt if needed

Garnish:
½ cup freshly grated, toasted
   bread crumbs

---

*Courtesy of the Virginia Historical Society

Hearth:
1. Put oysters in collander over a bowl to drain while preparing batter. Reserve oyster liquor.
2. Combine batter ingredients, blending together well.
3. Dip oysters into batter.
4. Heat 4 tablespoons lard in frying pan set over hot coals. Fry oysters until lightly browned on both sides. Add more lard if needed for frying. Drain and keep warm by the fire in serving dish.
5. To make sauce: Pour fat out of frying pan and return pan to hot coals. Stir in flour and let it cook briefly. Add butter and stir until melted. Add remaining sauce ingredients and stir constantly until it bubbles and thickens. Taste and add salt if needed.
6. Pour sauce over hot oysters, sprinkle with toasted bread crumbs, and serve immediately.

Modern:
Follow hearth directions 1 through 6, frying oysters over moderate heat.

To Feed Oysters

When it is necessary to keep oysters a day or two before they are cooked, they must be kept clean and fed, otherwise they will die and spoil. Put them into a large tub of clean water; wash from them the mud and sand, and scrub them with a birch broom. Then pour off that water, and give them a clean tubful, placing the oysters with the deep or large side downward, and sprinkling them well, with salt mixed with it, allowing about a pint of salt to every two gallons of water. But if you have a very large quantity of oysters, add to the salt and water several handfuls of indian meal. Repeat this every twelve hours, with fresh water and meal. Always at the time of high water, oysters may be seen to open their shells, as if in expectation of their accustomed food. If this is carefully continued, they will remain plump and healthy for two days.

Terrapins also, and other shell fish, should have the salt and water changed every twelve hours, and be fed with corn meal.

Turtle must also be well fed, and allowed salted water to swim in.

Eliza Leslie

To Roast a Goose

Chop a few sage leaves and two onions very fine, mix them with a good lump of butter, a teaspoonful of pepper and two of salt, put it in the goose, then spit it, lay it down, and dust it with flour; when it is thoroughly hot, baste it with nice lard; if it be a large one, it will require an hour and a half, before a good clear fire; when it is enough, dredge and baste it, pull out the spit, and pour in a little boiling water.

Mary Randolph

Serves 6 to 8

8- to 10-pound goose
2 teaspoons salt
2 large onions
2 cups tart apples (such as Granny Smith), peeled and chopped
1 hard-boiled egg, peeled and finely chopped
½ to ⅔ cup minced, fresh sage leaves
1 teaspoon pepper
1 tablespoon softened butter

Flour
Lard

Gravy
Pan juices from goose
Cooked giblets and broth
Salt and pepper
2 tablespoons softened butter
2 tablespoons flour

Hearth:

1. Remove neck and giblets from goose and set aside in saucepan. Cover with water and simmer, covered, until done. Remove from fire and cool. Discard neck and chop giblets. Set aside and keep warm by fire while goose is roasting.
2. Rinse goose thoroughly with clean water, pat dry, and rub outside and cavity of goose with salt.
3. Peel, quarter, and parboil onions for 5 minutes. Drain and set aside to cool. Finely chop onion and combine with apple, egg, sage, pepper, and butter. Mix well and stuff mixture into cavity of goose. Sew cavity together.

4. Carefully spit goose, dust all over with flour, and place in front of fire. After goose is hot and has begun to sizzle, baste with melted lard every half hour. Roast, following directions on pages 118–120. Roasting time will range from 1½ to 2½ hours depending on size of goose. Bird is done when legs move easily and juice from goose runs clear.
5. Dust again with flour, then baste with lard before removing spit. Keep warm near fire while preparing gravy.
6. To prepare gravy: Pour off juices from dripping pan and combine with cooked giblets. Add broth. Season with salt and pepper to taste. Set saucepan over hot coals and bring gravy to a simmer. Combine butter and flour & add to gravy. Stir until mixture bubbles and is slightly thickened. Cook briefly, pour into sauce boat, and serve with goose.
7. Accompany goose with applesauce (page 292).

Modern:
1. Follow hearth directions 1 through 3. Preheat oven to 450°. Put prepared goose in roasting pan, dust with flour, and roast 1½ to 2½ hours, depending on size of bird. Goose is done when legs move easily and juices run clear. Baste with melted lard every half hour, occasionally turning goose to assure even cooking.
2. Follow hearth direction 6, simmering gravy over moderately low heat.
3. Accompany with applesauce (page 292).

Blackford Family Fricaseed Rabbit

The best way of cooking rabbits is to fricasee them. Take a couple of fine ones, cut up and disjoint them. Put them into a stew pan. Season them with cayenne pepper, salt, chopped parsley and powdered mace. Pour in a pint of warm water, or veal broth if you have it, and stew it over a slow fire until the rabbits are quite tender; adding when they are about half done some butter in small lumps, rolled in flour. Just before you take it from the fire enrich the gravy with a gill or more of cream seasoned with nutmeg. Stir the gravy well but take care not to let it boil after the cream is put in lest it curdle.

Put the pieces of rabbit on a hot dish and pour the gravy over them.

Blackford Family Cookbook

Serves 4 to 6

2½ to 3 pounds rabbit, cut into serving pieces
¼ teaspoon cayenne pepper
1¼ teaspoons salt
2 tablespoons lard
4 tablespoons softened butter
Parsley

¼ teaspoon mace
2 cups veal or chicken broth
2 tablespoons softened butter
4 tablespoons flour
¼ cup cream
¼ teaspoon nutmeg

Hearth:
1. Lightly sprinkle rabbit with cayenne and salt.
2. Melt lard and butter in large frying pan set over hot coals. Carefully add rabbit and brown lightly on all sides. Remove from pan, pour off drippings, and rinse pan.
3. Return rabbit to pan. Sprinkle with parsley and mace, then pour on stock. Place over coals, cover, and bring to a simmer. Cook, turning rabbit occasionally and replenishing coals as necessary, until rabbit is fork tender, 45 to 50 minutes.

4. Combine butter and flour and stir into sauce. Cook 5 minutes, stirring often.

5. Combine cream and nutmeg. Stir into gravy and heat through, uncovered, about 5 minutes.

6. Sprinkle with additional chopped parsley before serving.

Modern:
Follow hearth directions 1 and 2, browning rabbit over high heat. After rinsing pan, add rabbit and cook following hearth directions 3 through 6 to complete.

Eliza Leslie's Haunch of Roast Venison

*"Venison is finest in autumn or early winter, and keeps longer than any
other fresh meat, no other care being necessary for keeping it from three to
four weeks than to hang it up in a cool, dry place. When bought at mar-
ket any taint may be best discovered by plunging a knife into the flesh
nearest the thigh bone, which is the part that would spoil first, and betray
its condition by bad odor."*

Mary Stuart Smith

To prepare a haunch of venison for roasting (we will suppose it to be
perfectly *good and well kept,) wipe it thoroughly all over with clean
cloths, dipped in lukewarm water, and then go over it with clean dry
cloths. Trim off all unsightly parts. Lay over the fat a large sheet of thick
brown paper, well buttered, and securely tied on with twine. Or else make
a coarse paste of brown meal, and cover it with that. Place it before a
good steady fire, and let it roast from three to four hours, according to its
size. After roasting well for three hours, remove the covering of paper or
paste, and baste the meat well all over; first with dripping or butter, and
then with its own gravy, dredging it very slightly with browned flour.
Skim the fat off the gravy, and send the venison to table plain, with sweet
sauce of black current jelly, or raspberry jam, in a glass dish with a spoon
in it.*

Eliza Leslie

Serves 4 to 6

5 to 6 pounds venison roast   Brown flour (page 319)
Softened butter

Hearth:
1. Rinse venison and pat dry.
2. Take a sheet of brown paper or baker's parchment paper
large enough to completely cover venison. Spread butter
thickly on paper, then wrap the venison with the buttered
side of the paper on the meat. Tie paper securely with
twine.
3. Carefully spit venison, set before the fire, and roast, following directions on pages 118–120.
4. After venison has roasted to your taste (do not overcook,
for venison is best slightly rare), remove paper. Baste meat
with pan drippings and additional butter, then dust lightly
with brown flour. Turn meat on spit briefly to cook flour.

5. Carefully remove meat from spit, place on platter, and send to table. Miss Leslie suggests black currant jelly or raspberry jam to accompany venison roast.

Modern:
1. Follow hearth directions 1 and 2.
2. Preheat oven to 500°. Put prepared venison on rack in baking pan and roast 15 minutes. Reduce temperature to 350° and roast until done as desired (venison should be somewhat rare).
3. Follow hearth directions 4 and 5 to complete recipe.

Miss Leslie's Hashed Venison

Take the remains of cold roast venison, from which sufficient gravy or dripping has been saved to cook the meat again, without any water at all. It would be well if this were done in all hashes made from cold meat. For want of drippings, use butter or lard. Cold meat stewed in water is weak and unpalatable.

Two or three large spoonfuls of mushroom, or tomato catchup, are improvements to all hashes. If nothing better can be obtained use onions, always previously boiled to render them less strong.

Minced sweet herbs are excellent seasoning for hashes. Also minced tarragon leaves; they give a peculiar flavor that is very generally liked. Fresh tarragon is in season in July, August, and September.

French mustard (to be obtained at all the best grocery stores) is a great improvement to hashes and stews. Stir in at the last, one or two large table-spoonfuls. The chief ingredient of French mustard is tarragon.

Eliza Leslie

Serves 4 to 6

2 to 4 tablespoons butter
½ cup chopped onion
3 to 4 cups chopped cooked
   leftover venison
2 tablespoons mushroom
   catchup (page 313)
½ teaspoon marjoram
½ teaspoon thyme

¼ teaspoon summer savory
1 tablespoon fresh minced
   parsley
2 or more cups leftover venison
   gravy
2 tablespoons Dijon mustard
   (or Fine French Mustard,
   page 316)
Hot cooked rice

Hearth:

1. Melt butter in skillet set on trivet over hot coals. Add onions and sauté until soft.
2. Add venison, mushroom catchup, herbs, and gravy. Cover and cook over hot coals, stirring occasionally, for about 20 minutes or until mixture is bubbling hot. Stir in mustard and heat through. Correct seasonings if necessary.
3. Pour over hot cooked rice and serve immediately.

Modern:

1. Melt butter over low heat. Add chopped onion and sauté until soft.
2. Follow hearth directions 2 through 3 to complete, cooking hash covered over low heat 20 to 30 minutes.

Mrs. Peyton Randolph's Wild Duck

". . . if your fire be very hot, they will roast in twenty minutes, and the quicker they are roasted the better they will taste."

Mary Randolph

Roast the duck 25 minutes before a clear fire & send to the table with its drippings—Pour into your lighted chafing dish 3 (?) glasses of port wine, a good pinch of cayenne pepper, a sprinkle of salt, and let come to a boil—The duck must be carved in pieces & put into the boiling sauce, then serve from the chafing dish.

Jean Lloyd French Collection

Serves 2 to 4

1 wild duck	Drippings from roasted duck
Salt	¾ cups port wine
Melted lard for basting	⅛ teaspoon cayenne pepper

Hearth:

1. Dress and clean duck thoroughly. Sprinkle with salt. Spit and roast before hot, clear fire, following directions on pages 118–120, about 20 minutes, basting occasionally with melted lard.

2. Carefully remove duck from spit, put on platter, and keep warm while preparing sauce.

3. Pour off up to 1 cup of the drippings and combine in a saucepan with wine and cayenne pepper. Set pan on trivet over coals and bring to a boil. Taste, adding salt if needed. Boil briefly to reduce sauce. Pour into chafing dish.

4. To serve, carve duck in pieces at table and put in bubbling sauce. Serve from chafing dish.

Modern:

1. Dress and clean duck thoroughly. Sprinkle with salt. Put on rack in roasting pan. Brush with melted lard.

2. Preheat oven to 500°. Put bird in oven and immediately reduce heat to 350°. Roast about 20 minutes, basting occasionally with melted lard (butter may be substituted).

3. Follow hearth directions 3 and 4, boiling sauce over medium heat to reduce.

Elizabeth Nicholson's Omelette

The great merit of an omelette is, that it should not be greasy, burnt, or overdone; if too much of the white is used it becomes hard. To dress an omelette, the fire should not be too hot, as it is an object to have the whole substance heated without too much browning on the outside; the omelette must not be too thin, therefore it must be thick and have a full, rich, moist flavour. They should be fried in a small pan, with a small quantity of good butter. Five or six eggs will make a good sized omelette. Break them into a basin, separating the whites from the yolks, mince very finely a tablespoonful of fresh parsley, beat up the yolks well, and to it add the parsley and a little salt, and a very little cayenne, then whip the whites to a stiff froth; put about a large spoonful of butter into the hot pan, and while it is melting mix with the yolks two tablespoonsful of good cream, then beat in the whites when well mixed, and pour it into the pan; shake it in the pan until the eggs begin to set, then turn up the edges, and when a nice brown, it is done. Then have a hot dish and lay it on the pan and turn it upside down on the dish. Never make it until it is wanted at table, as it must be eaten as soon as made. They can be flavoured with finely chopped onions, or oysters, or cooked and chopped ham. The above is the basis of all omelets, only omitting the cream if anything else is used.

Elizabeth Nicholson

Serves 4

6 eggs, separated
2 tablespoons cream
1 tablespoon fresh minced
   parsley

½ to 1 teaspoon salt
⅛ teaspoon cayenne pepper
2 to 4 tablespoons butter for
   frying

Hearth:

1. Beat egg yolks with cream until frothy. Add parsley, salt, and cayenne pepper, blending well.
2. Beat egg whites until stiff and fold into egg yolks.
3. Melt butter in frying pan set over warm coals until bottom of omelette begins to set. Lift up edges of omelette so that eggs on top can run into bottom of pan to cook.
4. Have ready a hot serving dish. Turn eggs into it and serve immediately.

Modern:

1. Follow hearth directions 1 through 4, cooking eggs over moderate to moderately low heat.

Friar's Omelet

12 apples,
4 eggs,
¾ large or 1 small nutmeg,

2 ounces butter,
3 ounces bread crumbs,
¾ pound sugar.

To make: Steam the apples and pass them through a colander; stir in the butter, and add the grated nutmeg while hot. Separate the eggs; beat both whites and yolks very light; beat the sugar into the yolks; add the prepared apples. Give the whole a good beating before adding the whites. Butter a pudding dish; strew the bottom and sides with bread crumbs; fill the dish with the mixture; strew bread crumbs over the top; dot with little bits of butter, and put in a moderate oven to bake until a nice, light brown. Serve hot or cold.

Mrs. John W. Cringan

Serves 4 to 6

6 tart apples, such as Granny Smith
3 tablespoons softened butter, divided
1 teaspoon nutmeg

2 eggs, separated
¾ cup sugar
½ cup freshly grated bread crumbs

Hearth:

1. Peel, core, and quarter apples. Over saucepan of hot water set on hot coals, steam apples until soft.
2. Remove apples from heat and force through a colander or sieve. Add 2 tablespoons butter and nutmeg while apples are hot. Set aside to cool.
3. Beat egg yolks until thick. Beat in sugar, then add cooled apple mixture. Blend well.
4. Beat egg whites until stiff and gently fold into egg mixture.
5. Butter a heatproof dish and shake all but 2 tablespoons of bread crumbs around bottom and sides of dish.
6. Pour in apple mixture. Sprinkle remaining bread crumbs over top, then dot with remaining butter cut into small pieces.

7. Put dish on trivet in preheated Dutch oven with about 1 inch of water in bottom. Set Dutch oven on hot coals and bake, following directions on pages 216–217.

8. Remove from heat. Omelet may be served warm or cold, as desired. Serve, accompanied by Vanilla Sauce (page 302) if desired.

Modern:

1. Follow hearth direction 1, steaming apples over simmering water until soft.

2. Follow hearth directions 2 through 6.

3. Bake omelet in preheated 350° oven until knife inserted in center comes out clean and top is a light golden brown, 45 to 50 minutes.

4. Remove from oven. Follow hearthside direction 8 to complete.

Vegetables

The common belief, perpetrated by many historians, is that vegetables in the early days were neglected or were cooked in quantities of water to a sodden, colorless mass. It is true that by the last quarter of the 19th century vegetables were being done to death. Perhaps this was a natural outgrowth of the canning process with its lengthy boiling, which became common as a means of preservation after the Civil War.

Early cookbooks, however, tell a different story. Hannah Glasse, the most influential 18th-century cookbook author, told her readers: "Most people spoil garden things by over-boiling them. All things that are green should have a little crispness, for if they are over-boiled, they neither have any sweetness or beauty."[1]

Mary Randolph, whose book, *The Virginia House-wife*, superseded those written by Mrs. Glasse, was just as emphatic. In her instructions for asparagus she stated: "Great care must be taken to watch the exact time of their becoming tender; take them just at that instant, and they will have their true flavour and colour; a minute or two more boiling destroys both."[2]

Eliza Leslie, writing cookbooks until the middle of the 19th century, was even more determined to get the point across. "In France, so little water is used in cooking vegetables, that they are rather stewed than boiled, and are the better for it. A puddle of greasy water in the bottom of every vegetable dish is a disgusting sight . . . it is a certain indication of a bad cook, or an inefficient mistress, or both."[3]

Nancy Carter Crump treats vegetables as early Virginians did, with love and respect. She does not overcook or oversalt.

A wide array of vegetables were available in early Virginia. Many of them, such as leeks and broccoli, virtually disappeared over time, only to be rediscovered in the mid-20th century as "new" entries on the culinary scene. A number of vegetables popular then are all but impossible to find now—salsify, corn salad, and sorrel, for instance—and their loss is to be mourned.

"Pease ought to be preferred they being a more succulent Vegetable . . ." noted Robert Carter III in his journal entry for April 25, 1788.[4] Peas were undoubtedly one of the most popular vegetables of the day, and gentlemen farmers vied with one another each spring to bring the first dish of peas to table.[5] Green corn—the young, tender ears—was also relished. Good cooks knew the importance of cooking these vegetables as soon as possible after they were picked.

Certain vegetables, particularly tomatoes and white potatoes, were unfamiliar in the early days. Potatoes were introduced to England during the late Tudor period, brought there by Sir Francis Drake who had encountered them on one of his voyages. It took years for potatoes, now so much a part of Western cuisine, to be accepted. They were long thought to be poisonous. In America they became popular only after Thomas Jefferson began cultivating them at Monticello.

The same held true with the tomato, also thought to be poisonous by the British. For years it was grown in England as an ornamental plant, even though other nations had made it a part of their culinary traditions. Again, Jefferson is credited for planting in 1781 the first tomatoes in this country.

Gardening was of tremendous importance to the Virginia gentry, who exchanged seeds, plants, and advice on methods. Jefferson especially loved the pastime and meticulously recorded his gardening activities throughout most of his life. Despite long years as a statesman, Jefferson's happiest moments were spent in his Monticello gardens. He was convinced that those "who labour in the earth are the Chosen people of God."[6]

Directions from the early cookbooks for preparing vegetables still apply. "Use but very little salt in cooking vegetables," cautioned Eliza Leslie[7], and certainly in today's diet- and health-conscious age that is still valid.

A Ragoo of Asparagus

Scrape a hundred of grass* very clean, and throw them into cold water; when you have scraped all, cut as far as is good and green about an inch long, and take two heads of endive clean washed and picked, cut it very small, a young lettuce clean washed and cut small, a large onion peeled and cut small, put a quarter of a pound of butter into a stew-pan, when it is melted throw in the above things: toss them about, and fry them ten minutes; then season them with a little pepper and salt, shake in a little flour, toss them about, then pour in half a pint of gravy; let them stew till the sauce is very thick and good; then pour all into your dish. Save a few of the little tops of the grass to garnish the dish.

N.B. You must not fry the asparagus: boil it in a little water and put them in your ragoo, and then they will look green.

Hannah Glasse

Serves 4

1½ pounds fresh asparagus	½ cup diced onion
4 tablespoons butter	¼ teaspoon pepper
1 endive, sliced	¼ teaspoon salt
1½ cups shredded, loosely packed Boston lettuce	2 tablespoons flour
	1½ cups chicken stock

Hearth:

1. Rinse asparagus. Trim off and discard tough portions of stalk. Quarter and reserve remainder.

2. Pour 2 cups water in small pot. Set over coals and bring to a boil. Add asparagus. Cover and simmer 7 to 10 minutes or until asparagus is just tender. Remove from heat and drain thoroughly. Reserve about half the asparagus tips in a small bowl and keep them, along with the remaining asparagus, warm by the fire.

3. While asparagus is cooking, melt butter in skillet set on warm coals. Add endive, lettuce, and onion. Cook, stirring often, for about 10 minutes or until vegetables are barely tender. Season with pepper and salt.

4. Sprinkle on flour. Stir until mixture is well blended. Gradually blend in stock, stirring until mixture bubbles and begins to thicken. Allow to simmer briefly.

---

*"Sparrow grass" or "grass" was a commonly used corruption of asparagus.

5. Put reserved asparagus in serving bowl and pour in sauce and vegetables. Top with reserved asparagus tips and serve piping hot.

Modern:
Follow hearth directions 1 through 5, simmering quartered asparagus over low heat until barely tender.

Mrs. Randolph's Artichokes

Soak them in cold water, wash them well, then put them into plenty of boiling water, with a handful of salt, and let them boil gently till they are tender, which will take an hour and a half, or two hours; the surest way to know when they are done enough, is to draw out a leaf; trim them and drain them on a sieve, and send up melted butter with them; which some put into small cups so that each guest may have one.

Mary Randolph

Serves 4 to 6

4 to 6 artichokes (1 per person)
Lemon juice
2 tablespoons salt
Mrs. Randolph's Melted Butter
   (page 290)

Hearth:
1. Rinse and remove stems and tough bottom leaves of artichokes. Trim points of remaining leaves, then dip points in lemon juice to prevent darkening.
2. Fill an iron pot with water and set it on a crane. Add salt and bring to a boil over flames.
3. When water boils, add artichokes. Cover. Adjust height of pot on crane to gently boil artichokes until they are tender, 45 to 60 minutes. Artichokes are ready when leaves pull away easily. Remove from fire and drain thoroughly.
4. Serve hot with Mrs. Randolph's Melted Butter.

Modern:
1. Follow hearth directions 1 through 4, boiling artichokes over moderate heat.

To Ragou French Beans Mrs. Bradley's Way

Boil some young French Beans till they are tender, then set them by to drain. Set a Stewpan over the Fire, throw in a Piece of Butter, let it melt, then drudge in a little Flour, peel a large Onion, cut it into thin Slices, throw it in, and fry it till it is very brown. Beat up the Yolk of an Egg in half a Teacup of Cream, let this stand by, put the drained French Beans into the Stewpan, and grate in a little nutmeg; strew over them a little Pepper and Salt, and then shake them well about. When they are well mixed, and thoroughly hot, put in the Egg and Cream, and then shake them about over the Fire two minutes. They will thus mix thoroughly together, and be well heated; then dish them up for the Table.

Martha Bradley

2½ pounds fresh tender green beans
1 teaspoon granulated sugar
4 tablespoons butter
2 tablespoons flour
½ cup thinly sliced onion
2 teaspoons salt
½ teaspoon pepper
¼ teaspoon nutmeg
2 egg yolks, lightly beaten
½ cup cream

Hearth:
1. Trim ends from green beans, break in half, and rinse well.
2. Put beans in iron pot. Add sugar. Barely cover beans with water. Cover, place pot on crane, and bring to boil over flames. Adjust height of pot on crane and simmer beans gently until just tender, 10 to 15 minutes. Drain beans thoroughly, then refresh with cold water. Set aside in colander.
3. Melt butter in saucepan set over warm coals. Blend in flour, then cook and stir briefly. Add sliced onion. Cook until soft but not brown, stirring often.
4. Add green beans, along with salt, pepper, and nutmeg. Cook and stir until heated through.
5. Mix together egg yolks and cream and stir into green bean mixture. Let simmer for about 5 minutes, stirring frequently, until thickened.
6. Correct seasoning, pour into dish, and serve immediately.

Modern:

1. Follow hearth directions 1 and 2, simmering beans in a covered pot over low heat until just tender, 10 to 15 minutes.

2. Melt butter over low heat. Follow hearth directions 3 through 6 to complete recipe.

To Stew Beets

Wash the beets, but do not scrape or cut them while they are raw; for if a knife enters them before they are boiled they will lose their colour. Boil them from two to three hours, according to their size.

Boil them first, and then scrape and slice them. Put them into a stew-pan with a piece of butter rolled in flour, some boiled onion and parsley chopped fine, and a little vinegar, salt and pepper. Set the pan on hot coals, and let the beets stew for a quarter of an hour.

Eliza Leslie

Serves 4 to 6

2 pounds fresh beets, trimmed leaving 1″ of stem, and rinsed	½ teaspoon salt
	¼ teaspoon pepper
	½ cup cider vinegar
½ cup peeled, chopped onion	2 tablespoons softened butter
2 tablespoons fresh minced parsley	2 tablespoons flour

Hearth:

1. Barely cover beets with water in iron pot. Set on crane, cover, and bring to a boil. Adjust height of pot on crane and simmer beets until tender, about 30 to 60 minutes depending on size and age of beets. Remove from fire, drain thoroughly, and set beets aside to cool.
2. Put about 1 cup water in saucepan set on hot coals, bring to boil, and add onions. Cook 5 minutes, drain, and set aside.
3. When beets are cool enough to handle, peel and slice them. There should be about 3 cups.
4. Put the beets in a saucepan with onion, parsley, salt, pepper, and vinegar. Cover and set pan over hot coals. Cook beets gently to just heat through, about 5 minutes.
5. Combine butter and flour. Stir into beets and cook gently 10 minutes longer, stirring often to prevent sticking. Serve hot or cold.

Modern:

1. Follow hearth direction 1, simmering beets over moderate heat until tender. Parboil onions over moderate heat for 5 minutes.
2. Complete recipe following hearth directions 2 through 5, simmering beets with other ingredients over low heat.

Carrots or French Beans Dressed the Dutch Way

Slice the carrots very thin, and just cover them with water, season them with pepper and salt, cut a good many onions and parsley small, a piece of butter; let them simmer over a slow fire till done. Do French beans the same way.

Hannah Glasse

Serves 6 to 8

4 cups pared, thinly sliced
  carrots
1 cup finely chopped onion
¾ teaspoon salt
½ teaspoon pepper

3 tablespoons fresh, minced
  parsley
2 tablespoons softened butter
Additional chopped parsley for
  garnish

Hearth:

1. Put carrots in a saucepan and barely cover them with water. Add onion, salt, pepper, and parsley.
2. Set pan on trivet over hot coals. Cover and simmer until carrots are barely tender, 15 to 20 minutes. Remove from heat and drain thoroughly.
3. Put carrots in serving dish and add butter. Cover and keep warm by the fire until ready to serve. Just before sending to table, garnish with chopped parsley.

Modern:

1. Follow hearth directions 1 through 3, cooking over moderately low heat until carrots are tender, 15 to 20 minutes.

Note: Green beans can be done the same way using the same proportions.

Cabbage A-La-Creme

Take two good heads of cabbage, cut out the stalks, boil it tender with a little salt in the water, have ready one large spoonful of butter and a small one of flour rubbed into it, half a pint of milk, with pepper and salt, make it hot, put the cabbage in after pressing out the water, and stew it till quite tender.

Mary Randolph

Serves 4 to 6

2 large cabbages	1 tablespoon flour
1½ teaspoons salt, divided	, ¼ teaspoon pepper
2 tablespoons butter	1 cup half and half

Hearth:

1. Remove and discard stalks and outer leaves from cabbages. Quarter cabbages and put in an iron pot. Cover with water, add 1 teaspoon salt, put pot on crane, and bring to a boil over flames. Adjust height of pot and simmer cabbage until barely tender, about 15 minutes. Remove from crane and drain thoroughly, pressing down on cabbage with spoon to extract as much water as possible. Keep warm by fire.

2. Combine butter and flour. Set a saucepan over warm coals, add butter and flour, and stir until butter melts and mixture begins to simmer. Add pepper and remaining ½ teaspoon salt.

3. Gradually add half and half stirring constantly until well blended and slightly thickened. Correct seasoning if necessary.

4. Add cabbage, cover, and simmer for about 5 minutes, stirring occasionally. Serve piping hot.

Modern:

1. Follow hearth direction 1, boiling cabbage over moderate heat.

2. Complete, following hearth directions 2 through 4. Simmer creamed cabbage over low heat.

Miss Leslie's Stewed Carrots

Half-boil the carrots; then scrape them nicely, and cut them into thick slices. Put them into a stew-pan with as much milk as will barely cover them; a very little salt and pepper; and a sprig or two of chopped parsley. Simmer them till they are perfectly tender. When nearly done, add a piece of fresh butter rolled in flour. Send them to table hot. Carrots require long cooking; longer than any other vegetable.

Parsnips and salsify may be stewed in the above manner, substituting a little chopped celery for the parsley.

Eliza Leslie

Serves 4 to 6

3 cups carrots, scraped, trimmed, and cut into 1½" slices
½ cup milk
½ teaspoon salt
¼ teaspoon pepper
1 tablespoon fresh, minced parsley
2 tablespoons softened butter
1 tablespoon flour

Hearth:
1. Barely cover carrots with water in an iron pot. Cover, place pot on crane, and bring to a boil. Adjust height of pot on crane and simmer carrots until nearly done, 15 to 20 minutes. Remove from heat and drain thoroughly.
2. Put drained carrots in saucepan. Add milk, salt, pepper, and parsley. Cover and set pan on trivet over warm coals. Simmer until carrots are just cooked through.
3. Combine butter and flour and stir into carrots. Continue to stir until mixture is well blended and slightly thickened. Pour into bowl and serve piping hot.

Modern:
1. Follow hearth directions 1 and 2, simmering carrots over low heat.
2. Prepare sauce over moderate heat following hearth direction 3. Add carrots and cook gently over low heat until tender.

Cauliflower and Broccoli

CAULIFLOWERS

Choose large fine white cauliflowers. Wash them well, and lay them in a pan of cold water, having divided each cauliflower into quarters. Trim off the outside green leaves. Put on the cauliflowers in boiling water with a little salt in it. It is still better to boil them in milk. Let them cook till tender throughout, flower and stalk. When quite done, put some bits of fresh butter among the flowers, or pour over them drawn butter sauce, made with milk and seasoned with powdered nutmeg or mace. Serve them up hot, and covered.

BROCCOLI

Is drest in the same manner. It is very good with toast under, though inferior to cauliflower.

Eliza Leslie

Serves 4 to 6

1 pound cauliflower	2 tablespoons flour
1 pound broccoli	1 cup milk
Salt	¼ teaspoon nutmeg
4 tablespoons butter	

Hearth:

1. Put cauliflower and broccoli in separate pots. Cover with water, add about 1 teaspoon salt to each pot, and put pots on crane. Cover and bring to a boil. Adjust height of pots and simmer vegetables until barely tender. Drain thoroughly.
2. Slowly melt butter in saucepan and set over warm coals. Stir in flour and a little more salt, if desired. Slowly add milk, then nutmeg, and simmer until well blended and somewhat reduced.
3. Add cauliflower and broccoli. Heat through and serve immediately.

Modern:

1. Follow hearthside direction 1, simmering cauliflower and broccoli in separate pots over moderately low heat.
2. Follow hearth directions 2 and 3 to complete recipe, preparing sauce over moderately low heat.

Shirley Plantation Corn Fritters

Grate 6 ears of corn, mix yolks of 2 eggs, ½ cup milk, ½ cup flour, salt & pepper. Beat the whites stiff & fold in last. Drop spoonfuls in hot fat & fry brown on both sides.

Shirley Plantation Collection

Serves 4 to 6

Enough fresh corn to equal 2 cups
2 eggs, separated
¼ cup cream
¼ cup flour

½ teaspoon salt
⅛ teaspoon pepper
½ cup lard

Hearth:
1. Grate corn into large bowl to equal 2 cups.
2. Beat egg yolks until frothy. Combine with cream, flour, salt, and pepper to make batter. Stir in grated corn.
3. Beat egg whites until stiff. Gently fold into corn mixture.
4. Melt lard in frying pan set over hot coals.
5. When lard is sizzling, drop in fritters by tablespoonfuls and fry on both sides until golden brown. Drain and serve piping hot.

Modern:
1. Follow hearth directions 1 through 5, frying fritters over moderate high heat.

Photo by Marler

Oatlands, home of Kate Powell Carter, in Loudoun County, VA.

Oatlands Corn Pudding

Scrape with a strong knife the grains from 12 years of corn to this add a quarter of a pound of butter 4 eggs well beaten with pepper and salt to your taste, add nice milk or cream, if the milk from the corn does not make it liquid enough, it generally requires some, stir all well together and bake in a baking dish

Kate Powell Carter

Serves 6 to 8

10 to 12 ears young, tender corn, enough for 4 cups grated
Cream
4 eggs lightly beaten

1½ teaspoons salt
½ teaspoon pepper
2 tablespoons sugar
6 tablespoons melted butter

Hearth:
1. Strip leaves and silk from corn and discard. Rinse corn. Put an ear of corn in a colander set over a bowl. With a sharp knife, carefully slice off tops of kernels, then scrape each ear to extract the pulp. Prepare each ear of corn in the same way.
2. Leave the scraped corn in colander set over bowl for about half an hour, stirring occasionally so that "milk" from corn can drip into bowl.
3. Measure the milk and add enough cream to make 1 cup. Combine with remaining ingredients. Fold in corn.
4. Butter a heatproof dish. Pour in corn mixture.
5. Carefully place filled dish on trivet in preheated Dutch oven. Cover, set on coals, and bake following directions on pages 216–217 for 45 to 60 minutes, or until knife inserted in center comes out clean.

Modern:
Follow hearth directions 1 through 5. Bake corn pudding in preheated 350° oven 45 to 60 minutes or until knife inserted in center comes out clean.

Mrs. Tebbs' Dried Corn

*Take young roasting ears—parboil them in salt water, take them out, cut
the corn off from the cob—put on dishes—then dried in an oven with
great care, Then to be put in a linen bag, and hung in the air. When
intended for use to be soaked 4 to 5 hours in boiling water before it is
cooked. Requires much boiling—When put on for dinner, boil in new
milk and water—the water to be changed.—*

M. H. D. Tebbs Receipt Book

Serves 4 to 6

2 cups dried corn (follow Mrs.
  Tebbs' original recipe)
4 cups boiling water
2 teaspoons sugar
Salt to taste

Pepper to taste
2 to 4 tablespoons butter
½ cup cream
½ cup milk

Hearth:
1. Roughly crush and rinse dried corn. Put in a large sauce-pan.
2. Pour over boiling water, cover, and soak corn 2 to 3 hours.
3. Bring corn and water to a boil over hot coals. Add remaining ingredients and cook until tender, 45 to 60 minutes.

Modern:
Follow hearth directions 1 through 3, simmering corn over low heat.

Indian Corn

Corn for boiling should be full grown but young and tender. When the grains become yellow it is too old. Strip it of the outside leaves and the silk, but let the inner leaves remain, as they will keep in the sweetness. Put it into a large pot with plenty of water, and boil it rather fast for half an hour. When done, drain off the water, and remove the leaves.

You may either lay the ears on a large flat dish and send them to table whole, or broken in half; or you may cut all the corn off the cob, and serve it up in a deep dish, mixed with butter, pepper and salt.

Eliza Leslie

Serves 6

12 ears very fresh, tender corn
2 to 4 tablespoons sugar

Salt and pepper to taste
Plenty of softened butter

Hearth:
1. Strip outer leaves and silk from corn, leaving a few inner leaves attached. Rinse corn.
2. Fill an iron pot with water and set it on crane over flames. Add sugar.
3. When water boils, throw in corn and boil until tender, 20 to 30 minutes.
4. Carefully remove corn from water and drain thoroughly. Strip off remaining leaves.
5. Serve with salt, pepper, and plenty of butter.

Modern:
Follow hearth directions 1 through 5.

Mrs. Robert E. Lee declared Mushrooms au beurre "delicious" in her cookbook.

Mrs. Robert E. Lee's Mushrooms au beurre*

Cut the stems from some fine meadow mushroom-buttons, & clean them with a bit of new flannel & some fine salt; then either wipe them dry with a soft cloth, or rinse them in fresh water, drain them quickly, spread them in a clean cloth, fold it over them, & leave them ten minutes, or more to dry. For every pint of them thus prepared, put an ounce & a half of fresh butter into a thick iron saucepan, shake it over the fire until it just begins to brown, throw in the mushrooms, continue to shake the

---

*Courtesy of the Virginia Historical Society

saucepan over a clear fire, that they may not stick to it, nor burn, & when they have simmerd [sic] three or four minutes, Strew over them a little salt, some cayenne, & pounded mace; stew them until they are perfectly tender, heap them on a dish & seson [sic] them with their own sauce only, for breakfast, supper, or luncheon. Nothing can be finer than the flavor of the mushroom thus prepared, & the addition of any liquid is far from an improvement. They are very good, when drained from the butter & served cold, & in a cool larder may be kept for several days. The butter in wʰ they are stewed is admirable for flavouring gravies, sauces, or potted meats, small flaps, freed from the fur & skin, may be stewed in the same way, & either those, or the bottoms, servd [sic] under roast poultry or partridges, will give a dish of very superior relish.

Mrs. Robert E. Lee

Serves 4 to 6

6 tablespoons butter	¼ teaspoon cayenne pepper
6 cups fresh mushrooms, sliced	¼ teaspoon mace
1½ teaspoons salt	

Hearth:
1. Melt butter in a saucepan set on trivet over hot coals. When it sizzles, stir in mushrooms.
2. Cook mushrooms 3 or 4 minutes, stirring often. Stir in seasonings and continue cooking until mushrooms are very tender.
3. Pour into dish and keep warm by the fire until ready to serve.

Modern:
Follow hearth directions 1 through 3, cooking mushrooms over moderate heat.

Mrs. Banister's Way to Make a Ragoo of Onions

Take a pint of little young onions, peel them, and take four large ones, peel them and cut them very small; put a quarter of a pound of good butter into a stew-pan, when it is melted and done making a noise, throw in your onions, and fry them till they begin to look a little brown; Then shake in a little flour, and shake them round till they are thick; throw in a little salt, a little beaten pepper, a gill of good gravy, and a tea-spoonful of mustard. Stir all together and when it is well tasted and of a good thickness pour it into your dish, and garnish it with fried crumbs of bread and raspings. They make a pretty little dish, and are very good.

Mary Bolling Banister, who makes slight changes in this
Hannah Glasse receipt

Serves 4

4 tablespoons butter	¼ cup chicken stock
3 cups chopped onion	1 rounded teaspoon Fine
2 tablespoons flour	French Mustard (page ooo)
½ teaspoon salt	¼ cup browned, freshly grated
¼ teaspoon pepper	bread crumbs

Hearth:
1. Melt butter in saucepan in skillet set over coals.
2. Add onion and cook, stirring often, until tender and light brown.
3. Sprinkle on flour, salt, and pepper. Stir until mixture is well blended. Simmer briefly.
4. Blend in stock and mustard, stirring until mixture thickens.
5. Pour into serving dish and sprinkle with bread crumbs before serving.

Modern:
Follow hearth directions 1 through 5, cooking over moderately low heat.

---

*Courtesy of the Virginia Historical Society

To Roast Onions

Select fine large onions; do not peel them, but place them in a bake-pan, and set them in an oven. Bake them slowly till tender all through. When done, peel off the outer skin, and send them hot to table, to eat with pepper and cold butter.

They are very good when covered up and roasted under hot ashes, taking care that they are done quite through to the heart.

Eliza Leslie

Serves 6

6 large onions, unpeeled
Freshly ground pepper
Softened butter

Hearth:
1. Roast onions under hot ashes in fireplace until easily pierced with a fork, 45 to 60 minutes.
2. Peel off outer skin and serve hot, accompanied with pepper and softened butter.

Modern:
1. Follow hearth directions 1 and 2, roasting onions on a cookie sheet in preheated 400° oven until done, 45 to 50 minutes.

Hannah Glasse's Parsnips

Boil them tender, scrape them from the dust, cut them into slices, put them into a sauce-pan with cream enough; for sauce, a piece of butter rolled in flour, a little salt, and shake the sauce-pan often; when the cream boils; pour them into a plate for a corner-dish, or a side-dish at supper.

Hannah Glasse

Serves 4 to 6

1½ pounds parsnips	1 teaspoon salt
3 tablespoons softened butter	1 cup cream
2 tablespoons flour	

Hearth:
1. Scrape and trim off ends of fresh parsnips. Slice cross-wise 1″ thick and put in cold water to prevent parsnips from darkening.
2. Drain parsnips, put in an iron pot, and just cover with fresh water. Set pot on crane, cover, and bring to boil. Adjust height of pot to simmer parsnips until barely tender, 20 to 30 minutes. Remove from fire and drain thoroughly.
3. Combine butter and flour. Set a saucepan over warm coals, add butter and flour, and stir until butter melts and mixture begins to simmer. Stir in salt.
4. Gradually add cream, stirring constantly until well blended and slightly thickened.
5. Add parsnips and cook about 5 minutes, stirring often. Correct seasoning and serve hot.

Modern:
1. Follow hearth directions 1 and 2, simmering parsnips over moderate heat until barely tender.
2. Complete hearth directions 3 through 5, cooking parsnips over low heat.

Field Peas

There are many varieties of these peas, the smaller kind are the most deli-
cate.—Have them young and newly gathered, shell and boil them tender,
pour them in a colander to drain; put some lard in a frying-pan, when it
boils, mash the peas, and fry them in a cake of a light brown; put it in the
dish with the crust uppermost, garnish with thin bits of fried bacon. They
are very nice when fried whole, so that each pea is distinct from the other,
but they must be boiled less, and fried with great care. Plain boiling is a
very common way of dressing them.

Mary Randolph

Serves 6

2 pounds fresh field peas or
  black-eyed peas

1 tablespoon salt
2 or more tablespoons lard

Hearth:
1. Shell peas and rinse in colander. You should have 4 to
4½ cups of peas.
2. Put peas and salt in iron pot. Cover with water. Set pot
on crane, cover, and bring to a boil. Adjust height of pot
and simmer peas until barely tender, 30 to 45 minutes. Remove from heat and drain thoroughly. Set by fire to keep
warm and to evaporate any remaining moisture.
3. Melt lard in saucepan and set over hot coals. Add peas
and fry while stirring, until piping hot. Serve immediately.

Modern:
1. Follow hearth directions 1 and 2, simmering peas over
medium-low heat.
2. Fry in melted lard over moderate heat until tender.

Eliza Leslie's Lettuce Peas

Having washed four lettuces, and stripped off the outside leaves, take the hearts, and (having chopped them well) put them into a stew-pan with two quarts of young green peas, freshly shelled; a lump or two of loaf-sugar; and three or four leaves of green mint minced as finely as possible. Then put in four slices of cold ham, and a quarter of a pound of butter divided into four bits, and rolled in flour; and two table-spoonfuls of water. Add a little cayenne, and let the whole stew for about twenty-five minutes, or till the peas are thoroughly done. Next take out the ham, and add to the stew half a pint of cream. Let it continue stewing for five minutes longer. Then send it to table.

Eliza Leslie

Serves 4 to 6

4 to 5 pounds unshelled young green peas
1 tablespoon sugar
½ to 1 teaspoon fresh minced mint leaves
⅛ teaspoon cayenne pepper
¼ pound sliced ham
¼ cup water
4 to 6 tablespoons softened butter
2 tablespoons flour
1 cup shredded Boston lettuce
½ cup cream

Hearth:
1. Choose very young and tender green peas which, when shelled, will equal 4 cups peas.
2. Combine peas with sugar, mint, cayenne pepper, ham, and water in saucepan. Cover and bring to a simmer over hot coals.
3. Combine butter and flour. Stir into peas, cover, and simmer gently until peas are tender, 25 to 30 minutes. Stir occasionally, adding more butter if necessary.
4. When peas are done, remove ham and add Boston lettuce. Stir and cook briefly, just until lettuce is wilted.

5. Stir in cream and heat through.
6. Correct seasoning if necessary. Pour into bowl and serve immediately.

Modern:
1. Follow hearth directions 1 through 6, simmering peas over low heat until tender.

Mary Randolph's Peas with Mint

To have them in perfection, they must be quite young, gathered early in the morning, kept in a cool place, and not shelled until they are to be dressed; put salt in the water, and when it boils, put in the peas; boil them quick twenty or thirty minutes, according to their age; just before they are taken up, add a little mint chopped very fine, drain all the water from the peas, put in a bit of butter, and serve them up quite hot.

Mary Randolph

Serves 4 to 6

4 to 5 pounds young unshelled peas	2 teaspoons fresh, finely chopped mint
Salt to taste	2 to 3 tablespoons softened butter
1 to 2 teaspoons sugar	

Hearth:
1. Shell peas just before they are to be cooked.
2. Fill iron pot with water, add salt and sugar, and put pot on crane over flames.
3. Bring water to a boil and add peas. Keep them at a steady boil until they are tender, 20 to 30 minutes. During the last 5 minutes of cooking add mint.
4. Drain peas thoroughly. Put peas in serving dish and stir in butter. Cover and keep warm until ready to serve.

Modern:
Follow hearth directions 1 through 4, boiling peas over moderate heat until done.

Boiled New Potatoes

Rub each one with a coarse cloth to clear off the skin, it being too thin for paring. Wash them well, and cut a small piece off the top and bottom of each potato, to make them boil tender all through. Put no salt in the water, and boil them till soft. Serve them plain, and eat them with cold butter—or put them into a sauce-pan, and stew them in butter.

Eliza Leslie

Serves 4 to 6

2 pounds small new potatoes
Softened butter
Salt and pepper to taste

Hearth:
1. Scrub potatoes well. Trim ends of potatoes and put them in an iron pot. Place on crane. Cover, bring to a boil, then adjust height of pot on crane and simmer until potatoes are tender, 25 to 30 minutes. Drain well. Keep warm by fire until ready to serve.
2. Put potatoes in warmed bowl and serve with softened butter and salt and pepper to taste.

Modern:
1. Follow hearth directions 1 and 2, simmering potatoes over low heat.

Roasted Potatoes

Take large fine potatoes; wash and dry them, and either lay them on the hearth and keep them buried in hot wood ashes, or bake them slowly in a Dutch oven. They will not be done in less than two hours. It will save time to half-boil them before they are roasted. Send them to table with the skins on, and eat them with cold butter and salt. They are introduced with cold meat at supper.

Potatoes keep best buried in sand or earth. They should never be wetted till they are washed for cooking. If you have them in the cellar, see that they are well covered with matting or old carpet, as the frost injures them greatly.

Eliza Leslie

Serves 6

6 large baking potatoes   Softened butter
Salt and pepper

Hearth:
1. Wash and dry potatoes.
2. Roast until done in fireplace covered with hot coals, or in a covered Dutch oven set over hot coals, 1½ to 2 hours.
3. Carefully remove from ashes, using fireplace tongs. Wipe off potatoes and serve them, unpeeled, with salt, pepper, and butter as desired.

Modern:
Follow hearth directions 1 through 3. Bake potatoes in 450° oven for 1 hour.

Mrs. Cringan's Sweet Potatoes Baked with Wine

4 large sweet potatoes,　　　*½ pint sugar,*
2 tablespoons butter,　　　*2 gills wine,*
½ teaspoon salt,　　　*½ pint water.*

*To Cook: Boil or steam the potatoes; when cold, peel and slice them. But-
ter a baking-dish, put a layer of potatoes in the bottom, sprinkle with
sugar and butter; then put another layer of potatoes, and so continue until the dish is full, having sugar and butter on top. Stir the salt into the
water and pour it over the potatoes, and put the dish into a moderate
oven. Cook until brown on top. Just before taking the dish from the oven
pour over the wine. Serve hot.*

Mrs. John W. Cringan

Serves 6

4 large sweet potatoes　　　¼ teaspoon salt
4 to 6 tablespoons butter, cut　　　½ cup water
　　into small pieces　　　½ cup Madeira wine
¾ cup granulated sugar

Hearth:
1. Scrub potatoes. Put in an iron pot and cover with water.
Cover and bring to a boil over flames. Adjust height of pot
on crane and simmer potatoes until they can easily be
pierced with a fork. Remove potatoes from heat, drain
thoroughly in colander, and cool until they can be easily
handled.
2. Peel potatoes and slice crosswise into 1″ pieces. Layer
with butter and sugar in buttered heatproof dish. Top with
last of butter and sugar. Sprinkle with salt.
3. Combine water and Madeira wine. Pour over prepared
potatoes.
4. Place filled dish on trivet in warmed Dutch oven. Cover
and set over hot coals. Bake about 30 to 45 minutes or until
most of liquid is absorbed and tops of sweet potatoes are a
light brown.

Modern:
1. Follow hearth directions 1 through 3, simmering potatoes over low heat until tender.
2. Preheat oven to 375° and bake potatoes in a 2-quart buttered casserole until done, as in hearth direction 4.

Roasted Sweet Potatoes

They should all be large. Wash them, dry them, and cut off the ends. Then bake them in an oven, laying side by side, not piling one on another. Or else (which is better) roast them in hot ashes. They will not be done in less than an hour and a half, perhaps longer. Then wipe them clean, and serve them up in the skins. Eat them from the skins, with cold butter and tea-spoon.

Eliza Leslie

Serves 6

6 large sweet potatoes   Softened butter

Hearth:
1. Wash, dry, and trim ends from sweet potatoes.
2. Roast until done in fireplace covered with hot ashes, or in a covered Dutch oven set over hot coals, about 1½ hours.
3. Carefully remove from ashes, using fireplace tongs. Wipe off potatoes and serve them, unpeeled, with butter as desired.

Modern:
Follow hearth directions 1 through 3, baking potatoes in 450° oven for 1 hour.

To Dress Salsify

Salsify, also known as oyster plant, was an extremely popular root vegetable which, unfortunately, is rarely seen now. Seeds are still available through certain seed catalogs and gardeners may wish to grow their own.

Boil them till they are very tender then lay them in a pan & mash them fine and smooth season with pepper & salt to your taste beat up one egg and add to it a little flour just to bind it make it in the shape and size of oysters and fry in lard

Gray Family Papers

Serves 4 to 6

2 to 3 pounds salsify	¾ cups freshly grated bread crumbs
¼ teaspoon pepper	
¼ teaspoon salt	Flour
1 tablespoon softened butter	2 to 3 tablespoons lard

Hearth:

1. Scrape and trim off ends of fresh salsify. As they are scraped and trimmed, put the salsify into cold water to prevent darkening.
2. Drain and quarter salsify. Put in iron pot and cover with water. Set pot on crane and bring to a boil over flames. Cover, adjust height of pot on crane, and let salsify simmer until tender, 20 to 30 minutes.
3. Remove salsify from fire, drain well in a colander, and coarsely mash. There should be about 3½ cups. Combine salsify with pepper, salt, butter, and bread crumbs. Shape into patties and dust lightly with flour.
4. Melt 2 tablespoons lard in frying pan over hot coals. Fry salsify patties on both sides until they are light brown, turning often and adding more lard if needed.
5. Serve immediately or keep warm by the fire until ready to serve.

Modern:

1. Canned salsify may replace fresh.
2. Follow hearth directions 1 through 5, frying salsify patties over moderate heat until lightly browned.

Note: Cooked salsify is delicious simply dressed with a little butter, salt, and pepper.

Mrs. Moncure's Spinach

Pick off the stems and wash it through several waters—put it in boiling water with a little salt—when done, squeeze the water out, chop it very fine, and put it in a sauce-pan with either butter or cream, garnish with poached eggs, or hard boiled eggs chopped fine.

Mrs. M. B. Moncure

Serves 2 to 4

1 ½ to 2 pounds spinach	2 hard-boiled eggs, yolks and
⅓ cup cream	whites separated and finely
Salt	chopped

Hearth:

1. Rinse spinach thoroughly in clear water to remove any sand. Stem and break into coarse pieces. Put into large saucepan, cover, and bring to a boil over hot coals. It is not necessary to add water—the water that clings to leaves after rinsing is sufficient.

2. As soon as spinach reaches boiling point, remove from coals; it will wilt quickly and be sufficiently cooked without any prolonged cooking time.

3. Drain and return to pan. Add cream and salt to taste. Stir just until cream is hot and blended into spinach.

4. Pour into serving bowl. Sprinkle with chopped hard-boiled eggs and serve immediately.

Modern:

Follow hearth directions 1 through 4, cooking spinach over moderately high heat.

Squash (Cymlins)

MRS. CRINGAN'S CYMLINS

Boil and mash as above directed. Beat into the cymlins, after passing through a colander, one egg, one gill of milk, one tablespoon melted butter, one teaspoon salt, one-fourth teaspoon pepper. Put into a buttered dish and bake until brown.

Mrs. John W. Cringan

Serves 4 to 6

3 ½ cups yellow squash, cooked
    and coarsley mashed (2 ½
    pounds raw squash)
1 egg
¼ cup milk

2 tablespoons butter
1 teaspoon salt
¼ teaspoon pepper

Hearth:
1. Combine squash with remaining ingredients.
2. Pour into a buttered heatproof dish.
3. Carefully place on trivet in preheated Dutch oven. Bake over hot coals for about 30 minutes or until mixture is bubbly and lightly browned.

Modern:
Follow hearth directions 1 through 3. Bake in preheated oven at 350° for 30 minutes.

MRS. RANDOLPH'S SQUASH

Gather young squashes, peel, and cut them in two; take out the seeds, and boil them till tender; put them into a colander, drain off the water, and rub them with a wooden spoon through the colander; then put them into a stew-pan, with a cupful of cream, a small piece of butter, some pepper and salt, stew them, stirring very frequently until dry. This is the most delicate way of preparing squashes.

Mary Randolph

Hearth:
1. Use same ingredients as for Mrs. Cringan's Cymlins, eliminating egg.
2. Combine all ingredients in saucepan set on trivet over hot coals.
3. Cook and stir until squash is tender, 10 to 15 minutes.

Modern:
1. Follow hearth direction 1.
2. After combining ingredients, cook over moderately low heat, stirring often until squash is tender.

Mrs. Glasse's Stewed "Spinage" and Eggs

Pick and wash your spinage very clean, put it into a sauce-pan with a little salt, cover it close, shake the pan often; when it is just tender and whilst it is green throw it into a sieve to drain, lay it into your dish: in the mean time have a stew-pan of water boiling, break as many eggs into cups as you would poach; when the water boils put in the eggs, have an egg slice ready to take them out with, lay them on the spinage, and garnish the dish with orange cut into quarters, with melted butter in a cup.

Hannah Glasse

Serves 4

1 ½ pounds spinach
1 teaspoon salt
water for poaching
4 eggs

Salt and pepper
2 tablespoons melted butter
Fresh quartered orange slices

Hearth:

1. Wash spinach thoroughly in clear water. Break off and discard tough stalks. Put in frying pan with salt. Cover.
2. Fill a small saucepan half full of water and set on trivet over hot coals. Bring water to a simmer. Crack open eggs and slide into simmering water. Sprinkle lightly with salt and pepper. Cover and continue with recipe.
3. Put pan with spinach over hot coals. Shake pan briefly until spinach is just tender but has not lost its color. Drain, put in serving dish, and keep warm by fire.
4. When eggs are poached sufficiently, take them out of hot water with a slotted spoon. Arrange on spinach and pour over melted butter.
5. Squeeze on a little orange juice and garnish with quartered orange slices. Serve immediately.

Modern:

Follow hearth directions 1 and 2, simmering eggs over moderate heat. Cook spinach briefly over medium heat and complete recipe following hearth directions 3 through 5.

Scolloped Tomatos

Take fine large tomatos, perfectly ripe. Scald them to loosen the skins, and then peel them. Cover the bottom of a deep dish thickly with grated bread-crumbs, adding a few bits of fresh butter. Then put in a layer of tomatos, seasoned slightly with a little salt and cayenne, and some powdered mace or nutmeg. Cover them with another layer of bread-crumbs and butter; then another layer of seasoned tomatos; and proceed thus until the dish is full, finishing at the top with bread-crumbs. Set the dish into a moderate oven, and bake it near three hours. Tomatos require long cooking, otherwise they will have a raw taste, that to most persons is unpleasant.

Eliza Leslie

Serves 4 to 6

2 ½ pounds ripe tomatoes
1 teaspoon salt
2 to 3 teaspoons sugar
¼ teaspoon cayenne pepper

¼ teaspoon mace
2 cups freshly grated bread crumbs
½ cup butter, softened and cut in small pieces

Hearth:
1. Scald and peel tomatoes. Combine with salt, sugar, cayenne pepper, and mace.
2. Butter a heatproof dish. Put in a thick layer of bread crumbs and dot with butter.
3. Cover with a layer of seasoned tomatoes. Continue alternating layers of bread crumbs and butter with tomatoes, ending with bread crumbs.
4. Put filled dish on trivet in Dutch oven. Cover and set on hot coals. Bake 45 to 50 minutes or until bubbly and bread crumbs are golden brown. Keep warm by fire until ready to serve.

Modern:
Follow hearth directions 1 through 4, baking scalloped tomatoes in a 2- to 4-quart casserole in preheated 350° oven for about 45 to 60 minutes.

Stewed Tomatoes and Corn

These vegetables are so generally liked together that an enterprising house-keeper projected the plan of mixing them, half and half, after they had been stewed separately, with the usual seasoning of butter, sugar, pepper, and salt, putting them in a baking-dish and serving hot. It proved to be a very nice dish, if the rapidity of its disappearance be the criterion for judgment.

Mary Stuart Smith

Serves 4 to 6

4 cups peeled, quartered ripe
  tomatoes
2 cups freshly grated corn
1 teaspoon salt

¼ teaspoon pepper
1 to 2 teaspoons sugar
3 tablespoons softened butter

Hearth:
1. Simmer tomatoes and corn in separate covered saucepans set over fire. If needed, add just enough milk to corn to prevent sticking. Cover and cook until both vegetables are tender. Remove from heat.
2. Combine corn and tomatoes in one saucepan. Add seasonings and butter. Return to heat and simmer mixture gently for about 10 minutes. Serve hot.

Modern:
Follow hearth directions 1 and 2, simmering vegetables over low heat.

Mashed Turnips

When they are boiled quite tender, squeeze them as dry as possible, put them into a sauce pan, mash them with a wooden spoon, and rub them through a colander; add a little bit of butter, keep stirring them till the butter is melted and well mixed with them, and they are ready for table.

Mary Randolph

Serves 4 to 6

3 cups peeled, diced turnips
3 tablespoons butter, softened

Salt and pepper to taste

Hearth:
1. Put turnips in small iron pot and barely cover with water. Set pan on crane, cover, and bring to a boil. Adjust height of pot on crane and simmer turnips until fork tender, about 15 minutes. Remove from heat and drain thoroughly.
2. Put turnips in bowl. Cut butter into turnips and stir to melt. Season to taste with salt and pepper. Keep warm by fire until ready to serve.

Modern:
1. Follow hearth direction 1, simmering turnips over moderately low heat until tender. Drain.
2. Complete following hearth direction 2.

EOT 47—12.1 M ch

Cakes and Little Cakes (Cookies)

Cakes of all kinds were popular desserts, and recipes for them occupy a great deal of space in early cookbooks.

Leavening agents in Colonial time were liquid yeast or eggs, which were beaten at length to produce the aerating necessary for cakes to rise. Although this required time and some endurance, the result was a cake free from a certain metallic taste endured by modern palates accustomed to baking powders foisted upon us in the name of progress.

Around 1790 pearl ash, obtained from leaching wood ashes, was discovered to have leavening qualities. This was followed by saleratus, a form of baking soda developed and used during part of the 19th century. An acid such as buttermilk was added to activate saleratus; by the mid-19th century the acid being used was cream of tartar. In 1856 baking powder was introduced, a combination of the two. It was downhill from then on.

The cake recipes on the following pages contain no baking powder. If saleratus was called for in an original recipe, soda has been substituted; otherwise, the only leavening agents are yeast and eggs, which must be beaten thoroughly to produce a well-aerated batter.

Instructions for baking cakes on the hearth are once again from early writers. For those who wish to maintain historical accuracy, as in a museum setting, please return to the last part of Chapter 2.

BAKING

1. Before baking a cake, "every ingredient necessary for it must be ready: when the process is retarded by neglecting to have them prepared, the article is injured,"[1] All ingredients should be at room temperature.

2. It is important to beat in the eggs thoroughly after each addition.

3. To bake in a Dutch oven, first preheat both the container and the lid by setting them in front of the fire, covering the "inside of the bottom with sand or ashes to temper the heat."[2]

4. "Earthen pans or molds, with a hollow tube in the middle, are best for cakes. If large cakes are baked in tin pans, the bottom and sides should be covered with sheets of paper, before the mixture is put in. The paper must be well

buttered."[3] Fill the prepared pans no more than two thirds full.

5. Put the filled pan on a rack or trivet inside the Dutch oven to keep it suspended above the hot bottom surface of the oven. Set the covered Dutch oven on hot coals and top with more hot coals.

6. "For all cakes the heat should be regular and even. While baking, no air should be admitted to it, except for a moment, now and then, when it is necessary to examine if it is baking properly . . . *the best guide is practice and experience;* so much depending on the state of the fire, that it is impossible to lay down any infallible rules" (emphasis mine).[4]

7. Generally the cakes are done "when they cease to make a simmering noise; and when on probing them to the bottom with a twig from a broom, or with the blade of the knife, it comes out quite clean."[5] See individual recipes for approximate times. When the cake tests done, remove it from the Dutch oven to cool.

8. Little cakes (cookies) are baked following the same method. When baked, remove from the pan to cool on a rack.

9. Eliza Leslie suggests that "novices in the art of baking" try everything in shallow pans until more experience is gained.[6] The preceding instructions are still valid.

French Almond Cake

Six ounces of shelled sweet almonds.
Three ounces of shelled, bitter almonds, or peach kernels.
Three ounces of sifted flour, dried near the fire.
Fourteen eggs.
One pound of powdered loaf-sugar
Twelve drops of essence of lemon.

Blanch the almonds, by scalding them in hot water. Put them in a bowl of cold water, and wipe them dry, when you take them out. Pound them, one at a time, in a mortar, till they are perfectly smooth. Mix the sweet and bitter almonds together. Prepare them, if possible, the day before the cake is made. While pounding the almonds pour in occasionally a little rose water.* It makes them much lighter.

Put the whites and yolks of the eggs, into separate pans. Beat the whites till they stand alone, and then the yolks till they are very thick.

Put the sugar gradually to the yolks, beating it in very hard. Add, by degrees, the almonds, still beating very hard. Then put in the essence of lemon. Next, beat in, gradually, the whites of the eggs, continuing to beat for some time after they are all in. Lastly, stir in the flour, as slowly and lightly, as possible.

Butter a large tin mould or pan. Put the cake in and bake it in a very quick oven, an hour or more according to its thickness.

The oven must on no account be hotter at the top, than at the bottom.

When done, set it on a sieve to cool.

Ice it, and ornament it with nonpareils.

These almond cakes are generally baked in a turban shaped mould, and the nonpareils put on, in spots or sprigs.

A pound of almonds in the shells (if the shells are soft and thin,) will generally yield half a pound when shelled. Hard, thick-shelled almonds, seldom yield much more than a quarter of a pound, and should therefore never be bought for cakes or puddings.

Bitter almonds and peach-kernels can always be purchased with the shells off.

Eliza Leslie

Makes one 7-cup tube cake

1½ cups whole almonds
1 tablespoon rose water (or more as needed)*
6 eggs, separated

1½ cups sugar
1 tablespoon lemon extract
½ teaspoon almond extract
¾ cup sifted flour

Hearth:

1. Blanch almonds, then remove skins. With a mortar and pestle, pulverize the almonds to a fine powder in small batches, adding a little rose water to each batch to prevent oiling. Set aside. (This may be done day before preparing cake.)
2. Beat egg yolks until very thick and a pale lemon color. In a steady stream, very slowly pour in sugar, beating constantly until it is all incorporated into the egg yolks.
3. Sprinkle in ground almonds, a little at a time, incorporating each addition before adding the next.
4. Add extracts.
5. Beat egg whites until very stiff, then gradually add to batter. Beat batter for several minutes.
6. Very gently fold in flour, a little at a time. Incorporate well, but use a light touch and do not overbeat.
7. Butter a tube pan and pour in cake batter. Set pan on trivet in preheated Dutch oven. Set oven on hot coals and bake covered 30 to 40 minutes following directions on pages 216–217.
8. Remove from heat. Allow cake to sit in pan uncovered about 10 minutes, then unmold and set on rack to cool.

Modern:

1. Blanch and skin almonds. Dry thoroughly on paper towels.
2. Grind almonds with ½ cup of the sugar to a fine powder, using a food processor.
3. Follow hearth directions 2 through 6, using an electric mixer. Add rose water with extracts.
4. Preheat oven to 350°. Pour batter into a buttered tube pan and bake about 45 minutes or until cake tests done.
5. Complete, following hearth direction 8.

---

*Rose water, a fragrant preparation made by steeping or distilling rose petals in water, is used in cosmetics and in cookery. This was a favorite condiment during the Tudor and the Stuart periods and was still in use into the 19th century, when it was gradually replaced by vanilla. Orange flower water was sometimes used as a substitute for rose water.

Kate Powell Carter, 1839–1903, at her home, Oatlands.

Kate Powell Carter's Black Cake

Prepare 2 pounds of currants by washing picking them and setting them in the sun, or by the fire to dry, then stone 2 pounds of raisins, rub them in flour to prevent their sticking, pound 2 nutmegs and a table spoon full of cinnamon and mace mixed, cut up a pound of citron in strips, sift a pound of sugar in one pan and a pound of flour in another, stir a pound of butter with the sugar to a cream, beat 24 eggs light, then stir them alternately into the butter and sugar with the flour then add the fruit spice and 2 wine glasses of wine or one of french brandy   beat the whole well together, put it into a moderate oven and bake 4 hours, some persons who wish the cake very black carefully brown *not* burn *the flour they make it of in an oven, some use brown sugar instead of white, and some add a teacup of molasses—*

Kate Powell Carter

Makes one large tube cake or two loaf cakes

3 cups currants
3 cups raisins
1 cup diced citron
1¾ cups sifted flour, divided
1 cup softened butter
1 cup brown sugar, firmly
  packed
5 eggs

2 teaspoons freshly grated
  nutmeg
1½ teaspoons cinnamon
1½ teaspoons mace
¼ cup Madeira or sweet sherry
  wine
2 tablespoons brandy

Hearth:

1. Combine currants, raisins, and citron in large bowl. Add ¼ cup flour and mix well. Set aside.
2. Cream butter and sugar until light. Add eggs one at a time, beating in each egg well before adding another.
3. Sift remaining flour together with spices. Gradually blend into creamed mixture.
4. Blend in Madeira and brandy, combining until well mixed.
5. Fold in fruit and mix well.
6. Butter a large tube pan or two smaller pans. Pour in batter and smooth with a knife. Set on trivet in preheated Dutch oven. Cover, set on coals, and bake following directions on pages 216–217, until done, 2 to 2½ hours.
7. Remove from Dutch oven and turn out on rack to cool.

Modern:

1. Follow hearth directions 1 through 5.
2. Preheat oven to 300°. Grease a large tube pan or two 9″ × 5″ × 3″ loaf pans. Pour in batter and smooth with a knife.
3. Bake until cake tests done, 2 to 2½ hours.
4. Remove. Turn out on rack to cool.

Note: Wrap cake in brandy-soaked cloth and store in air-tight container for two to three weeks to allow flavors to mellow. Moisten cloth with additional brandy every few days.

Hopkins Family Cocoanut Pound Cake*

1 lb of sugar ¾ of a lb of butter 10 eggs 1 lb of flour 1 lb of grated cocoanut ½ a wine glass of Rose Water, 1 grated nutmeg   Beat the butter and sugar very light, then stir in the Rose water   beat in one fourth of the flour   Whisk the eggs until very thick which stir in by degrees; then add the remainder of the flour half at a time   lastly the cocoanut mix all well together

(Hopkins?) Family Cookbook

Makes two 7-cup tube cakes or one 7-cup tube cake and one loaf cake or one 13-cup tube cake

1½ cups butter	1 tablespoon freshly grated
2 cups sugar	nutmeg
3 tablespoons rose water	6 eggs
3½ cups sifted flour	4½ cups freshly grated coconut

Hearth:

1. Cream butter until very light. Add sugar, ½ cup at a time, beating in each addition thoroughly before adding the next. Blend in rosewater.
2. Stir together flour and nutmeg. Add 1 cup to creamed mixture, blending in thoroughly.
3. Add eggs, one at a time, beating in each one completely before adding the next.
4. Gradually add remainder of dry mixture, blending in each addition thoroughly.
5. Fold in coconut.
6. Pour into greased pans. Place in preheated Dutch ovens and bake, following Dutch oven directions on pages 216–217, for 1½ hours or until cake tests done.
7. Carefully remove cake pans from Dutch ovens. Cool about 10 minutes, then run a knife around edges and turn cakes out to cool before slicing.

---

*Courtesy of the Virginia Historical Society

Modern:
1. Use a mixer to prepare cake, following hearth directions 1 through 5. Preheat oven to 325° and bake for 1½ hours or until cake tests done.
2. Allow cakes to cool on rack for about 10 minutes. Run knife around edges and turn out onto rack to finish cooling.

Miss Leslie's Indian Pound Cake

Eight eggs.
The weight of eight eggs in powdered sugar.
The weight of six eggs in Indian meal, sifted.
Half a pound of butter.
One nutmeg, grated,—or a tea-spoonful of cinnamon.

Stir the butter and sugar to a cream. Beat the eggs very light. Stir the meal and eggs, alternately, into the butter and sugar. Grate in the nutmeg. Stir all well. Butter a tin pan, put in the mixture, and bake it in a moderate oven.

Eliza Leslie

Makes 1 7-cup tube cake

5 eggs
1 cup butter
2 cups granulated sugar
2 cups white cornmeal

1 cup flour
2 teaspoons freshly grated
  nutmeg
1 teaspoon cinnamon

Hearth:
1. Beat eggs until very foamy. Set aside.
2. Cream butter until fluffy. Gradually add sugar, beating in each addition well before adding the next. Beat creamed mixture until light and fluffy.
3. Combine cornmeal and flour with spices. Blend into creamed butter and sugar, alternating with eggs, one third at a time. Again beat in each addition thoroughly before adding the next.
4. Pour batter into greased 7-cup tube pan. Put pan on trivet in preheated Dutch oven and bake, following directions on pages 216–217, for 1½ hours. Turn oven occasionally to assure even cooking. Cake is done when straw inserted in middle comes out clean and cake pulls away from sides of pan.
5. Carefully remove cake from Dutch oven and cool about 10 minutes. Run a sharp knife around sides of pan to loosen cake. Turn out and allow to cool thoroughly before slicing.

Modern:

1. Use electric mixer to beat eggs. Then pour them into a small bowl and set aside.

2. In same mixer bowl, cream butter and sugar as instructed in hearth direction 2.

3. Follow hearth directions 3 and 4. Preheat oven to 325°. Bake cake 1½ hours or until it tests done. Remove from oven and cool on rack 10 minutes. Loosen edges and turn onto rack to cool completely before slicing.

Note: Changing tastes have eliminated this once popular cake from the American dessert scene. It is given here to illustrate another of the many uses for cornmeal during the 18th and early 19th centuries. Surprisingly good, although somewhat heavy in texture, it is best eaten on the day in which it is made.

Paul Family Pound Cake

Beat a pound of butter to a cream and mix with it the whites and Yolks of eight eggs beaten apart. Have ready warm by the fire a pound of flour and the same of sifted sugar; mix them and a few cloves, a little nutmeg and cinnamon in fine powder together. Then by degrees work the dry ingridients [sic] into the butter and eggs, When well beaten add a glass of wine. It must be beaten a full hour—butter a pan and bake an hour in a quick oven.

Araminta G. Paul

Makes 1 large tube cake (13-cup) or 2 loaf cakes

2 cups unsweetened butter
2 cups granulated sugar
6 eggs
3½ cups flour

1½ teaspoons freshly grated nutmeg
¼ teaspoon cloves, ground
1¼ teaspoon ground cinnamon
¼ cup sherry

Hearth:

1. Cream butter until light. Add sugar, ½ cup at a time, beating in each addition thoroughly before adding the next.
2. Add eggs one at a time, beating in each one thoroughly before adding the next.
3. Sift flour with nutmeg, cloves, and cinnamon.
4. Gradually add dry mixture to creamed butter, sugar, and eggs. Beat in each addition thoroughly before adding the next.
5. Mix in sherry until well blended.
6. Pour batter into greased pan. Bake in preheated Dutch oven, following directions on pages 216–217, for 1½ hours or until cake tests done.
7. Carefully remove cake from Dutch oven and cool about 10 minutes. Run knife around edges and turn cake out to cool before slicing.

Modern:

1. Use a mixer to prepare cake, following hearth directions 1 through 5.

2. Pour batter into greased pan. Preheat oven to 325° and bake cake 1½ hours or until cake tests done.

3. Allow cake to cool on rack for about 10 minutes. Run knife around edges and turn out onto rack to finish cooling.

Hannah Glasse's Seed or Saffron Cake

You must take a quarter of a peck of fine flour, a pound and a half of butter, three ounces of carraway-seeds, six eggs beat well, a quarter of an ounce of cloves and mace beat together very fine, a pennyworth of cinnamon beat, a pound of sugar, a pennyworth of rose-water, a pennyworth of saffron, a pint and a half of yeast, and a quart of milk; mix it all together lightly with your hands thus: first boil your milk and butter, then skim off the butter and mix with your flour, and a little of the milk; stir the yeast into the rest and strain it, mix it with flour, put in your seed and spice, rose-water, tincture of saffron, sugar, and eggs; beat it all up well with your hands lightly, and bake it in a hoop or pan, but be sure to butter the pan well: it will take an hour and half in a quick oven. You may leave out the seed if you choose it, and I think it rather better without it; but that you may do as you like.

Hannah Glasse

Makes 1 7-cup tube cake

1 cup milk, divided	¼ teaspoon cinnamon
½ teaspoon crushed saffron	½ cup sugar
¾ cup softened butter	2 teaspoons yeast
2¼ cups sifted flour	1 egg
¼ teaspoon cloves	1 tablespoon rose water
¼ teaspoon mace	1 tablespoon caraway seeds

Hearth:

1. Heat cup milk over warm coals until very warm. Pour ½ cup over saffron and set aside.

2. Combine remaining ½ cup milk with butter and set aside to cool to lukewarm.

3. While milk is cooling, sift flour with spices and sugar into a large bowl. Stir in yeast.

4. Beat egg until frothy and combine with rose water.

5. When milk and butter are lukewarm gradually add to dry mixture, beating until well blended.

6. Stir in egg and rose water, then milk and saffron, blending thoroughly. Batter will be very soft.

7. Coarsely crush caraway seeds and fold into batter.

8. Beat mixture vigorously for a few minutes. Cover and set in a warm place to rise until doubled in bulk, about 2 hours.

9. Beat batter down and pour into greased 7-cup tube pan. Again cover and set to rise in a warm place, about 1 hour.

10. Place pan on rack or trivet in preheated Dutch oven and bake, following directions on pages 216–217 until done, about 45 minutes. Carefully remove from Dutch oven and turn cake out on rack to cool before slicing.

Modern:

1. Follow hearth direction 1, warming milk over moderate heat until very warm.

2. Follow hearth directions 2 through 9.

3. Preheat oven to 375° and bake cake 30 minutes, then reduce oven temperature to 350° and continue baking 15 minutes or until cake is done. Remove from oven and turn out on rack to cool.

Notes: (1) Seed cakes were popular during the 18th century, but the addition of caraway seeds to this spicy batter may not be agreeable to everyone's taste. Indeed, as the 18th-century cookbook writer Hannah Glasse added at the end of her recipe, "You may leave out the seed if you choose it, and I think it rather better without it; but that you may do as you like." Her instructions apply to this modernized version. (2) This cake is even better when slightly "aged." After baking, allow flavors to blend for about 24 hours before serving.

Elizabeth Eppes' Washington Cake*

1¾ lbs of flour ¾ of butter 1½ of sugar, 6 eggs, one pint of milk 1 nutmeg 12 cloves, 1 lb currants 1 of Raisins 1 tea spoon of pearl ash dissolved in a wine glass of Brandy.

Elizabeth Eppes

Makes 1 large tube cake or 2 loaf cakes

¾ cup butter, softened	1 teaspoon soda
1½ cups sugar	1½ teaspoons nutmeg
3 eggs	1 teaspoon cloves
3 cups flour, sifted	¾ cup half-and-half
1½ cups currants	¼ cup brandy
1½ cups raisins	

Hearth:

1. Cream butter until very light. Add sugar, ½ cup at a time, beating in each addition thoroughly before adding the next.
2. Add eggs one at a time, beating in each one before adding the next.
3. Mix ¼ cup of the flour with currants and raisins and set aside. Stir remaining flour together with soda, nutmeg, and cloves.
4. Gradually add dry mixture to creamed butter, sugar, and eggs, alternating with half-and-half. Beat in each addition thoroughly before adding the next.
5. Mix in brandy until well blended. Then fold in raisins and currants.
6. Pour batter into greased pan. Bake in preheated Dutch oven, following directions on pages 216–217, for 1½ hours or until cake tests done.
7. Carefully remove cake from Dutch oven and cool about 10 minutes. Run knife around edges of cake and turn out to cool before slicing.

---

*Courtesy of Virginia Historical Society

Modern:

1. Use a mixer to prepare cake, following hearth directions 1 through 5. Fold in raisins and currants by hand.

2. Pour batter into greased pan. Preheat oven to 325° and bake cake 1½ hours or until cake tests done.

3. Allow cake to cool on rack for about 10 minutes. Run knife around edges and turn out onto rack to finish cooling.

Virginia Gray's Icing

1½ lbs best loaf sugar; 3 gills water gently stew until it ropes—then throw it into a bowl keep stirring until warmer than new milk have ready the whites of 8 eggs beat to a strong froth, add by the spoonful beating all the time until the eggs are in—flavor it & beat unceasingly 1 hour.

Gray Family Papers

Makes about 3 cups

3 cups sugar
1 cup water
3 egg whites
Dash of salt

1½ to 2 teaspoons flavoring of choice (almond, lemon, rose water, or vanilla)

1. Combine sugar and water. Cover and simmer over moderately low heat until sugar crystals are dissolved. Do not stir. Uncover and keep at a simmer until mixture spins a thread when dropped from the end of a spoon.
2. Whip egg whites until frothy. Add salt. Add sugar syrup in a thin stream, beating eggs whites continually. Beat until nearly cool. Add flavoring and continue beating for several more minutes.

Mrs. Tebbs' Chocolate Nuts

The whites of two eggs beaten to a froth—mix in two ounces of Chocolate or a third of a cake of chocolate and one pound of Loaf sugar well beaten—Bake on white paper in an oven.
Sift the Chocolate and Sugar, let the oven be barely warm.

M. H. D. Tebbs Receipt Book

Makes about 1½ to 2 dozen

3 egg whites
6 tablespoons sifted
   unsweetened cocoa

¾ cup superfine sugar

Hearth:
1. Stir together cocoa and sugar. Set aside.
2. Beat egg whites until soft peaks form. Gradually add sifted cocoa and sugar, beating until stiff peaks form.
3. Preheat Dutch oven, then set away from hearth to cool slightly.
4. Put a sheet of parchment paper on a tin baking pan. Drop meringue by tablespoonfuls onto parchment paper, spacing about 1½ inches apart.
5. Put tin on trivet in warm Dutch oven. Cover and set aside for meringues to bake 1 hour or longer. Do not set Dutch oven on hot coals; heat from warmed oven should be sufficient to bake meringues.
6. When meringues are baked, immediatly remove from paper and set on rack to cool.

Modern:
1. Follow hearth directions 1 through 4.
2. Preheat oven to 250°. Bake meringues 1 hour, then turn off oven and let meringues remain until oven is cold.
3. Remove from paper, cool completely on rack, and store in air-tight container.

Mrs. Robert E. Lee's Gingerbread*

6 cups of flour 1 of lard with a table spoonfull of butter two tea spoonfuls salt, a cup of butter milk teaspoonful of soda sifted with the flour half a cup of brown sugar as much molasses as will make a dough which must be rolled out & baked in a moderate oven. The dough should be well worked out & rolled with flour enough to make the cakes smooth but not to have any on the outside when baked

Mrs. R. E. Lee

Makes about 3 dozen

½ cup softened lard	3½ cups sifted flour (or more)
1 tablespoon softened butter	1 teaspoon salt
½ cup brown sugar	1 teaspoon soda
½ cup buttermilk	2½ teaspoons ginger
½ cup molasses	

Hearth:

1. Cream lard and butter. Add sugar and beat together well.
2. Blend in buttermilk and molasses.
3. Sift together dry ingredients and gradually add to liquids. Blend well.
4. Turn dough out onto lightly floured surface and knead briefly to thoroughly incorporate ingredients, blending in extra flour if needed.
5. Roll out dough to ¼″ thickness. Cut with round cutter.
6. Put cakes on greased tins and set on trivet in preheated Dutch oven. Cover and set Dutch oven on hot coals. Bake, following directions on pages 216–217, for 12 to 15 minutes.
7. Remove from tins and cool on racks.

Modern:

1. Follow hearth directions 1 through 5.
2. Preheat oven to 350°. Put cakes on greased cookie sheets and bake 12 to 15 minutes. Remove to a rack and cool.

---

*Courtesy of the Virginia Historical Society

Mrs. Tebbs' Naples Biscuit

5 eggs beat very well ½ lb sugar beat them very light together.—½ lb of flour—rose water, cinnamon, nutmeg & six drops of essence of Lemon.—
Mrs. Humphreys in M. H. D. Tebbs Receipt Book

Makes 20 to 24

3 eggs
1 cup sugar
2 cups flour
¼ teaspoon freshly grated
   nutmeg

½ teaspoon cinnamon
1 teaspoon rose water
¼ teaspoon lemon extract

Hearth:
1. Beat eggs until very light and foamy. Gradually add sugar, continuing to beat until mixture is very fluffy.
2. Combine flour and spices. Blend into egg and sugar mixture. When thoroughly combined, add rose water and lemon extract.
3. Butter French roll pans. Fill about half full. Bake in hearth, following directions on pages 216–217, until a delicate brown, 12 to 15 minutes.
4. Remove from pan and cool on rack.

Modern:
1. Follow hearth directions 1 and 2.
2. Preheat oven to 375°. Fill buttered ladyfinger pans half full with batter and bake 12 to 15 minutes.
3. Remove from pan and cool on rack.

Jumbles

Three eggs.
Half a pound of flour, sifted.
Half a pound of butter.
Half a pound of powdered loaf-sugar.
A table-spoonful of rose-water.
A nutmeg grated.
A tea-spoonful of mixed mace and cinnamon.

Stir the sugar and butter to a cream. Beat the eggs very light. Throw them, all at once, into the pan of flour. Put in, at once, the butter and sugar, and then add the spice and rose-water. If you have no rose-water, substitute six or seven drops of strong essence of lemon, or more if the essence is weak. Stir the whole very hard, with a knife.

Spread some flour on your paste-board, and flour your hands well. Take up with your knife, a portion of the dough, and lay it on the board. Roll it lightly with your hands, into long thin rolls, which must be cut into equal lengths, curled up into rings, and laid gently into an iron or tin pan, buttered, not too close to each other, as they spread in baking. Bake them in a quick oven about five minutes and grate loaf-sugar over them when cool.

Eliza Leslie

Makes about 3 dozen

1 cup butter	2 teaspoons freshly grated
1 cup sugar	nutmeg
1 egg	½ teaspoon mace
1 tablespoon rose water	½ teaspoon cinnamon
3 cups sifted flour	Additional granulated sugar

Hearth:

1. Cream butter and sugar until very light. Add egg and rose water, blending thoroughly.
2. Sift flour with spices. Add all at once to creamed mixture, blending well.
3. Wrap dough and chill at least 2 hours.
4. On lightly floured surface, roll out dough to ¼″ thickness.

5. Cut with wine glass or cut into strips 1" × 8" and shape into rings.

6. Put on tins. Bake in preheated Dutch oven over hot coals, following directions on pages 216–217, 10 to 12 minutes. Remove, sprinkle with sugar, and cool.

Modern:

Follow hearth directions 1 through 4. Cookies may be cut with doughnut cutter. For step 6, preheat oven to 375°. Bake cookies on ungreased sheets 10 to 12 minutes or until lightly browned around edges. Remove to rack, sprinkle with sugar and cool.

Note: These cookies may be varied by adding one of the following: 1 to 2 tablespoons caraway seeds, crushed; ½ cup chopped almonds; ½ cup currants; ½ cup coconut.

Mrs. Tucker's Naples Biscuit

1ᵇ Flour 1 D° Sugar—12 Whites & 10 Yolks of eggs 2 Glasses Wine—
These should gradually harden in the oven till quite crisp & be frequently
turned in the pan—

Tucker Family Cookbook

Makes 3 to 4 dozen

4 eggs, separated (4 whites, 3 yolks)
1 cup sugar

1⅔ cups sifted flour
¼ cup Madeira wine

Hearth:
1. Beat egg yolks until thick. Very gradually add sugar, beating in each addition completely before adding the next.
2. Sift flour again and add, alternating with wine, a little at a time, beating well.
3. Whip egg whites until very stiff and fold them into the batter.
4. Pour into buttered French roll pans or muffin tins. Carefully put filled tins on trivet in preheated Dutch oven. Cover and set on hot coals. Bake, following directions on pages 216–217, until light golden brown, 10 to 15 minutes.
5. Remove biscuits and cool thoroughly on rack. Then return them to a warmed Dutch oven, cover, and let them crisp in the oven, turning occasionally, 3 hours or longer. Biscuits will be very dry.

Modern:
1. Follow hearth directions 1 through 3.
2. Preheat oven to 325°. Fill buttered ladyfinger pans. Bake until light golden brown, 10 to 15 minutes, then remove to racks to cool.
3. Return biscuits to warm oven until they are crisp, turning occasionally, as in hearth direction 5.

Note: Store in air-tight container.

Mrs. Randolph's Shrewsbury Cakes

Cream one pound of butter, add a pound of powdered sugar, with a pound and a half of flour, six eggs, a grated nutmeg, and a gill of brandy; work it well, roll it thin, and cut it in shapes; put them on tin sheets, and bake without discolouring them.

Mary Randolph

Makes about 3 dozen

1 cup softened butter	2 eggs
3¼ cups sifted flour	1 tablespoon rose water
1 cup sugar	2 tablespoons cream

Hearth:
1. Cream butter.
2. Combine flour and sugar. Work into butter, mixing well.
3. Beat eggs until light. Add rose water and cream, blending together well.
4. Blend liquids into butter mixture, combining well.
5. Turn dough onto lightly floured surface. Roll out ⅛″ thick and cut into rounds with glass or cutter.
6. Put on greased tin pans. Set on trivet in preheated Dutch oven. Cover and set over hot coals. Bake, following directions on pages 216–217, until edges of cookies are a light golden brown.
7. Remove from tins and place on rack to cool.

Modern:
1. Follow hearth directions 1 through 5.
2. Preheat oven to 350°. Put cakes on greased cookie sheets and bake 12 to 15 minutes or until a light golden brown. Remove from sheets and place on rack to cool.

EOT 50—7.6 M ch

Queen Cake

One pound of powdered white sugar.
One pound of fresh butter—washed.
Fourteen ounces of sifted flour.
Ten eggs.
One wine-glass of wine and brandy, mixed.
Half a glass of rose-water, or twelve drops of essence of lemon.
One tea-spoonful of mace and cinnamon, mixed.
One nutmeg, beaten or grated.

Pound the spice to a fine powder, in a marble mortar, and sift it well.

Put the sugar into a deep earthen pan, and cut the butter into it. Stir them together, till very light.

Beat the eggs in a broad shallow pan, till they are perfectly smooth and thick.

Stir into the butter and sugar, a little of the beaten egg, and then a little flour, and so on alternately, a little egg and a little flour, till the whole is in; continuing all the time to beat the eggs, and stirring the mixture very hard. Add by degrees, the spice, and then the liquor, a little at a time. Finally, put in the rose-water, or essence of lemon.* Stir the whole very hard at the last.

Take about two dozen little tins, or more, if you have room for them in the oven. Rub them very well with fresh butter. With a spoon, put some of the mixture in each tin, but do not fill them to the top as the cakes will rise high in baking. Bake them in a quick oven, about a quarter of an hour. When they are done they will shrink a little from the sides of the tins.

Before you fill the tins again, scrape them well with a knife, and wash or wipe them clean.

If the cakes are scorched by too hot a fire, do not scrape off the burnt parts till they have grown cold.

Make an icing with the whites of three eggs, beaten till it stands alone, and twenty-four tea-spoonfuls of the best loaf-sugar, powdered, and beaten gradually into the white of egg. Flavour it with a tea-spoonful of rose-water or eight drops of essence of lemon, stirred in at the last. Spread it evenly with a broad knife, over the top of each queen-cake, ornamenting them, (while the icing is quite wet) with red and green nonpareils, or fine sugar-sand, dropped on carefully, with the thumb and finger.

When the cakes are iced, set them in a warm place to dry; but not too near the fire, as that will cause the icing to crack.

Eliza Leslie

Makes about 3 dozen standard cupcakes or about 5 dozen miniature cupcakes

2 cups softened butter
2 cups granulated sugar
4 eggs
2 tablespoons white wine
2 tablespoons brandy
2 tablespoons rose water
3 cups sifted flour
1 tablespoon cinnamon

1 teaspoon mace
1 teaspoon lemon extract

Glaze:
2 cups sifted confectioner's
  sugar
3 tablespoons milk
2 teaspoons lemon extract

Hearth:

1. Cream butter until light. Gradually add sugar, beating in each addition thoroughly until light and fluffy.
2. Beat in eggs one at a time, blending in each well before adding the next.
3. Combine wine, brandy, and rose water.
4. Sift flour with spices and add alternately with liquid to creamed mixture, beating well after each addition. Blend in lemon extract.
5. Lightly butter patty pans. Fill half full with batter. Very carefully set them on rack or trivet in preheated Dutch oven. Bake over hot coals, according to directions on pages 216–217, about 15 minutes. Watch carefully; they are ready when cakes pull away from sides of pans and top springs back when lightly pushed.
6. Carefully remove cakes from Dutch oven and turn out of tins. Glaze tops lightly while still warm. When first glaze has hardened slightly, glaze again.

Modern:

1. Follow hearth directions 1 through 4.
2. Pour batter into lightly greased miniature tart pans or cupcake pans. Bake in preheated 375° oven 12 to 15 minutes or until done. Follow hearth directions 5 and 6 to complete.

Sweet Pies, Puddings, and Cheesecakes

Sweet pies and puddings were dearly loved by Virginians and were very much a part of their British heritage. Their evolution from ancient times is complicated and often confusing, beginning when pie crusts were known as "coffins," used primarily as containers in which sweetened fish or meat were baked, to modern times and their principal function as dessert. There was a fine line between pies and puddings that is difficult to define, a link that developed over time.

Puddings were uniquely English in character and evidently filled a real need in the British diet. "Rich in fat and carbohydrates to keep out the cold, and in sugar and fruit to build up energy, the Englishman's pudding filled his stomach and satisfied his appetite."[1]

There were several types of puddings—boiled, baked, and stirred—made from a variety of ingredients. A visitor to England in the 1690's summed it up: "The pudding is a dish very difficult to be described, because of the several sorts there are of it; flour, milk, eggs, butter, sugar, suet, marrow, raisins, etc., etc., are the most common ingredients of a pudding. They bake them in an oven, they boil them with meat, they make them fifty several ways: BLESSED BE HE THAT INVENTED PUDDING, for it is a manna that hits the palates of all sorts of people."[2]

Boiled puddings were at first encased in bags made from the entrails of sheep or pigs, filled with a combination of chopped animal organs, bread crumbs, seasonings, and binders (the Scottish *haggis* is a holdover from this medieval practice). At best this was a messy procedure. Experiments with other containers finally led to the pudding cloth, which was in use by the early 17th century. Main dish and sweet puddings to be boiled in cloths, such as the traditional Christmas plum pudding, became a regular part of the British diet.

Another type of pudding was stirred as it cooked over the fire—really a custard to be spooned or used as a pie filling. This was part of the crossover in the convoluted story.

A third type provided the strongest connection between puddings and pies. In looking for a container other than animal stomachs to hold prepared puddings, English cooks began pouring the filling into a pan, then topping it with a crust.[3] Later cooks began using "paste" (pastry) as a decorative rim around the edge of the dish. Recipes appeared instructing the cook to "lay a puff-paste all over the dish, pour in the ingredients and bake it."[4] And so the pie as we know it today was born.

Early 18th-century cookbooks contained receipts for baked bread and batter puddings that included Yorkshire and rice puddings. All were dear to the hearts of the English. "Ah, what an excellent thing is an English pudding! To come in pudding-time, is as much as to say, to come in the most lucky moment in the world. Give an English man a pudding, and he shall think it a noble treat in any part of the world."[5]

Pies and baked puddings can be cooked on the hearth following the instructions given for cake baking on pages 216–217.

To boil puddings, a cloth is needed. Choose a sturdy material such as the heavy linen used for crewel embroidery or a firm muslin. Two notes of caution: Be sure that the cloth is *not* permanent press, and *always* prewash the fabric to remove any sizing or chemicals added by manufacturers.

Making the cloth is a simple procedure. Cut a 24-inch square of material. You may either seam the edges together to form a bag or put the cloth into a large bowl and use it as a mold to shape the prepared pudding. Pull the cloth up around the pudding and tie it firmly at the top, leaving several inches of space for it to expand.

Each time after using the cloth, dip it in very hot water, then spread it with butter and sprinkle it with flour before adding the filling. This helps to "seal in" the mixture. Be sure that the pudding cloths are washed and stored away for further use.

The pudding is boiled in a large pot of water on the crane or on top of the stove. It is important that once the pudding is put in the water remains at a steady boil. Keep a kettle of hot water on hand to add more to the pot if necessary so that the pudding remains well covered and cooking steadily. Occasionally turn the pudding in the boiling water to assure even cooking. Cooking times are lengthy, but the results are delicious when served with one of the sweet sauces beginning on page 299.

Cheesecakes are another confusing development in the history of cooking. Evolving from early times when curds were eaten with sugar, spices, and cream, cheesecakes became more like those with which we are familiar today, somewhere between a cake and a pie baked in a crust. These cheese pies often contained currants as part of the filling. By the middle of the 17th century, the same basic filling, although still referred to as cheesecake, was often made without the curds. The cream, spices, and sugars were combined with eggs to form a delectable custard filling, still called cheesecake or chess (a corruption of *cheese*) pie. Still later, lemon juice and peel were added to the basic filling, creating lemon cheese (or chess) cakes or pies, also known as lemon curd.[6] These terms carried over, as seen in the following recipe.

Miss Leslie's Common Pie Crust

Sift two quarts of superfine flour into a pan. Divide one pound of fresh butter into two equal parts, and cut up one half in the flour, rubbing it fine. Mix it with a very little cold water, and make it into a round lump. Knead it a little. Then flour your paste-board, and roll the dough out into a large thin sheet. Spread it all over with the remainder of the butter. Flour it, fold it up, and rol it out again. Then fold it again, or roll it into a scroll. Cut it into as many pieces as you want sheets of paste, and roll each not quite an inch thick. Butter your pie-dish.

This paste will do for family use, when covered pies are wanted. Also for apple dumplings, pot-pies, &c.; though all boiled paste is best when made of suet instead of butter. Short cakes may be made of this, cut out with the edge of a tumbler. It should always be eaten fresh.

Eliza Leslie

Makes enough pastry for tops and bottoms of two 9″ pies

4 cups sifted flour
1 teaspoon salt

1 cup softened unsalted butter, divided
¼ to ⅓ cup cold water

1. Sift flour and salt together into a large bowl.
2. Rub in ½ cup butter by hand until mixture is crumbly.
3. Add enough cold water to bind dough together, sprinkling it on and gathering dough together lightly.
4. Shape into a ball. Turn out on lightly floured surface. Roll out into thin sheet.
5. Spread remaining ½ cup butter over sheet of dough. Lightly sprinkle with flour.
6. Fold up dough by bringing long edges together in middle, then folding short ends together in middle to form an envelope. Roll out again into a thin sheet.
7. Fold dough again as in step 6. Roll out again and use as needed.

Miss Leslie's Lard Paste

Lard for paste should never be used without an equal quantity of butter. Take half a pound of nice lard, and half a pound of fresh butter; rub them together into two pounds and a quarter of flour, and mix it with a little cold water to a stiff dough. Roll it out twice. Use it for common pies. Lard should always be kept in tin.

Eliza Leslie

Makes enough pastry for top and bottom of one 9″ pie or about 20 3-inch patty pans

2½ cups sifted flour
1 teaspoon salt
¼ cup lard

½ cup butter
5 tablespoons cold water, or as needed

1. Sift flour and salt together into a bowl.
2. Rub in lard and butter by hand until mixture is crumbly.
3. Sprinkle on 5 tablespoons water, gathering dough together and adding a little more water if necessary. Form into a ball and roll out on lightly floured surface. Use as directed for a variety of recipes.

Sweet Paste (Pastry)

*Sift a pound and a quarter of the finest flour, and three ounces of pow-
dered loaf-sugar into a deep dish. Cut up in it one pound of the best fresh
butter, and rub it fine with your hands. Make a hole in the middle, pour
in the yolks of two beaten eggs, and mix them with the flour, &c. Then
wet the whole to a stiff paste with half a pint of rich milk. Knead it well,
and roll it out.*

*This paste is intended for tarts of the finest sweetmeats. If used as
shells, they should be baked empty, and filled when cool. If made into covered tarts, they may be iced all over, in the manner of cakes, with beaten
white of egg and powdered loaf-sugar. To make puffs of it, roll it out and
cut it into round pieces with the edges of a large tumbler, or with a tin
cutter. Lay the sweetmeat on one half of the paste, fold the other over it in
the form of a half-moon, and unite the edges by notching them together.
Bake them in a brisk oven, and when cool, send them to table handsomely
arranged, several on a dish.*

*Sweet paste is rarely used except for very handsome entertainments. You
may add some rose water in mixing it.*

Eliza Leslie

Enough for one 10″ pie

2 cups sifted flour	1 egg
¼ cup sugar	1 tablespoon rose water
1 teaspoon salt	¼ cup half-and-half
½ cup butter, softened	

Hearth:
1. Resift flour with sugar and salt.
2. Dice butter into dry ingredients. Rub in by hand until
thoroughly blended and mixture is crumbly.
3. Blend in egg and rose water.
4. Gradually add half-and-half, combining with other ingredients.
5. Gather mixture into a ball and turn out onto lightly
floured board. Knead briefly, just enough to blend ingredients. Wrap and chill dough 1 hour or longer.
6. When ready to use, place dough on lightly floured
board. Using a light but firm touch, roll out dough until
thin. Lift and turn dough, always rolling away from you, to
assure even crust.

7. Ease dough gently into greased pie or quiche pan. Allow it to rest about 10 minutes, then press into pan and flute edge.

8. To partially bake crust (necessary for some recipes), prick dough all over with a fork. Fill another pie tin with dried beans and set it on top of dough to prevent it from shrinking.

9. Carefully place in very hot Dutch oven and cover. Allow to sit by fire about 10 minutes or until just beginning to brown. Remove from Dutch oven and carefully take out bean-filled tin. Set crust aside to cool completely before filling.

Modern:

1. Follow hearth directions 1 through 8.

2. Bake crust at 400° following hearth direction 9 to complete recipe.

Mr. Carter's Apple Tart

*Take eight large Pippens, pare them, and core them, and cut them in
pretty thick Slices; lay them in a broad Stew-pan, and put to them some
clarify'd Sugar, and some Slices of Orange-peel, and stove them very
gently till they are clear; then sheet a Dish, or Petit-pan with Sugar-
paste; lay in the Bottom some slices candy'd Citron; lay over your Apples
in Rows, and some more Citron on them; then boil a Pint of Cream, and
draw it up thick with the Yolks of four or five Eggs, a little Sugar, and a
Blade of Mace; pour it over the Apples, and bake it, and when the Crust
is enough, it is ready.*

Another Way is,
*To stew the Apples, and bruise them into Pulp, and put to them some
Cream, and some Naples Bisket grated, and work it together with the
Yolks of Eggs and a little Orange-flower Water; sheet your Dish; put them
in, cross-bar them, and ice them over, and bake it; so serve it.*

Charles Carter

Makes one 10″ tart

6 to 7 cups peeled, cored, and
   sliced tart apples (Granny
   Smiths are best)
1 cup sugar, divided
2 tablespoons freshly grated
   orange peel
1½ cups cream

3 eggs, lightly beaten
½ teaspoon mace
¼ cup diced citron
10″ Sweet Pastry Shell (page
   248), partially baked

Hearth:
1. Put apples in heavy frying pan set on trivet over hot
coals. Add ⅔ cup sugar and orange peel. Cover and cook,
stirring often, until apples are just tender. Remove from
heat and set aside to cool.
2. Combine cream with remaining ⅓ cup sugar, eggs, and
mace. Beat together well.
3. Sprinkle bottom of tart shell with diced citron. Arrange
cooked apple mixture over citron. Pour on cream mixture.
4. Carefully put filled tart on trivet in preheated Dutch
oven with about 1″ hot water in bottom. Cover and gently
put oven over hot coals. Bake, following directions on pages

216–217, for 45 minutes or until knife inserted in center comes out clean. Remove from fire.

5. Carefully remove baked tart pan from Dutch oven. Set aside to cool completely before slicing.

Modern:
1. Follow hearth directions 1 through 3, cooking apples over moderately low heat.
2. Bake apple tart in preheated 375° oven for 30 minutes, then reduce heat to 350° and continue baking until knife inserted in center comes out clean, another 20 to 30 minutes. Cool completely before slicing.

Mrs. W. H. F. Lee's Mincemeat Pie Filling

Boil one beefs heart—peel & chop fine—It will make about 6 cups full when chopped. Add the same—i.e. 6 cups of chopped apples & chopped suet, mix & cover the whole with cider. Add 1 qt. wine. 1 qt. packed, seeded raisins 1 pt. brandy, 1 pt. currants—Cloves, nutmeg, allspice, sugar, salt & pepper to taste.

6 cups meat weighed 1¼ lbs
6 cups suet weighed 18 oz —*both chopped*
1 qt. raisins 2 lbs light. 1 pt. currants 14 oz.

Shirley Plantation Collection

Makes enough mincemeat for 6 to 8 pies

6 cups cooked, chopped beef heart (approximately 1¼ pounds)
6 cups peeled, cored, and chopped tart apples, such as Granny Smith
6 cups finely chopped beef suet
Apple cider to cover
4 cups raisins
2 cups currants
1 teaspoon cloves (or more to taste)
2 teaspoons nutmeg (or more to taste)
1 teaspoon allspice (or more to taste)
½ teaspoon salt
¼ teaspoon pepper
1 cup sugar (or more to taste)
4 cups red wine
2 cups brandy
Pie Crust (page 246)

1. Combine beef heart, apples, and suet in large pot. Cover with cider.
2. Combine raisins, currants, cloves, nutmeg, allspice, salt, pepper, and sugar. Mix into beef mixture, stirring well.
3. Combine wine and brandy. Pour over beef mixture and stir well to blend.
4. Cover and cook mixture 2 to 3 hours, stirring often. Pack while hot into hot sterile jars and set aside to age at least one month before using.
5. Use to fill any of the pie crusts in this section.
6. If baking on the hearth, follow directions on pages 216–217.
7. If baking in conventional oven, preheat oven to 425° and bake pie 40 to 50 minutes.

Randolph Pumpkin Pudding (Pie)

Stew a fine sweet pumpkin till soft and dry, rub it through a sieve, mix with the pulp six eggs quite light, a quarter of a pound of butter, half a pint of new milk, some pounded ginger and nutmeg, a wine glass of brandy, and sugar to your taste. Should it be too liquid, stew it a little dryer; put a paste round the edges and in the bottom of a shallow dish or plate, pour in the mixture, cut some thin bits of paste, twist them and lay them across the top and bake it nicely.

Mary Randolph

Serves 6 to 8

About 1½ pounds pumpkin (to equal 2 cups cooked and mashed)
¼ cup butter, melted
3 eggs, beaten
1 cup half and half

1¼ teaspoons ginger
¾ teaspoon nutmeg
1 cup sugar
¼ cup brandy
Pie Crust (page 246)
Whipped cream

Hearth:
1. Boil pumpkin in pot on crane until fork tender. Cool, peel, and mash.
2. Add butter, eggs, and half and half. Beat together well.
3. Add ginger, nutmeg, and sugar. Blend well, then mix in brandy.
4. Pour into prepared pie crust.
5. Set pie on trivet in preheated Dutch oven. Set Dutch oven on hot coals and bake, following directions on pages 216–217, about 60 minutes or until knife inserted in center comes out clean.
6. Cool and serve with whipped cream.

Modern:
1. May use canned, cooked pumpkin.
2. Follow hearth directions 2 through 4.
3. Preheat oven to 425°. Bake pie for 10 minutes. Reduce heat to 350° and continue baking pie for 45 to 50 minutes longer, or until knife inserted in center comes out clean. Follow hearth direction 6 to complete.

Southall Family Sweet Potato Pie

Take [?] a pound of Potato roasted and picked clean from the brown Skin, put to it half a pound of fresh Butter & beat it well in a Stone Mortar take 12 eggs well beaten to a froth, a wine glass of Orange flower water a little Mace beat it all together in the Mortar half pound of double refined [?] Sugar mix it well & when light put it in a China or Earthen Dish & bake it with or without Paste Citron is a great improvement to this Pudding Dish with Puff Paste round the Brim pour in your Pudding Ornament it with large ____ [sliced?] Citron & Blanched Almonds

Southall Family

Serves 6 to 8

About 2 pounds sweet potatoes
(to equal 2 cups cooked and
mashed)
¼ cup butter, melted
5 eggs
2 tablespoons plus 1 teaspoon
orange flower water
1 teaspoon mace

½ to ¾ cup sugar
¼ teaspoon salt
Pie Crust (page 246)
¼ cup diced citron
¼ cup blanched, slivered
almonds
Whipped cream

Hearth:

1. Roast or boil potatoes until fork tender. Cool, peel, and mash.
2. Beat in softened butter.
3. Beat eggs until light and frothy. Add to sweet potato mixture, beating well.
4. Add orange flower water, mace, sugar to taste, and salt. Blend all together thoroughly.
5. Prepare pie crust and line a greased heatproof pie dish. Pour in sweet potato mixture. Sprinkle with citron and almonds.
6. Put pie on trivet in Dutch oven. Cover, set on hot coals, and bake following directions on pages 216–217 until knife inserted in center comes out clean, about 60 minutes.
7. Remove from heat and cool before serving.
8. Serve with whipped cream.

Modern:

1. Can use unsweetened canned sweet potatoes
2. Follow hearth directions 2 through 5.
3. Preheat oven to 375° and bake for about 1 hour or until knife inserted in center comes out clean.

An Ordinary Bread Pudding

Quarter of a pound of grated stale bread. One quart of milk boiled with two or three sticks of cinnamon slightly broken. Eight eggs Quarter of a pound of mace & little grated lemonpeel. Two ounces of butter. Boil the milk with the cinnamon strain it and set it away till quite cold. Mix the butter and sugar. Grate as much crumb of the bread as will weigh a quarter of a pound. Beat the eggs and when the milk is cold stir them into it in turn with the bread and sugar. Add the lemonpeel and if you choose a tablespoonful of rose-water. Bake it in a buttered dish and grate nutmeg over it when done. Do not send it to the table hot. Baked puddings should never be eaten till they have become cold or at least cool.

Virginia Gearhart Gray Collection

Serves 6 to 8

1 cup milk
1 cup cream
2 sticks cinnamon, broken in 3 or 4 pieces
2 teaspoons freshly grated lemon peel
2 eggs, lightly beaten

½ cup sugar
¼ teaspoon nutmeg
¼ cup melted butter
4 cups coarse bread crumbs
2 teaspoons rose water (optional)

Hearth:

1. Scald milk and cream with cinnamon sticks and lemon peel on trivet over hot coals. Add butter and set aside to cool. When cool, strain into eggs, combining well.

2. Add sugar and nutmeg to bread crumbs. Pour in milk and egg mixture. Add rose water, if desired, and stir mixture well.

3. Pour mixture into buttered heatproof dish. Carefully place on rack in preheated Dutch oven with about 1″ hot water in bottom. Cover and bake on hot coals 45 to 60 minutes or until knife inserted in middle comes out clean.

4. Serve at room temperature or cold with cream, Vanilla Sauce (page 302), or Wine Sauce (page 303).

Modern:

Follow hearth directions 1 through 4, baking pudding in 1½-quart buttered casserole in preheated 350° oven for 45 to 60 minutes.

Note: ½ cup raisins or currants may be added.

Mrs. Alexander Cameron's Fig Pudding

½ lb stale bread crumbs. ½ lb figs put through meat chopper. 2 eggs. 6 oz. brown sugar, 2 oz. flour ¼ lb suet, a little milk, about half a cup. flavor with nutmeg. Boil 2 hours & serve with or without sauce.

Shirley Plantation Collection

Serves 6 to 8

1 egg, slightly beaten
½ cup milk
1 cup brown sugar, firmly
  packed
1 cup finely chopped suet
4 cups stale bread crumbs

2 teaspoons nutmeg
½ cup flour
2 cups chopped fresh figs (or
  ¾ cups dried)
Sweet Sauce (pages 299–303)

Hearth:

1. Combine egg, milk, and brown sugar, blending well.
2. Combine suet, bread crumbs, and nutmeg in a bowl. Add liquid and mix thoroughly.
3. Combine flour with figs, mixing well. Fold into batter.
4. Wet and butter a pudding cloth (see pages 244–245) and gather around batter. Tie securely with string, leaving room for pudding to expand.
5. Set an iron pot of water on crane and bring to a boil over flames. Drop in pudding and boil 2 hours, turning occasionally and keeping water at a boil. Replenish with additional boiling water as needed.
6. Pull crane away from fire and carefully remove pudding. Drain thoroughly in colander, then cut away string and put pudding in serving dish.
7. Serve hot, with or without sauce.

Modern:

Follow hearth directions 1 through 7, boiling pudding in uncovered pot for 2 hours as in hearth direction 5.

Note: Best cooked a week or two before use. Wrap and store in air-tight container. Warm through before serving.

Centre Hill Plum Pudding

1½ lbs bread crumbs (too much)
1 lb raisins
1 lb currants
¼ lb citron
¾ lb brown sugar
½ lb suet, or butter, suet is best
9 eggs—beaten separately
½ pint flour to roll the fruit in.
1 teaspoonful each cloves, mace and cinnamon

This allows about 1 qt. & a kitchen spoonful to each pudding. Boil 3 hours. Hang up in a dry place & use as required.

Shirley Plantation Collection

Makes 1 large or 2 small puddings, enough for 8 to 10 people.

1⅓ cup finely chopped suet
1½ cups brown sugar, firmly packed
5 cups bread crumbs
1 teaspoon ground cloves
1 teaspoon ground cinnamon
1 teaspoon mace
4 eggs
¼ cup flour
1½ cups raisins
1½ cups currants
⅔ cup diced citron
Plum Pudding Sauce (page 301) or Wine Sauce (page 303)

Hearth:
1. Combine suet, brown sugar, bread crumbs, and spices in large bowl.
2. Beat eggs until frothy. Add to dry mixture and mix thoroughly.
3. Sprinkle flour over fruit in separate bowl, then blend together well. Fold fruit into batter.
4. Butter and flour a wet pudding cloth (two if you are making two small puddings). Put cloth into bowl and add batter. Gather edges of cloth around pudding and tie securely, leaving room for puddings to expand.
5. Fill an iron pot with water. Place on crane and bring to boil over flames. Put pudding into boiling water and con-

tinue boiling for 3 hours, turning pudding occasionally. Replenish with additional boiling water as needed.

6. At end of cooking time, carefully remove pudding from water. Set aside to drain thoroughly in colander. When cool, carefully remove string and pudding cloth.

7. Serve pudding with Kate Powell Carter's Plum Pudding Sauce or Shirley Plantation Wine Sauce.

Modern:
Follow hearth directions 1 through 7, boiling pudding gently over moderately high heat.

Note: Make plum pudding several weeks before use. Wrap and store in an airtight container. Warm through before serving.

Kate Powell Carter's Rice Pudding

Take half a pint of rice boil it and while hot stir into it half a pound of butter, set it away to cool then add a heaping teacup of either brown or loaf sugar and six eggs well beaten, with a teacup of rich milk and some pounded nutmeg or mace put it into a baking dish and bake till quite done which may be told by running a straw in

Kate Powell Carter

Serves 6-8

2½ cups hot cooked rice
5 tablespoons butter
1 cup brown sugar, packed

4 eggs, well beaten
2 cups milk or half and half
½ teaspoon freshly grated nutmeg
Cream or Vanilla Sauce (page 302)

Hearth:
1. While rice is hot, stir in butter and allow mixture to cool to room temperature. Add sugar.
2. Beat together eggs, milk, and nutmeg just until well blended. Combine with rice mixture.
3. Pour into buttered 2½ quart baking dish. Carefully place on trivet in preheated Dutch oven, with about 1″ hot water in bottom. Cover and put oven on hot coals. Bake, following directions on pages 216–217, 1¼ hours or until knife inserted in center comes out clean.
4. Serve warm or cold with a pitcher of cream or Vanilla Sauce.

Modern:
Follow hearth directions 1 through 4. Bake uncovered in preheated 325° oven for 1¼ hours or until done.

Mrs. Humphrey's Whortleberry Pudding

¾ lb flour. ½ lb butter. 1 lb sugar. 1 qt. berries mashed & dried. 6 eggs, beaten separately. Cream butter & sugar together, add flour & eggs, lastly berries rolled in some of the flour. Serve hot with Fairy sauce.

Shirley Plantation Collection

Serves 8 to 10

1 cup softened butter
2 cups sugar
4 eggs, separated
2¾ cups sifted flour

4 cups blueberries, coarsely
  mashed
Fairy Butter (page 299)

Hearth:
1. Cream butter and sugar together until light and fluffy.
2. Beat egg yolks until light and gradually add to creamed mixture, blending well.
3. Reserve ¼ cup of the flour and add remainder to creamed mixture, blending well.
4. Beat egg whites until stiff. Gently fold into mixture.
5. Combine remaining ¼ cup flour with berries. Fold into batter.
6. Pour into buttered heatproof dish. Set on trivet in preheated Dutch oven. Cover, set on hot coals, and bake according to directions on pages 216–217, 50 to 60 minutes.
7. Serve hot with Fairy Butter.

Modern:
1. Follow hearth directions 1 through 7.
2. Preheat oven to 350° and bake pudding until knife inserted in center comes out clean, about 60 minutes.

Note: The whortleberry, also called hurtleberry or bilberry, is the blackish fruit of a small European shrub, *Vaccinium myrtillus.*

Mrs. Cringan's Cheese Cakes

Yolks of 9 eggs,
whites of 5 eggs,
juice and grated rind of 3 lemons,

½ pound butter,
¾ pound sugar.

To Make: *Cream the butter and sugar together. Beat the eggs, without separating, until very light. Beat the eggs, rind, and juice of the lemons into the butter and sugar. Give the whole a good beating, and bake in little fluted tins, lined with puff pastry.*

Mrs. John W. Cringan

Fills one 9″ pie or 12 tarts

1 cup butter
1½ cups sugar
6 eggs, divided (yolks of 6,
   whites of 3)

Juice and freshly grated peel of
   3 large lemons
Pie Crust (page 246)

1. Cream butter and sugar together until light and fluffy.
2. Beat egg yolks and whites together. Add lemon juice and peel.
3. Beat into creamed butter and sugar. Beat together several minutes.
4. Make pie crust and fill greased pie pan or patty pans. Partially bake, following directions on page 249.
5. Pour lemon filling into pie crust.
6. If baking on the hearth, follow directions on pages 216–217.
7. If baking in conventional oven, preheat oven to 425°. Bake pie 20 minutes, then reduce heat to 350° and bake until knife inserted in center comes out clean, 35 to 40 minutes longer.

Tucker Family Quire of Paper Pancakes

Take yᵉ Yolks of 4 Eggs wellbeat—mix in half a pint rich milk 3 spoon-fuls fine flour—3 oz Sugar 4 oz fresh Butter melted and cooled (this must not be put in until the others are well mixed)—4 table spoonsful of Madeira wine—& ¼ of a Nutmeg   Grease your pan once with fresh Butter which will be sufficient for all   The above quantity sufficient for 6 or 7 persons—

The Tucker Family Cookbook

Serves 4 to 6

½ cup sifted flour
6 tablespoons granulated sugar
¾ teaspoon freshly grated
   nutmeg
2 eggs
1 cup milk
4 tablespoons melted butter

4 tablespoons Madeira wine
Additional granulated sugar
Stewed pears or apples (pages
   286, 284) or fruit preserves
Stiffly beaten cream or sweet
   sauce (pages 299–303)

Hearth:
1. Stir together flour, sugar, and nutmeg.
2. In a separate bowl slightly beat eggs, then combine with cream and melted butter. Gradually blend into dry mixture.
3. Add Madeira wine and stir well.
4. Set a small frying pan over warm coals. Butter lightly. For each pancake pour in about ¼ cup of the batter, tilting pan to cover bottom. Cook until set, slightly puffy, and pale yellow. Slide out of pan onto plate, sprinkle with granulated sugar, and keep warm by fire while preparing other pancakes.
5. Fill center of each pancake with stewed fruit or preserves. Fold over each side and then top with whipped cream or dessert sauce. Serve immediately.

Modern:
1. Follow hearth directions 1 through 3 to prepare batter.
2. Melt a small amount of butter in a small frying pan or crepe pan over moderate heat. Follow hearth directions 4 and 5, keeping pancakes warm in 200° oven while preparing others.

Custards, Creams, Ices, and Fruit

Creams, ices, and jellies delighted the fancy of early Virginians. These delicacies were served as part of the second course or were displayed at a lavish side table filled with fancy desserts, which would also have included tarts, cookies ("little cakes"), great elaborately iced cakes, and candied as well as fresh fruit.

Creams or custards were combined with stewed fruit such as gooseberries to make a "fool," a title Eliza Leslie obviously felt undignified. She began her receipt by stating, "This foolish name signifies an excellent preparation of gooseberries . . ." and concludes, "We hope somebody will think of a better name for it."[1]

Isinglass—a transparent, almost pure gelatin prepared from the air bladder of certain fishes, such as the sturgeon—or calves' feet were boiled to jelly, strained, and added as thickener to other ingredients for jellies, flummeries, and blanc manges. These dishes were often colored with vegetable dye such as spinach juice and arranged in designs to please the eye.

Dessert puddings such as Trifle and Charlotte Russe were luscious concoctions of rich custards and sweet wine, poured over Naples or Savoy biscuits, both of which evolved into the lady fingers we know today.

Ice creams were viewed as exotic desserts to be consumed only by the wealthy who could afford the equipment needed to make them. George Washington is credited for importing the first ice cream maker in 1784. Jefferson often served ice cream, and recipes for it appear in his manuscripts.

The time and effort that went into making these desserts was part of the elaborate show expected of Virginia hostesses, who often made the elegant confections themselves rather than trust them to their cooks. Anne Blair Banister wrote her cousin to request that when butchering time came, "spare his feet for Jellies,"[2] which would provide the essential ingredient (calves' feet) needed to prepare many of the fanciful desserts so much a part of the early culinary scene.

Fresh fruit, abundant in Virginia, was enjoyed as a part of the last course, along with nuts and sweet wine, or was eaten for snacks just as we do today. Philip Fithian wrote of eating watermelon, peaches, and nectarines, among other things, and Virginia strawberries were choice.

The warm months meant a supply of all sorts of fruit, and they were consumed in quantity while they lasted. "Made myself sick with Ice-Creams, Water melons, Plumbs, &c,"[3] Mrs. Banister wrote candidly. For winter use, fruits were kept by putting them between heavy layers of sugar, or they were made into preserves, or brandied, or dried. These were also activities that might be undertaken or at least overseen by the mistress of the house.

Several recipes for these desserts follow.

Mrs. Bouvier's Boiled Custard

Eight eggs,
One quart of milk,
Sugar to the taste.

Add the sugar to the milk with any thing to flavor it you choose. Set it over the fire, and as soon as it begins to boil stir in the beaten eggs very gradually—stir all the time one way; as soon as it is thick take it off the fire, or it will curdle. Fill your cups and stand it away to cool. Grate nutmeg over before they are sent to table.

Hannah Moore Bouvier

Serves 6 to 8

2 cups cream	6 eggs, well beaten
2 cups milk	Freshly grated nutmeg
½ to ¾ cup sugar	

Hearth:
1. In a saucepan combine cream, milk, and sugar. Set over warm coals and stir until mixture reaches boiling point.
2. Immediately remove from fire. Slowly pour about ½ cup of the hot liquid into eggs, stirring constantly. Pour eggs into rest of liquid, stirring constantly.
3. Return mixture to heat and continue to stir until mixture begins to thicken.
4. Immediately remove from fire and pour into bowl or individual cups. Set away to cool.
5. Sprinkle nutmeg over custard before sending to table.

Modern:
Follow hearth directions 1 through 4, simmering mixture over low heat.

Mrs. William B. Taliaferro's Charlotte Russe

Boil together a pint of Milk & an ounce of Isinglass—Beat the yolks of 4 eggs with a gill of Milk and stir into it, while boiling—add half p of fine sugar—let the whole simmer a few minutes (It must not boil), stirring it constantly. Strain it & set it aside to cool. Take 1 qt of Rich Cream add to it 1 glass of Wine & a Tablespoon of Vanilla—Whip it to a froth & lay it on an inverted sieve to drain—When the custard is cold (before it hardens) stir in the cream beat them together for a minute—It is ready for the Molds lined with Lady Fingers—

Mrs. William B. Taliaferro

Serves 6 to 8

1 ¼ cups milk
2 tablespoons gelatine
4 egg yolks, slightly beaten
½ cup sugar
2 cups cream

¼ cup cream sherry
1 teaspoon vanilla
Naples Biscuit (Page 238) or
    purchased ladyfingers

Hearth:
1. Put milk in a saucepan and heat until lukewarm over warm coals. Remove and combine ¼ cup of the warm milk with gelatine, stirring until dissolved. Set aside.
2. Combine rest of milk with sugar and reheat to scalding, stirring until sugar is dissolved. Blend a small amount of the hot milk into the egg yolks, stirring constantly. Combine with gelatine mixture and blend well. Stir egg, milk, and gelatine mixture back into remaining milk in saucepan. Return to coals and again heat to scalding point.
3. Remove mixture from heat and strain into bowl. Stir in cream sherry and vanilla and set mixture aside to cool.
4. Rinse 6-cup mold in cold water. Line with biscuits, pressing in well. Carefully pour in cooled Charlotte mixture. Cover and chill until completely set.
5. When ready to serve, quickly dip mold in very hot water. Unmold onto serving dish.

Modern:
1. Follow hearth directions 1 through 4, heating mixture over medium heat.
2. Refrigerate Charlotte, covered, until completely set, 4 hours or overnight.
3. When ready to serve, unmold following hearth direction 5.

Mrs. Tebbs' Trifle

Lay Naples Biscuit in the bottom of your dish and pour in as much wine as they will soak up—Pour on cold rich custard. On that a layer of Raspberry Jam & cover the whole with a high whip made of rich cream
M. H. D. Tebbs Receipt Book

Serves 6

Naples Biscuit (page 235)	Boiled custard (page 267)
⅓ cup Madeira wine	1 cup cream
Raspberry jam	2 to 4 tablespoons sugar

1. Split Naples biscuits and put on bottom and around edges of medium-size glass bowl.
2. Pour wine over biscuits and let stand 10 to 15 minutes to absorb.
3. Spread on thick layer of raspberry jam. Cover with cooled boiled custard.
4. Whip cream until stiff, adding sugar to taste. Spread over custard, covering completely.
5. Cover and chill until ready to serve.

Northern Neck Orange Pudding

5 sweet juicy oranges
1 coffee cup sugar
1 pint of milk
1 Tablespoon of corn starch
3 eggs
1 tsp vanilla

Slice the oranges and put about half of the sugar—Let stand while making the custard—

Scald the milk, then slowly add the yolks so well beaten to which has been added the cornstarch dissolved in a portion of the remaining sugar stir rapidly as it is easy to curdle. When this begins to bubble pour over oranges—

Then make a meringue of the remaining sugar & egg whites Spread over oranges—& brown lightly in oven—Better when cold—

Carter/Mason Families

Serves 4 to 6

5 sweet, juicy oranges	3 eggs, separated
1 cup sugar, divided	1 tablespoon cornstarch
2 cups milk	1 teaspoon vanilla

Hearth:

1. Peel, seed, and slice oranges into a heatproof bowl. Be sure to remove all of the tough membrane. Add ½ cup of the sugar, stir together, and set aside while making the custard.

2. Scald milk in pan set over hot coals. Combine egg yolks with cornstarch and add about half of the hot milk, stirring constantly to prevent curdling.

3. Return mixture to rest of hot milk in pan. Add ¼ cup of remaining sugar. Set pan back over warm coals and cook, stirring constantly, just until mixture bubbles and begins to thicken. Remove from heat and pour over oranges.

4. Whip egg whites until stiff, gradually adding last ¼ cup of the sugar. Spread over custard, completely covering it.

5. Carefully put bowl of custard into Dutch oven that has *not* been heated. Warm top of oven and cover pudding. Put hot coals only on top of oven to brown meringue. Check after about 5 minutes, carefully lifting top from oven. When meringue has browned, ease pudding out of Dutch oven and set away to cool thoroughly before serving.

Modern:

1. Follow hearth directions 1 through 4, scalding milk over moderate heat and preparing pudding on moderate low heat.

2. After covering pudding with meringue, set pudding in preheated 450° oven until lightly browned, 5 to 10 minutes. Remove and set aside to cool before serving.

Note: Best served at cool room temperature.

Miss Leslie's Finest Blanc Mange

Break up a half pound of the best double-refined loaf sugar. On some of the pieces rub off the yellow rind of two large lemons, having rolled them under your hand to increase the juice. Then powder all the sugar, and mix with it, gradually, the juice of the lemons, a pint of rich cream, and a large half pint (not less) of sherry or madeira. Stir the mixture very hard till all the articles are thoroughly amalgamated. Then stir in, gradually, a second pint of cream. Put into a small sauce-pan an ounce of the best Russia isinglass, with one jill (or two common-sized wineglasses) of cold water. Boil it till the isinglass is completely dissolved, stirring it several times down to the bottom. When the melted isinglass has become luke-warm, stir it gradually into the mixture, and then give the whole a hard stirring. Have ready some whiteware moulds that have just been dipped and rinsed in cold water. Fill them with the mixture, set them on ice, and in two or three hours the blancmange will be congealed. When it is per-fectly firm, dip the moulds for a minute in luke warm water, and turn out the blancmange on glass dishes. This, if accurately made, is the finest of blancmange. For company, you must have double, or treble, or four times the quantity of ingredients; each article in due proportion.

Eliza Leslie

Serves 6

2 tablespoons gelatine
¼ cup lukewarm water
Juice and peel of one large
　lemon
2 cups cream

1 cup granulated sugar
½ cup Madeira wine or sherry
Fresh fruit for garnish, such as
　green and purple grapes, or
　Glazed Strawberries (p. 287)

Hearth:
1. Dissolve gelatine in ¼ cup water and set aside.
2. In a saucepan combine lemon peel, cream, and sugar. Heat over warm coals, stirring constantly, until mixture reaches scalding point. Do not boil.
3. Remove from heat and strain into gelatine mixture. Blend well and set aside to cool. When mixture is cooled to room temperature, stir in lemon juice and wine.
4. Rinse 4- to 5-cup mold in cold water. Pour in cooled blanc mange mixture. Cover and chill until firmly set.

5. Quickly dip mold in very hot water. Unmold blanc mange onto serving platter, garnish as desired, and keep cold until ready to serve.

Modern:
1. Follow hearthside directions 1 through 4, warming cream, lemon peel, and sugar over medium heat.
2. Refrigerate completed mixture until firm, at least 6 hours.
3. Follow hearth direction 5 to complete recipe.

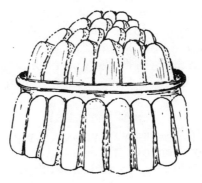

Araminta G. Paul's Blanc Mange

May be made by using at least 1 ounce of the Isinglass for two quarts of milk or cream, the peel of two lemons, sugar and spice to suit the taste—bring the whole to a boiling heat, strain it, and when nearly cool stir it well to mix the cream that will rise while cooling, pour it in moulds, and when perfectly cold, it may be turned out and ready for use. The moulds should be first wet with cold water, which will prevent it from sticking to them—

Araminta G. Paul

Serves 6

2 cups milk
2 tablespoons gelatine
½ to ¾ cup granulated sugar

Grated peel of two large
  lemons
½ teaspoon mace
1 cup cream

Hearth:
1. Put milk in saucepan and set it over warm coals. When it is lukewarm, combine ¼ cup of the milk with gelatine in a small bowl. Stir until gelatine is dissolved. Set aside.
2. Add sugar, lemon peel, and mace to remainder of milk. Return pan to warm coals and heat to scalding, stirring continually. Do not boil.
3. Remove milk mixture from heat. Strain into dissolved gelatine. Stir until completely blended. Blend in cream and set aside to cool to room temperature.
4. Rinse 4- to 5-cup mold in cold water. Pour in cooled mixture. Cover and chill until firmly set.
5. Quickly dip mold in very hot water. Unmold blanc mange into serving dish. Keep cold until ready to serve.

Modern:
1. Follow hearth directions 1 through 4, warming milk, sugar, and lemon peel over medium heat.
2. Refrigerate completed mixture until firm, at least 6 hours.
3. Follow hearth direction 5 to complete recipe.

Gooseberry Fool

Take two quarts of gooseberries, set them on the fire in about a quart of water; when they begin to simmer, turn yellow, and begin to plump, throw them into a cullender to drain the water out, then with the back of a spoon carefully squeeze the pulp, throw the sieve into a dish, make them pretty sweet, and let them stand till they are cold: in the meantime take two quarts of new milk, and the yolks of four eggs beat up with a little grated nutmeg; stir it softly over a slow fire; when it begins to simmer take it off, and by degrees stir it into the gooseberries; let it stand till it is cold, and serve it up: if you make it with cream, you need not put any eggs in; and if it is not thick enough, it is only boiling more gooseberries: but that you must do as you think proper.

Hannah Glasse

Serves 4 to 6

1 quart ripe gooseberries
1 cup sugar
½ teaspoon nutmeg

1 tablespoon rose water
2 cups cream

Hearth:
1. Combine gooseberries with ½ cup water in a saucepan set over hot coals. Cover and simmer until fruit is very tender, stirring occasionally to prevent sticking. Remove from heat and drain berries thoroughly.
2. Mash berries through a sieve, extracting as much pulp as possible. Stir in sugar, nutmeg, and rose water. Set aside to cool.
3. Stiffly beat cream. Fold in cooked fruit mixture. Pour into serving bowl, cover, and chill until ready to serve.

Modern:
Follow hearth directions 1 through 3, simmering berries over low heat.

Notes: Fresh raspberries or strawberries may be used instead of gooseberries. Canned or preserved gooseberries may be used if fresh ones are unavailable. Add a few drops of green food coloring to fruit mixture, if desired.

Charles Carter's Rasberry Cream

Take half a Pound of preserv'd Rasberries, wet, and bruise them, and boil them gently up in a Quart of Cream; put in a Blade of Mace; season them with fine Sugar, Orange-flower or Rose-water; strain it, and force it through your Strainer, and then draw it up with the Yolks of three Eggs, and put it in Basons or Glasses.

Another Way is
  When the Rasberries are ripe, bruise a Quart, and boil them up in a Quart of Cream; season them as before, and strain and force them through a Strainer; keep out the Seeds, and then draw them up with three Yolks of Eggs, and dish them as you please: You may use Mulberries, Strawberries or Damsons the same Way.

Charles Carter

Serves 4

1 pint fresh raspberries, rinsed
2 cups cream
¼ teaspoon mace
¼ cup sugar (or more to taste)

1 to 2 teaspoons orangeflower water
3 egg yolks, slightly beaten
Additional raspberries and fresh mint for garnish, if desired

Hearth:

1. Mash raspberries in a saucepan. Add cream, mace, and sugar.
2. Set pan on trivet over very warm coals. Cook, stirring constantly, until mixture begins to bubble. Simmer and stir mixture for about 5 minutes. Remove from fire and stir in orangeflower water. Strain mixture to remove raspberry seeds.
3. Very slowly pour about ½ cup of the hot raspberry mixture into egg yolks, stirring constantly. Return to rest of mixture in saucepan.
4. Replace on trivet and cook over warm coals, continuing to stir, until mixture coats spoon, about 10 to 15 minutes. Correct seasoning. Pour into a serving bowl and set on ice to chill completely before serving. Garnish with additional berries and sprigs of mint, if desired.

Modern:

1. Follow hearth directions 1 through 3, bringing raspberry mixture to boiling point. Reduce heat and simmer, stirring constantly, for about 5 minutes.

2. After egg yolks have been combined with rest of cream mixture, return to low heat and cook, stirring constantly, for 10 to 15 minutes, or until mixture coats a spoon. Pour into serving bowl, cover with plastic wrap, and refrigerate overnight.

Notes: Orange-flavored liquer may replace orangeflower water. This cream can also be made with raspberry preserves, using 1 cup of the preserves to 2 cups of cream. Or strawberries may be used. This recipe can be doubled, refrigerated overnight, and used as a base for ice cream.

Mrs. Randolph's Ice Creams

VANILLA CREAM

Boil a Vanilla bean in a quart of rich milk until it has imparted the fla-vour sufficiently; then take it out, and mix with the milk, eight eggs, yelks and whites, beaten well; let it boil a little longer—make it very sweet, for much of the sugar is lost in the operation of freezing.

CHOCOLATE CREAM

Scrape a quarter of a pound of chocolate very fine, put it in a quart of milk, boil it till the chocolate is dissolved, stirring it continually; thicken with six eggs. A vanilla bean boiled with the milk, will improve the fla-vour greatly.

COFFEE CREAM

Toast two gills of raw coffee till it is a light brown, and not a grain burnt; put it hot from the toaster, without grinding it, into a quart of rich, and perfectly sweet, milk; boil it, and add the yelks of eight eggs: when done, strain it through a sieve, and sweeten it—if properly done, it will not be discoloured. The coffee may be dried, and will answer for making in the usual way to drink, allowing more for the quantity of water, than if it had not gone through this process.

Mary Randolph

All make about 1½ quarts

Vanilla:

2 cups milk	1 cup sugar
1 vanilla bean (or 2 teaspoons vanilla extract)	4 eggs, slightly beaten
	2 cups cream

1. Scald milk and vanilla bean. Remove from heat and stir in sugar to dissolve. Set aside to cool to room temperature. When cooled, remove vanilla bean.
2. Beat eggs and cream together. Blend in milk mixture.
3. Chill and freeze.

Chocolate:
1. Add ½ cup sifted cocoa to above recipe, stirring into hot, scalded milk along with sugar.
2. When eggs and cream have been added, taste for sweetness and add more sugar if desired.
3. Chill and freeze.

Coffee
1. Add 1 to 2 tablespoons instant coffee to vanilla recipe, stirring into hot, scalded milk along with sugar.
2. When eggs and cream have been added, taste for sweetness and add more sugar if desired.
3. Chill and freeze.

Mrs. Cringan's Caramel Ice Cream

1 quart cream,   *4 ounces caramel,*
1 quart milk,   *½ pound sugar,*
1 tablespoon extract vanilla.

To Mix: Whip one pint of the cream, and put on ice; mix the milk and remainder of the cream with the sugar and vanilla. Make the caramel as directed, and stir it in while hot; stir until dissolved. Freeze to the consistency of firm sherbet; stir in the whipped cream; close the freezer carefully; repack and stand away until ready to serve. This makes three quarts of ice cream.

Mrs. John W. Cringan

Makes 1½ to 2 quarts

2 cups milk
¾ cup sugar
1 cup granulated sugar for
   caramel

1½ teaspoons vanilla extract
2 cups cream

1. Scald milk over moderate heat. Remove from heat and add sugar, stirring to dissolve completely. Set aside.
2. To make caramel: Put 1 cup sugar in a heavy frying pan. Melt slowly while stirring over medium heat until sugar is a golden caramel color. Pour into hot milk and stir until caramel is dissolved. Add vanilla. Chill mixture.
3. Beat cream until stiff. Combine with milk mixture and freeze.

Cousin Harriet's Lemon Ice Cream

2 quarts milk,   juice and grated rind of 6 lemons,
1 quart cream,   whites of 4 eggs,
3 tablespoons arrowroot,
                          2 pounds sugar.

*To Mix: Put the milk on the fire in a double boiler. Mix the arrowroot to
a paste with a little cold water. When the milk boils thicken it with the
arrowroot; stir over the fire until it is the consistency of thick custard.
Take from the fire and cool; take out the lemon peel, which was tied in a
muslin and boiled in the milk. Mix the lemon juice and sugar after
straining the juice. Whip the whites of the eggs and the cream together.
Put the milk in the freezer; with a long spoon or ladle stir in the cream
and whites. Add the lemon juice and sugar very slowly, stirring constantly. When thoroughly mixed freeze as directed.*

Mrs. John W. Cringan

Makes 1 quart

Freshly grated rind of 3 large   1 tablespoon arrowroot
   lemons   2 egg whites
1½ cups sugar   2 cups cream
2 cups milk   ⅓ cup fresh lemon juice

1. Add lemon rind and sugar to milk. Stir over moderate
heat until mixture reaches boiling point. Remove from heat
and cool to lukewarm.
2. Strain milk and mix with arrowroot that has been mixed
to a paste with a little water. Return to low heat and stir
constantly until mixture thickens. Again remove from heat
and cool.
3. Whip egg whites until foamy. Beat into cream, blending
thoroughly. Add cooled milk mixture.
4. Very slowly add lemon juice, stirring constantly to prevent mixture from curdling.
5. Cover and refrigerate overnight. Freeze.

The Misses Wards' Lemon Sherbet

2¾ quarts water—1 tumbler glassful lemon juice. 1 cup sugar to each quart water—Boil sugar and water together ten minutes with peel of one lemon. Beat to froth whites of six eggs (two to a quart)   Stir in eggs when freezing begins. When almost frozen take dasher out of freezer and stir well with a spoon.

Ward Family Collection

Makes about 1½ quarts

3 cups water
Peel of 1 lemon
1 cup sugar (or more to taste)

1 cup fresh lemon juice
2 egg whites

1. Simmer together water, lemon peel, and sugar, covered, 10 minutes. Remove from heat and set aside to cool, then strain and discard lemon peel.
2. Blend in lemon juice, stirring well.
3. Beat egg whites until frothy and fold into lemon base.
4. Freeze.

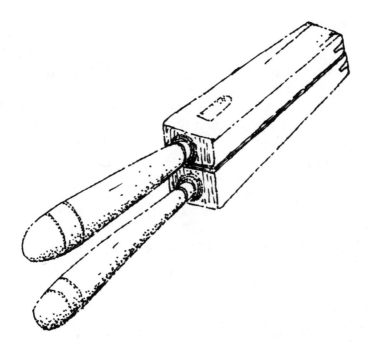

Kate Powell Carter's Orange Ice

The juice of one dozen oranges, the rinds of 2 and the juice of 2 lemons, put to 2 quarts of water, and the whites of 8 eggs well beaten sweeten to your taste—

Kate Powell Carter

Makes about 1 quart

2 cups water
Grated peel of 2 oranges
1 cup sugar (or more to taste)

1½ cups fresh orange juice
2 tablespoons fresh lemon juice
2 egg whites

1. Simmer water with orange peel and sugar, covered, 10 minutes. Remove from heat, cool, then strain and discard orange peel.
2. Combine with juices.
3. Beat egg whites until foamy and fold into orange base.
4. Freeze.

Note: If bases for sherbets and ices seem tart, remember that the flavor of the juices diminishes in the freezing process.

Mrs. Cringan's Stewed Apples

*1 dozen apples,
  yellow rind of 1 orange,*
*3/4 pound sugar,
  yellow rind of 1 lemon,*
3 pints cold water.

To Cook: Peel and core the apples; drop them in cold water to prevent their turning dark. Put into a saucepan the water, sugar, orange and lemon peel. Boil for fifteen minutes, then drop in the apples. Cook slowly until the apples are clear but not soft enough to break. Lift out carefully and put on dishes to cool. Cook the syrup until it begins to thicken (when it drops heavily from the spoon). Put the apples in a jar; scatter through them a little of the orange and lemon peel; pour over the syrup while hot. Stand aside to cool. Serve cold with rich cream or custard.

Mrs. John W. Cringan

Serves 6 to 8

6 to 8 large tart apples, such as
  Granny Smith
4 cups water
1 ½ cups sugar

Peel of 1 orange, quartered
Peel of 1 lemon, quartered
Cream or Vanilla Sauce (page
  302)

Hearth:

1. Peel and core apples. Drop in cold water to prevent their turning dark.
2. In a saucepan, combine water, sugar, and peels. Set pan over hot coals, cover, and boil for 15 minutes.
3. Drain apples and add to sugar syrup. Cover and simmer gently until apples are just tender but firm enough to hold a shape. Carefully lift out of syrup and put in serving bowl to cool.
4. Continue to cook syrup until it begins to thicken, then pour over apples.
5. Set aside to cool. Serve with cream or Vanilla Custard.

Modern:

Follow hearth directions 1 through 5, simmering apples over low heat.

Baked Pears

Take good-sized pears. Small ones are not worth the trouble of cooking. Peel them, split them in half, and remove the core, the stem, and the blossom end. Strew them well with brown sugar, and lay them on their backs in a large baking dish. A narrow slip of the yellow rind of lemon or orange, (cut so thin as to look transparent,) will be a great improvement, laid in the hollow of each pear. Also the juice squeezed. Put into the dish sufficient molasses or steam-syrup to well cover the pears. Place them in an oven, and bake them till they are soft, but not till they break. If you have no lemon or orange, season them with ground ginger or cinnamon.

The great pound pears are baked as above, with the addition of port wine and a few cloves, and colored red with a little cochineal.

Eliza Leslie

Serves 4 to 6

4 to 6 large, ripe, firm pears	Strained juice of 1 orange
Thinly pared strips of orange peel	½ to ¾ cup port wine
4 to 6 tablespoons brown sugar	2 whole cloves

Hearth:
1. Peel, halve, and core pears. Place them cut side up in a heatproof dish.
2. Lay one strip of orange peel in hollow of each pear. Sprinkle 1 tablespoon brown sugar over each pear. Sprinkle orange juice over and around pears.
3. Combine wine and cloves. Pour into dish with pears.
4. Put filled dish on rack in preheated Dutch oven with 2″ water in bottom. Cover, set on hot coals, and bake until pears are tender but still hold their shape, 20 to 30 minutes. Baste occasionally with wine. Do not put coals on top of Dutch oven.
5. Serve warm or cold.

Modern:
1. Follow hearth directions 1 through 3.
2. Preheat oven to 350°. Bake pears 20 to 30 minutes, basting occasionally.

Pears Stewed with Ginger Root

1 quart pears,	*3 pints cold water,*
½ pound sugar,	*3 ounces green ginger root,*

To Cook: Peel the pears and scrape the stems; throw them into cold water to prevent their turning dark. Put into a kettle the water, the scraped and sliced ginger root, and the pears. Cook slowly until the pears can be pierced with a straw; add the sugar, and cook until the syrup thickens, stirring occasionally to prevent scorching; serve cold, with cream or milk. One and one-half teaspoons of whole cloves may be substituted for ginger.

Mrs. John W. Cringan

Serves 4 to 6

4 cups peeled, halved, and sliced ripe pears	4 cups water
	1 cup sugar
⅓ cup fresh scraped, thinly sliced ginger root	Cream or Vanilla Sauce (page 302)

Hearth:

1. Combine pears and ginger root in saucepan. Pour on water, cover, and set pan over warm coals. Simmer pears until they are tender and can be easily pierced with a fork, about 20 minutes.
2. Add sugar, stirring gently to dissolve. Cook uncovered, stirring occasionally, until syrup is thickened, 15 to 20 minutes.
3. Serve cold with softly whipped cream or Vanilla Sauce.

Modern:

Follow hearth directions 1 through 3, simmering pears gently over low heat.

Glazed Strawberries

Choose large ripe strawberries, pick them off the vines so as the stems may all adhere to the fruit. Dip them one at a time in a vessel of cold water and place them on a sieve to dry. Beat the whites of two or three eggs, according to the quantity of fruit. The egg should be beaten very little or it will not adhere to the fruit, dip the berries in the egg one at a time, place them on a sieve so as not to touch each other, and sift powdered white sugar over them. They are very ornamental to a dinner table. Bunches of grapes, oranges peeled and quartered, or any small fruit may be done in the same manner.

Hannah Moore Bouvier

Serves 6 to 8

4 cups fresh strawberries, stems attached	2 to 3 egg whites
	Granulated sugar

1. Rinse berries but do not stem. Set aside in colander to dry.
2. Beat egg whites just until frothy. Do not overbeat.
3. Dip berries in egg white. Then set out on rack, not touching each other.
4. Sift sugar over berries, covering well. Let berries stand until dry.
5. Pile carefully in glass bowl and serve.

Note: Small bunches of grapes or other small fruit may be prepared in the same way.

Sauces

Savory sauces were intended to complement prepared entrées. Generally the juices ("gravy") from cooked produce were combined with seasonings and either poured over the food prior to serving or sent to the table in a separate sauce boat to accompany the main dishes.

Sauces were thinner than those of today. They were usually thickened slightly with beaten egg yolk or, beginning near the end of the 17th century, with a small amount of flour combined with butter and whipped into the seasoned stock. Brown flour (page 319) was kept on hand to be added to certain sauces (Mrs. Randolph's Veal Cutlets on page 136, for example) where a darkened sauce was appropriate. Bread crumbs were also used as a thickener, a holdover from medieval practices.

It was not until later in the 19th century that inordinate amounts of flour came into use as a thickener. Sauces of earlier times are rich and delicate, without the heavy starchiness familiar to us today. In working with the modernized versions of the savory sauces that follow, the amounts of flour are between the old and the new.

Mrs. Randolph's Melted Butter

Nothing is more simple than this process, and nothing so generally done badly. Keep a quart tin sauce pan with a cover to it exclusively for this purpose; weigh one quarter of a pound of good butter, rub into it two teaspoonsful of flour; when well mixed, put it in the sauce pan with one table spoonful of water, and a little salt; cover it, and set the sauce pan in a larger one of boiling water, shake it constantly till completely melted and beginning to boil. If the pan containing the butter be set on coals, it will oil the butter and spoil it. This quantity is sufficient for one sauce boat. A great variety of delicious sauces can be made, by adding different herbs to melted butter, all of which are excellent to eat with fish, poultry, or boiled butchers meat. To begin with parsley—wash a large bunch very clean, pick the leaves from the stems carefully, boil them ten minutes in salt and water, drain them perfectly dry, mince them exceedingly fine, and stir them in the butter when it begins to melt. When herbs are added to butter, you must put two spoonsful of water instead of one.

To Make Egg Sauce
Boil four eggs for ten minutes, chop half the whites, put them with the yelks, and chop them both together, but not very fine, put them into a quarter of a pound of good melted butter, and put it in a boat.

Mary Randolph

Makes approximately ⅔ cup

½ cup softened butter
2 teaspoons flour
1 tablespoon water

¼ teaspoon salt
Additions (see notes below)

Hearth:
1. Combine butter and flour. Put in a small saucepan with water and salt. Cover and set pan in a larger one of boiling water. Set over hot coals.
2. Shake pan constantly until butter is melted and begins to bubble.
3. Remove from heat, pour into sauce boat, and serve.

Modern:
Follow hearth directions 1 through 3, cooking sauce in top part of a double boiler set over boiling water.

Notes: 1. This sauce must be cooked over hot water, not directly over heat.
2. A variety of delicious sauces can be made from this basic butter sauce. Mrs. Randolph suggests adding *one* of the following minced herbs: ¼ cup parsley, chervil, fennel, burnet, tarragon, cress, or pepper grass. Herbs must be parboiled briefly in salted water, then thoroughly dried and minced before adding to butter sauce.
3. *Egg Sauce:* Add to butter sauce four hard-boiled eggs that have been finely chopped.

Mrs. Randolph's Sauce for a Goose (Applesauce)

Pare, core, and slice some apples, put them in a sauce pan, with as much water as will keep them from burning, set them over a very slow fire, keep them close covered till reduced to a pulp, then put in a lump of butter, and sugar to your taste, beat them well, and send them to the table in a china bowl.

Mary Randolph

Makes about 3½ cups

2 pounds tart, juicy apples, such as Granny Smith
Grated peel of 1 large lemon
¼ to ½ cup water
2 tablespoons softened butter

½ to 1 cup sugar (or to taste)
1 tablespoon rose water
½ teaspoon freshly grated nutmeg

Hearth:
1. Peel, core, and quarter apples. Put in saucepan with lemon peel and ¼ cup water. Cover, set on hot coals, and simmer mixture until apples are very soft. Stir often, adding more water if necessary to prevent sauce from scorching. If additional water is needed, add a little at a time; sauce should be thick.
2. When apples are soft, remove from heat and mash with a spoon, adding butter, ½ cup sugar, rose water, and nutmeg. Stir to blend ingredients, then taste and add more sugar if needed.
3. Serve as accompaniment to roast pork or goose.

Modern:
Follow hearth directions 1 through 3, simmering apples over low heat.

Note: Eliza Leslie recommends the addition of rose water, lemon, or nutmeg, or "all these if for company." These seasonings have been added to Mary Randolph's applesauce recipe.

Mrs. Tebbs' Celery Sauce

Take a large bunch of Celery wash & pare it very clean—cut it in small pieces, and boil it in water or milk & water—then add a little Mace, Nutmeg, Pepper and Salt, thickened with a piece of Butter rolled in Flour & stew it a little—This is a good Sauce for boiled fowls or Roasted partridges—

M. H. D. Tebbs Receipt Book,
(Taken from Hannah Glasse)

Makes approximately 2¼ cups

1½ cups diced celery
1 cup cream
⅔ cup water
⅛ teaspoon mace
¼ teaspoon freshly grated
    nutmeg

⅛ teaspoon pepper
¾ teaspoon salt
2 tablespoons softened butter
2 tablespoons flour

Hearth:
1. Combine celery, cream, and water in a small saucepan. Cover and set over hot coals. Bring to a simmer and cook, stirring occasionally, until celery is very tender, about 20 minutes. Stir in seasonings.
2. Combine butter and flour and stir into sauce. Cook while stirring for about 5 minutes or until sauce begins to bubble and thickens slightly.
3. Pour into sauce boat and use as accompaniment to meat and poultry dishes.

Modern:
Follow hearth directions 1 through 3, cooking sauce over moderate heat.

Mary Randolph's Sauce for a Turkey [Bread Sauce]

Cut the crumb of a loaf of bread in thin slices and put it in cold water, with a few pepper corns, a little salt and onion, then boil it till the bread is quite soft, beat it well, put in a quarter of a pound of butter, two spoonsful of thick cream, and put it in a bowl.

Mary Randolph

Makes about 1¾ cups

¼ cup chopped onion	1 cup finely crumbled fresh
½ teaspoon pepper (or to taste)	bread crumbs
½ teaspoon salt (or to taste)	4 tablespoons butter
½ cup water	⅓ cup cream (or more as
½ cup milk	needed)

Hearth:

1. In a saucepan combine onion, pepper, salt, water, and milk. Set on trivet over hot coals. Bring to a boil and add bread crumbs. Cover and simmer, stirring often, 10 to 15 minutes.

2. Add butter and stir until melted.

3. Add cream, stirring until sauce is well blended and smooth. If sauce is too thick, add more cream by tablespoonsful until of desired consistency.

4. Remove from heat, pour into sauce boat, and serve warm as an accompaniment to poultry.

Modern:

1. Follow hearth directions 1 through 4, simmering mixture over low heat.

Cabell Family Gravy for Wild Fowl*

To one wine glassful of port wine add a table spoonful each of walnut ketchup, mushroom ketchup, and lemon juice, one shalot [sic] sliced (or a little of the essence) a small piece lemon peel and a blade of mace. These should be all scalded, strained, and added to the gravy that comes from the fowl in roasting. The breast of the fowl should be scored in three or four places, and the gravy poured boiling hot over it before it is sent to table.

Jane Charity Alston Cabell Cookbook

Makes about 1 ½ cups

¼ cup port wine
1 tablespoon walnut catchup (page 314)
1 tablespoon mushroom catchup (page 313)
1 tablespoon fresh lemon juice

1 teaspoon freshly grated lemon peel
1 shallot, finely minced
⅛ teaspoon mace
1 cup juice from roasted fowl

Hearth:
1. In a small saucepan combine wine, catchups, lemon juice and peel, shallot, and mace. Set pan on trivet over hot coals and bring mixture to a boil.
2. Remove from heat, strain, and keep warm by fire.
3. When fowl is roasted, combine juices from bird with wine mixture. Stir well. Correct seasoning.
4. Slash breast of roasted fowl in three or four places. Pour sauce over bird and serve.

Modern:
Follow hearth directions 1 through 4, bringing to a boil over moderately high heat.

---

*Courtesy of the Virginia Historical Society.

Eliza Leslie's Mint Sauce

This is only used for roast lamb in the spring. When the lambs are grown into sheep, the mint is too old for sauce. But they harmonize very pleasantly when both are young.

Take a large bunch of fine fresh green mint, that has been washed well. Strip the leaves from the stems, and mince them small. Put it into a pint bowl, and mix with it gradually some of the best cider vinegar. This sauce must not be the least liquid, but as thick as horse-radish sauce or thicker. Make it very sweet, with the best brown sugar. Mix it well, and transfer to a small tureen, or a little deep dish with a tea-spoon in it. Serve it up always with roast lamb, putting a tea-spoonful on the rim of your plate.

A quart or more of mint sauce, made as above, but with a larger portion of sugar and vinegar, will keep very well for several weeks, in a jar well corked.

Eliza Leslie

Makes approximately 1 cup

½ cup cider vinegar
1 tablespoon brown sugar (or
  more to taste)

⅓ cup minced fresh mint
  leaves

Hearth:
1. Combine vinegar and brown sugar in small saucepan. Set on trivet over hot coals and heat until warm.
2. Remove from heat and add mint leaves. Stir well and set aside to cool.
3. Pour into sauce boat and serve as accompaniment to roast lamb.

Modern:
1. Follow hearth direction 1, heating vinegar and sugar over low heat.
2. Complete following hearth directions 2 and 3.

Mrs. Randolph's Mushroom Sauce

Clean and wash one quart of fresh mushrooms, cut them in two, and put them into a stew pan, with a little salt, a blade of mace, and a little butter. Stew them gently for half an hour, and then add a pint of cream and the yelks of two eggs beat very well; keep stirring it till it boils up, and then squeeze in a half a lemon. Put it over the fowls or turkies; or you may put it on a dish, with a piece of fried bread first buttered, then toasted brown, and just dipped into boiling water. This is a very good sauce for white fowls of all kinds.

Mary Randolph

Makes about 3 cups

4 tablespoon butter
2 cups fresh, quartered
   mushrooms
½ teaspoon salt
¼ teaspoon mace

1 cup cream
1 egg yolk, lightly beaten
1 tablespoon lemon juice

Hearth:
1. Melt butter in saucepan. Set over warm coals. Add mushrooms, salt, and mace. Cover and simmer, stirring occasionally, until mushrooms are very tender, 20 to 30 minutes.
2. Beat cream and egg yolk together and blend into mushroom mixture, stirring constantly until mixture bubbles and thickens slightly. Stir in lemon juice and heat through.
3. Serve hot.

Modern:
1. Follow hearth directions 1 through 3, cooking mushrooms over low heat.

Mrs. Bradley's Sauce Robert

Cut some large Onion into Dice, or small square pieces, but not so small as by mincing, cut some fat Bacon in the same Manner, and put both together into a Saucepan, set them over the Fire, and keep them continually stirring about.

When they begin to brown, pour off the Fat, and pour in some rich Veal Gravy, add a little Pepper and Salt, and let them boil gently together till the Onions are tender; then put in a little Mustard and some Vinegar, and serve it up hot.

This is excellent with roast Pork, and it eats very well with a roast Goose, and many other Things.

Martha Bradley

Makes approximately 2½ cups

½ cup finely chopped onion	Pepper
2 tablespoons finely chopped salt bacon	½ teaspoon powdered mustard (or more to taste)
2 cups veal or beef stock	¼ cup wine vinegar
Salt	

Hearth:

1. In a small saucepan combine onion and bacon. Set pan on a trivet over hot coals, stirring until they are lightly browned.
2. Remove from heat and drain off fat.
3. Return pan to hot coals and add stock and salt and pepper to taste. Simmer, stirring occasionally, until onions are tender, around 10 minutes.
4. Blend in mustard and wine vinegar. Stir until mixture begins to simmer, then remove from heat.
5. Pour into sauce boat and serve as accompaniment to roast goose, roast pork, or other meats.

Modern:

Follow hearthside directions 1 through 5, cooking sauce over moderately low heat.

Mrs. Bradley's Fairy Butter

Boil two Eggs hard, take out the Yolks and beat them in a Marble Mortar, put in by Degrees two Spoonfuls of Orange-Flower Water, and half a Spoonful of double-refined Sugar beat to a Powder, grind this to a kind of Paste, and then put in about an equal Quantity of Butter from the Churn; put it into a fine Strainer, and sit a Plate underneath; Force it all through into the Plate in Form of a Jelly.

Martha Bradley

Makes approximately ½ cup

2 hard-boiled eggs
2 teaspoons orangeflower water

1 tablespoon confectioner's
   sugar (or more to taste)
¼ cup softened butter

Hearth and Modern:
1. Shell eggs, remove yolks, and discard whites. Using a fork, mash yolks with orange flower water and sugar until mixture is a smooth paste.
2. Blend in butter until smooth.
Force mixture through a sieve into small bowl. Cover and chill until needed. Especially good with gingerbread, bread pudding, and Whortleberry Pudding.

Note: Orange-flavored liquer can replace orangeflower water.

Miss Leslie's Lemon Cream

Beat well together a quart of thick cream and the yolks of eight eggs. Then gradually beat in half a pound of powdered loaf-sugar, and the grated rind of three large lemons. Put the mixture into a porcelain skillet, and set it on hot coals till it comes to a boil; then take it off, and stir it till nearly cold. Squeeze the juice of the lemons into a bowl; pour the cream upon it, and continue to stir it till quite cold. You may serve it up in a glass bowl, in glass cups, or in jelly glasses. Eat it with tarts or sweet-meats.

Eliza Leslie

Makes about 3 cups

2 cups cream
4 egg yolks, slightly beaten
¼ cup sugar

Juice and freshly grated peel of
  3 lemons

Hearth:
1. Beat cream and egg yolks together thoroughly. Add sugar and lemon peel, mixing well.
2. Pour mixture in saucepan and set pan on a trivet over hot coals. Stir until mixture boils, then immediately remove from heat. Set aside to cool to lukewarm.
3. Pour lemon juice into bowl. When cream mixture has cooled, gradually stir it into lemon juice, stirring constantly. Blend well, cover, and chill until needed. Good with ginger-bread, bread pudding, and other baked or boiled puddings.

Modern:
1. Follow hearth directions 1 through 3, bringing mixture to a boil over moderate heat.

Kate Powell Carter's Sauce for Plum Pudding

For a large bowl of sauce take a pound of sugar and rub well into it half a pound of butter, then beat two eggs light and add them to the sugar & butter, put it on the fire and let it stew a short time, then add a pounded nutmeg and two wine glasses of wine

Kate Powell Carter

Makes approximately 3 cups

½ cup softened butter
1 cup sugar
1 egg

1 teaspoon freshly grated
  nutmeg (or more to taste)
¼ cup red wine

Hearth:

1. Cream butter and sugar until light and fluffy.
2. Beat egg until foamy and blend into sauce.
3. Pour into saucepan and set on trivet over hot coals. Cook, stirring constantly about 5 minutes.
4. Remove from heat and add nutmeg and wine, blending in well.
5. Pour into sauce bowl and serve warm or at room temperature.

Modern:

1. Follow hearth directions 1 and 2, simmering mixture over low heat.
2. Complete following hearth directions 3 and 4.

Mrs. Moncure's Vanilla Sauce

TO BE EATEN WITH A BAKED BATTER PUDDING.
   To three pints of milk stir in one table-spoonful of flour or arrow root, the yolks of six eggs well beaten, stir it until it boils, sweeten to your taste, and season with vanilla—use it when cold.

Mrs. M. B. Moncure

Makes about 2¼ cups

1 cup milk	2 egg yolks, well beaten
1 cup cream	¼ cup sugar
2 teaspoons arrowroot	1 teaspoon vanilla

Hearth:

1. In a small saucepan combine milk, cream, arrowroot, and beaten egg yolks. Set pan on trivet over warm coals.
2. Cook, stirring, until mixture begins to bubble and thickens slightly. Remove from heat.
3. Stir in sugar and vanilla, blending well. Cover and set aside to cool before using, stirring occasionally. Serve at room temperature or chilled.

Modern:

Follow hearth directions 1 through 3, cooking sauce over moderate heat.

Shirley Plantation Wine Sauce

Cream ½ lb. of butter with 10 tablespoonsful of brown sugar, yolks of 2 eggs, 10 wineglasses of wine & one of brandy, boil 5 minutes in the silver sauce pan.

Shirley Plantation Collection

Makes approximately 3 cups

½ cup softened butter
6 tablespoons brown sugar,
  firmly packed

1 egg yolk, lightly beaten
1 cup sherry wine
2 tablespoons brandy

Hearth:
1. Cream butter with brown sugar until fluffy.
2. Beat in egg, then gradually add wine and brandy, blending in well.
3. Pour sauce into small pan and set on trivet over hot coals. Bring to a boil, then cook and stir 5 minutes, being careful not to splatter hot sauce.
4. Remove from heat and serve warm or at room temperature.

Modern:
1. Follow hearth directions 1 through 4, cooking sauce over moderate heat.

Salad Dressings

The virtues of salads were appreciated by our ancestors going back to ancient times, for many salad ingredients were thought to have healing properties. Herbalists promoted this idea, defining the medicinal qualities of raw salad vegetables and herbs in print.

Aceteria: A Discourse on Sallets, published in 1699 by the English diarist John Evelyn, detailed the importance of many salad herbs as well as the proper method for making a classic vinaigrette dressing. Evelyn wrote that "Whole nations" of meat eaters had become "Heavy, Dull, Unactive, and much more Stupid . . ." than plant eaters who were "more Acute, Subtil, and of deeper Penetration . . ."[1], a statement with which many 20th-century vegetarians would agree.

Lettuce, over which Mr. Evelyn rhapsodized, "ever was . . . the principal Foundation of the universal Tribe of Sallets; which is to Cool and Refresh . . . it allays Heat [good for fevers] . . . extinguishes Thirst, excites Appetite . . . represses Vapours, conciliates Sleep, mitigates Pain; besides the effect it has upon the Morals, Temperance and Chastity. . . . In a Word, we meet with nothing among all . . . so proper to mingle with . . . the rest. . . ."[2]

In providing his readers with directions for dressing salads, Evelyn discussed everything from the right kind of oil—"a pallid Olive green, without Smell . . . smooth, light, and pleasant upon the tongue . . ."[3]—to the proper salad bowl "of Porcelane or of . . . Delft. . . ."[4]

"Skill and Judgment" are required to combine salad in-

gredients, asserted Mr. Evelyn, "as nothing should be suffer'd to domineer. . . ."[5]

Thomas Jefferson was avid about salads, saying that he
preferred them to most other foods. He grew many of the
necessary ingredients in his Monticello gardens. He recommended endive for winter use, also planting celery and
spinach for cold-weather consumption. His Williamsburg
cousin, John Randolph, authored a treatise on gardening
that gave details on planting seeds in successive crops that
would provide fresh vegetables at least through the late fall.
Many of the Virginia gentry built greenhouses as another
way to have the fresh produce needed for salad making.

The lettuces and salad herbs referred to in the old recipes did not include the insipid iceberg lettuces found today.
Leaf lettuces, cresses, parsley, salad burnet, and sorrel were
among the greens used, often topped in summer with fresh
nasturtiums or marigolds. Bear that in mind as you create
salads with which the following dressings are to be used.

Mason Family Lettuce Dressing

One-half pint of cream or rich milk, one-half pint of good vinegar, one small tea cupful of sugar, three eggs well beaten, a lump of butter the size of an egg, one fourth teaspoonful of ground mustard. Pepper and salt. Mix all together cold and cook until as thick as custard.

Mason Family Collection

Makes approximately 2¼ cups

3 eggs, well beaten
2 tablespoons softened butter
1 cup cream
2 tablespoons sugar

¼ teaspoon ground mustard
½ teaspoon pepper
¾ teaspoon salt
1 cup red wine vinegar

Hearth:

1. Beat eggs and butter together in a small saucepan. Add cream, sugar, mustard, pepper, and salt, beating until thoroughly blended. Very slowly add wine vinegar, stirring constantly to prevent mixture from curdling.
2. Set saucepan over warm coals. Cook, stirring, until mixture is hot and begins to thicken. Remove from heat, pour into bowl, and set away to cool.

Modern:

Follow hearth directions 1 and 2. Cook dressing over low heat, stirring constantly, until it thickens. Pour into bowl, cover, and refrigerate until cold.

Sydney Smith's Salad Dressing

The Reverend Sydney Smith (1771–1845) was a genial Anglican divine whose exuberance and wit, together with a shrewd intelligence, made him a favorite of English society. An epicure, Smith felt that character was affected by food, and so he spent a good part of his life preaching the virtues of a sound diet. He entertained weekly at lavish dinner parties and often traveled on the continent to sample different cuisines, which he then described in chatty letters to family and friends back in England. The Reverend Mr. Smith is remembered for his culinary skills, especially for his rhyming salad dressing recipe which begins:

> To make this condiment your poet begs
> The pounded yellow of two hard-boiled eggs;
> Two boiled potatoes, passed through kitchen sieve,
> Smoothness and softness to the salad give.[6]

By mid-19th century, his recipe was appearing in American cookbooks. Its modernized recipe follows.

Have ready two well-boiled potatoes, peeled and rubbed through a sieve; they will give peculiar smoothness to the mixture. Also, a very small portion of raw onion, not more than a quarter of a tea-spoonful, (as the presence of the onion is to be scarcely hinted,) and the pounded yolks of two hard-boiled eggs. Mix these ingredients on a deep plate with one tea-spoonful of salt, one of made mustard, three table-spoonfuls of olive oil, and one table-spoonful of vinegar. Add, lastly, a tea-spoonful of essence of anchovy; mash, and mix the whole together, (using a boxwood spoon) and see that all the articles are thoroughly amalgamated. Having cut up a sufficiency of lettuce that has been well washed in cold water, and drained, add to it the dressing immediately before dinner, mixing the lettuce through it with a boxwood fork.

This salad dressing was invented by the Rev. Sydney Smith, whose genius as a writer and a wit is well known on both sides the Atlantic. If exactly followed, it will be found very fine on trial; no peculiar flavor predominating, but excellent as a whole. The above directions are taken from a manuscript receipt given by Mr. Smith to an American gentleman then in London.

Eliza Leslie

Makes about ½ cup

2 small potatoes, boiled and
  peeled
1 teaspoon freshly minced
  onion
2 hard-boiled egg yolks
1 teaspoon salt

1 teaspoon prepared mustard
3 tablespoons olive oil
1 tablespoon red wine or cider
  vinegar
1 teaspoon anchovy paste

1. Rub potatoes through a sieve into a small bowl. Add onion.
2. Mash egg yolks and add to potato mixture.
3. Add salt and mustard, blending well.
4. Blend together olive oil and vinegar, then stir into potato mixture.
5. Add anchovy paste and mix all ingredients thoroughly until well blended and smooth.
6. Add to salad greens immediately before serving.

Mr. Evelyn's Vinaigrette Dressing

In preparing this, or any other salad-dressing, take care not to use that excessively pungent and deleterious combination of drugs which is now so frequently imposed upon the public as the best white wine vinegar. In reality, it has no vinous material about it; and it may be known by its violent and disagreeable sharpness, which overpowers and destroys the taste (and also the substance) of whatever it is mixed with. It is also very unwholesome. Its color is always pale, and it is nearly as clear as water. No one should buy or use it. The first quality of real cider vinegar is good for all purposes.

The above receipt may be tried for lobster dressing.

A Spanish proverb says, that for compounding a good salad, four persons are required—a spendthrift for oil; a miser for vinegar; a man of judgment for salt; and a madman for stirring the dressing

Eliza Leslie

Makes about 1⅔ cups

3 to 4 rounded teaspoons Dijon mustard	6 tablespoons red wine vinegar (or cider vinegar)
½ teaspoon sea salt	1½ cups olive oil
½ teaspoon freshly ground pepper	1 hard boiled egg, shelled and mashed

1. In a small bowl combine mustard, salt, pepper, and wine vinegar, blending together well (blender may be used).
2. While beating, very slowly blend in olive oil, incorporating ingredients thoroughly.
3. Stir in hard-boiled egg

Note: Fresh herbs such as tarragon, basil, marjoram, or thyme may be added to this basic dressing.

Catchups
and Condiments

Say the word "catchup" today and we think immediately of that gooey, red tomato stuff poured on hamburgers or used by one of our more recent Presidents to flavor his cottage cheese. *Tomato* catchup, however, is relatively new to the culinary scene, not even appearing in American cookbooks until Mary Randolph's *The Virginia House-wife* was published in 1824.[1]

The commercial product of today is far different from the diverse homemade versions dating back to the 17th century. Acquainted with Asian sauces through the East India trade (the Malay word *kechap* means soy sauce), British and American cooks began creating their own sauces, or *catchups,* from such ingredients as mushrooms, walnuts, lemons, grapes, and oysters. Combining one of these ingredients with vinegar and pungent seasonings, which included cloves, nutmeg, cayenne pepper, ginger, shallots, and horseradish, the mixture was simmered and reduced to create a spicy sauce that was then used as an essential flavoring for many made dishes.

Toward the end of the 18th century the appearance of commercially made seasoning sauces was a welcomed convenience to cooks of the period. Gradually the numerous published recipes for them disappeared. Three of the most popular early catchups are presented here.

Lemon Catchup or Pickle

Grate the peel of a dozen large fresh lemons. Prepare, by pounding them in a mortar, two ounces of mustard seed, half an ounce of black pepper, half an ounce of nutmeg, a quarter of an ounce of mace, and a quarter of an ounce of cloves. Slice thin two ounces of horseradish. Put all these ingredients together. Strew over them two ounces of fine salt. Add the juice of the lemons.

Boil the whole twenty minutes. Then put it warm into a jar, and let it stand three weeks closely covered. Stir it up daily.

Then strain it through a sieve, and put it up in small bottles to flavour fish and other sauces.

This is sometimes called lemon pickle.

Eliza Leslie

Makes about 1½ cups

12 large fresh lemons
4 tablespoons mustard seed
1 tablespoon peppercorns
2 teaspoons freshly grated
    nutmeg
1 teaspoon mace

1 teaspoon whole cloves (may
    use ½ teaspoon ground)
2 tablespoons minced
    horseradish
2 tablespoons salt

1. Grate peel from lemons into large bowl. Squeeze and reserve lemon juice.
2. Pound spices together until smooth. Add to lemon peel along with horseradish. Mix in salt, blending well. Mix in lemon juice.
3. Simmer mixture together, covered, for 20 minutes. Pour into jar, cover tightly, and let stand in cool dark place for 3 weeks. Stir daily.
4. Strain, mashing ingredients to extract as much of the liquid as possible. Bottle for use.

Anna R. Peck's Mushroom Ketchup

Take your mushrooms just as they are gathered, without washing, break them with y hands and between every of mushrooms put a large handfull of salt, let them lie thus all night, then squease them very dry from the liquor, and let it stand till it is very clear, then boil it up with garlick, spice, pepper, anchovies, Indian pepper, Bay leaf & shallot till half is consumed, and bottle it for use.*

Anna R. Peck Memorandum Book

Makes 3 cups

6 pounds mushrooms
6 tablespoons salt
Dry red wine (if needed)
4 cloves garlic, peeled and
  minced
1 tablespoon freshly ground
  nutmeg
1½ teaspoons whole allspice
  berries
1 teaspoon whole cloves

1 teaspoon mace
1 teaspoon ginger
1 teaspoon peppercorns
1 tablespoon cayenne pepper
2 to 3 bay leaves
¼ pound shallots, peeled and
  finely chopped

1. Break mushrooms into a large earthenware bowl, alternating each layer with 1 tablespoon salt. Top with last tablespoon of salt. Cover and set away for 24 hours, stirring and mashing mushrooms occasionally after the first 12 hours.
2. Strain mushrooms into a large bowl, squeezing out as much of the juice as possible from the mushrooms. Measure liquid and add wine, if necessary, to make 4 cups. Save mushrooms for powder (p. 315).
3. Combine mushroom juice with remaining ingredients. Pour into pot and bring to boil. Simmer mixture uncovered, stirring occasionally, until liquid is reduced, 1 hour or longer to blend flavors.
4. Remove from heat, cover, and let sit until cool.
5. Strain and bottle for use. Will keep indefinitely under refrigeration. Shake thoroughly before use.

Oatlands Walnut Catsup

*Gather the black walnuts in harvest, if you cannot get white ones, allow
12 walnuts to every quart of vinegar pound the walnuts in an iron pot
and leave them exposed to the air for several hours to make them black
pour on the vinegar and boil them well for near an hour, let them cool
then strain through a sieve, and to every gallon of the liquor, put a pint
of good vinegar, an oz of all spice the same of pepper a tablespoonful of
pounded mace and cloves, 2 of salt with 2 onions chopped fine, boil it a
few minutes longer, let it cool and bottle and seal it closely. (You must keep
all the catsups where they will not freeze in winter.)*

Kate Powell Carter

Makes about 1½ quarts

100 green walnuts, unshelled	1 tablespoon mace
5 cups cider vinegar, divided	1 tablespoon cloves
(or more as needed)	2 tablespoons salt
2 tablespoons allspice berries	2 cups peeled, chopped onion
2 tablespoons peppercorns	

1. Break up unshelled walnuts and set out in sun 4 to 6
hours to darken.
2. Put walnuts in a large pot. Add 4 cups vinegar. Boil, uncovered, 1 hour.
3. Cool and strain through cloth-lined colander, squeezing
cloth to extract as much of the juice as possible. Discard
walnuts.
4. Add 1 cup fresh vinegar to walnut and vinegar liquid.
Add seasonings and onion.
5. Bring to a boil, then simmer gently, uncovered, 30 to 45
minutes. Let cool, strain, and bottle for use. Will keep indefinitely under refrigeration.

Mrs. Bradley's Mushroom Powder

Take a Peck of Mushrooms, wash and rub them clean with a Flannel Rag, cutting out all the Worms; but do not peel off the Skins; put to them sixteen Blades of Mace, forty Cloves, six Bay-leaves, twice as much beaten Pepper as will lie on a half Crown, a good Handful of Salt, a Dozen Onions, a piece of Butter as big as an Egg, and half a Pint of Vinegar: Stew these as fast as you can; keep the Liquor for use, and dry the Mushrooms first on a broad Pan in the Oven; afterwards put them on Sieves, till they are dry enough to pound all together into Powder. This Quantity usually makes half a Pound

Eliza Smith

Makes about 1 cup

Use mushrooms left from making Mushroom Catchup (p. 313)

Hearth:
1. Spread squeezed-out mushrooms in one layer on pans, or in bottom of Dutch oven, or (if available) in a warm bake oven, or out in sun.
2. Dry mushrooms for 48 to 60 hours, stirring occasionally. When they are completely dry, rub the mushrooms with your hands to a coarse powder.
3. Store in covered jars to use as a seasoning for soups, stews, and other savory dishes.

Modern:
1. Follow hearth direction 1, layering mushrooms on cookie sheets.
2. Dry in oven set at lowest possible temperature for 48 to 60 hours, stirring occasionally, until all moisture is completely evaporated and mushrooms are completely dried out.
3. Rub dried mushrooms to a coarse powder and store in tightly capped jars.

Fine French Mustard

Take a jill or two large wine-glasses of tarragon vinegar, (strained from the leaves,) and mix with it an equal quantity of salad oil, stirring them well together. Pound in a mortar, two ounces of mustard seed till it becomes a fine smooth powder, and mix it thoroughly. Add to it one clove of garlic (not more) peeled, minced and pounded. Make the mixture in a deep white-ware dish. If the mustard affects your eyes, put on glasses till you have finished the mixture. When done, put it up in white bottles, or gallipots. Cork them tightly, and seal the corks. Send it to table in those bottles.

This mustard is far superior to any other, the tarragon imparting a peculiar and pleasant flavor. It is excellent to eat with any sort of roast meat, particularly beef or mutton, and an improvement to almost all plain sauces, stews, soups, &c.

French mustard is to be purchased very good at all the best grocery stores.

Eliza Leslie

Makes about 1 cup

3 tablespoons mustard seed
2 cloves garlic, peeled and
   minced

¼ cup plus 2 tablespoons
   tarragon vinegar (page 317)
¼ cup plus 2 tablespoons olive
   oil

1. Pound mustard seed in a mortar until powdery. Put mustard powder into a small bowl.
2. Add garlic, then gradually stir in tarragon vinegar, blending well.
3. Gradually blend in olive oil. Mix well.
4. Bottle for use.

Note: This very hot & spicy mustard may be used as an accompaniment to beef or lamb.

Tarragon Vinegar

The fresh leaves of the tarragon plant are in perfection in July and August, and impart a new and pleasant taste to soups, hashes, gravies, &c. To use it fresh, wash a bunch of tarragon in cold water. Afterwards strip off the green leaves, chop or mince them, and boil a tea-spoonful or more in the dish you intend to flavor. The best way of keeping tarragon is to strip off as many fresh leaves as will half fill a glass jar that holds a quart. Pour on as much real cider vinegar as will fill up the jar. Cover it closely, and let the tarragon infuse in it for a week, shaking the jar every day. Then pour off that vinegar carefully, and throw away the tarragon leaves that have been steeping in it. Wash that jar, or take another clean one, put into it the same quantity of fresh tarragon leaves, and fill up with the same vinegar in which you have infused the first supply. Let the second leaves remain in the jar of vinegar. A tarragon bush is well worth planting; even in a small city garden.

Tarragon is the chief ingredient of French mustard.

Eliza Leslie

Makes 1 quart

Fresh tarragon	1 quart cider vinegar

1. Wash and strip enough tarragon leaves to half fill a quart jar. Pour on vinegar. Cover and shake well.
2. Set vinegar in a cool, dry place for 1 week to let tarragon infuse. Shake jar every day.
3. At the end of a week, strain and reserve vinegar. Discard tarragon leaves.
4. Wash out jar and fill again with fresh tarragon leaves. Pour on reserved vinegar. Cover and shake well. Keep in cool dry place, using as needed.

Fried Parsley

Pick the small sprigs of parsley from the large stalks. Wash it, and then throw it into clean cold water. After the meat or fish that it is to accompany has been fried and taken out of the pan, give the fat that remains a boil up, and lay the parsley into it. It will crimp and still continue green, if not kept frying too long. Take it out, drain it, and place it before the fire a few minutes, to dry it from the fat. Dish it laid on the top of the fish or steaks.

Eliza Leslie

1 cup fresh parsley sprigs   Lard for frying

Hearth:
1. Rinse parsley sprigs and dry thoroughly on cloths until they are free of moisture.
2. Shortly before serving food that is to be garnished with fried parsley, melt 2″ to 3″ lard over hot coals.
3. When lard sizzles, drop in parsley sprigs and fry until crisp, about 2 to 3 minutes. Drain and use as garnish.

Modern:
Follow hearth directions 1 through 3. May use cooking oil for frying.

Brown Flour

There should always be a supply of brown flour kept in readiness to thicken brown gravies, which must be prepared in the following manner:—Put a pint of flour in a Dutch oven, with some coals under it; keep constantly stirring it until it is uniformly of a dark brown, but none of it burnt, which would look like dirt in the gravy.

Mary Randolph

Makes 1 cup

1 cup flour

Hearth:

1. Put flour in skillet over hot coals. Stir constantly until it is a dark golden brown. Watch closely to avoid burning.
2. Cool and store for use in sauces.

Modern:

Follow hearth directions 1 and 2, cooking and stirring flour over moderately low heat.

Source Notes

The Pleasures of Hearthside Cooking

1. Mary Stuart Smith, *Virginia Cookery-Book.* (New York: Harper & Brothers, 1885,) preface.

2. Mary Randolph, *The Virginia House-Wife* (Washington: printed by Davis & Force, 1824), p. 171.

3. Randolph, p. 168.

4. John Evelyn, *Acetaria, A Discourse of Sallets* (London, 1699; Facsimile, London, Prospect Books, 1982), p. 25.

5. Evelyn, p. 61.

Fires, Tools, and Techniques

1. Hannah Glasse, *The Art of Cookery Made Plain and Easy . . .* (new ed., London: 1796; facsimile, with introduction by Fanny Cradock, Hamden, Conn: Archon Books, 1971), p. 29.

2. Philip Vickers Fithian, *The Journal and Letters of Philip Vickers Fithian, 1773–1774,* edited by Hunter Dickinson Farish (Williamsburg: Colonial Williamsburg, 1957), p. 61.

3. Fithian, p. 60.

4. Rachael Feild, *Irons in the Fire* (Ramsbury, Marlborough, Great Britain: Crowood Press, 1984), p. 78. Ms. Feild's research on hearth death was centered primarily in the British Isles (letter from Rachael Feild, November 23, 1985).

Traditional Virginia Cuisine

1. John Smith, *Captain John Smith's History of Virginia, a Selection,* edited by David Freeman Hawke (Indianapolis: Bobbs-Merrill, 1978), p. 13.

2. Robert Beverley, *The History and Present State of Virginia, In Four Parts* (London: printed for R. Parker, 1705), Book I, p. 2.

3. Richard Hakluyt, *The Principall Navigations, Voiages, and Discoveries of the English Nation* (London: 1589. Facsimile. 2 vols. Cambridge: Cambridge University Press, 1965), vol. 2, pp. 728–733.

4. Richard Hakluyt, *Diverse Voyages Touching the Discoverie of America* (London: 1582; facsimile, reprinted 19–?). See the section entitled "Notes in writing besides more privie by mouth that were given by a gentleman, Anno 1580. . . ."

5. Hakluyt, see number 4.

6. Thomas Hariot, *A Briefe and True Report of the New found Land in Virginia* (London: Theodore de Bry, 1590. Facsimile, Ann Arbor, Mich.: University Microfilms, 1966).

7. Richard Lee Morton, *Colonial Virginia*, Vol. I (Chapel Hill: University of North Carolina Press, for the Virginia Historical Society, 1960), p. 14.

8. William Byrd, *William Byrd's Natural History of Virginia, or The Newly Discovered Eden* (Bern: 1737. Reprint, edited and translated from a German version by Richard Croom Beatty and William J. Malloy, Richmond: Dietz Press, 1940), p. 20.

9. C. Anne Wilson, *Food & Drink in Britain* (New York: Barnes & Noble, 1974), p. 362.

10. Beverley, Book IV, p. 56.

11. Helen Mendes, *The African Heritage Cookbook* (New York: Macmillan, 1971), p. 74.

12. Mendes, p. 31.

13. Beverley, Book IV, p. 54.

14. Philip Alexander Bruce, *Social Life of Virginia in the Seventeenth Century* (Richmond: 1907. Reprint, Williamstown, Mass.: Corner House Publishers, 1968), p. 220.

15. Robert ("King") Carter, "Robert Carter Diary" (Manuscripts Department, Alderman Library, University of Virginia, Charlottesville, Va.), p. 3.

16. Glasse, p. xxx.

17. Joanne Young, *Shirley Plantation* (Charles City, Va.: Shirley Plantation, 1981), p. 36.

18. Glasse, p. 18.

19. Eliza Leslie, *Seventy-five Receipts for Pastry, Cakes and Sweet-Meats,* 3rd ed., with appendix (Boston: Munroe & Francis, 1830), p. 45.

20. Marion Cabell Tyree, editor, *Housekeeping in Old Virginia* (New York: W. Carleton, 1877), p. 66.

21. Bert Greene, "Jefferson, the Great Gastronome." *Cuisine* 13 (March, 1984): p. 40.

22. Marie Kimball, *Thomas Jefferson's Cook Book* (Charlottesville: University of Virginia Press, 1976), p. vii.

23. Young, p. 50.

24. George W. Bagby, *The Old Virginia Gentleman and Other Sketches*, edited by Allen M. Bagby (5th ed., Richmond: Dietz Press, 1948), pp. 192–193.

Bills of Fare

1. Amariah Frost, "Diary," June 1797. Cited in Moncure D. Conway, "Footprints In Washingtonland," *Harper's New Monthly Magazine* 78 (April, 1889), p. 743.

2. Martha Bradley, *The British Housewife* . . . (London: S. Crower & H. Wardgate, 1770), p. 3.

3. Carter "Diary," January 6, 1725/26.

4. Carter "Diary," January 14, 1725/26.

5. John Page, letter to St. George Tucker, February 28, 1777. (Tucker-Coleman Papers, Earl Gregg Swem Library, College of William and Mary, Williamsburg, Va.).

6. Carter "Diary," March 28, 1726.

7. Fithian, April 3, 1774, p. 90.

8. Byrd, *Secret Diary*, May 5, 1709, p. 20.

9. John Harrower *The Journal of John Harrower* . . . , *1773–1776*, edited by Edward Miles Riley (Williamsburg: Colonial Williamsburg, 1963), May 20, 1776, p. 152.

10. Anne Blair, letter to "Dicky", June 14, 1769. (Blair, Banister, Braxton, Horner, Whiting Papers, Earl Gregg Swem Library, College of William and Mary, Williamsburg, Va.)

11. Harrower, June 14, 1774, p. 56.

12. Fithian, July 6, 1774, p. 132.

13. Carter "Diary," August 31, 1727.

14. Anne Blair, letter to Eliza Whiting, August 16, 1799. (Blair, Banister, Braxton, Horner, Whiting Papers. Earl Gregg Swem Library, College of William and Mary, Williamsburg, Va.)

15. Carter "Diary," August 31, 1723.

16. Carter "Diary," September 4, 1727.

17. Fithian, October 20, 1774, p. 208.

18. Harrower, October 27, 1774, p. 67.

19. Byrd, *Secret Diary*, November 21, 1710, p. 113.

20. Carter "Diary," November 18, 1727.

21. Sally Cary Fairfax, "Diary," December 26, 1771. *Virginia Magazine of History and Biography,* Vol. 11 (June, 1904), p. 212.

22. Mira Rosanna Barraud, letter to Mrs. Ann Barraud, December 22, 1832. (Barraud Family Papers, Earl Gregg Swem Library, College of William and Mary, Williamsburg, Va.).

23. Joshua Brooks, "Journal" (unpublished). In *Mount Vernon Ladies' Association of the Union. Annual Report,* 1947, p. 22.

24. Ralph Hamor, *A Trve Discovrse of the Present Estate of Virginia . . .* (London: 1615. Facsimile, Albany: J. Munsell, 1860), May, 1615, p. 43.

25. William Dunlap, *History of the Rise and Progress of the Arts of Design in the United States* (New York: 1834. Reprint, New York: Dover Publications, 1969), Winter 1822, p. 286.

Recipes

Breads

1. Hugh Jones, *The Present State of Virginia* (London: 1724. Reprint. New York: Joseph Sabin, 1865), p. 40.

2. Mary Stuart Smith, *Virginia Cookery-Book* (New York: Harper, 1885), p. 19.

3. Dunlap, p. 286.

4. Mary S. Smith, p. 3.

5. Mary S. Smith, p. 5.

6. Eliza Leslie, *Directions for Cookery . . . ,* 31st ed. (Philadelphia: 1848. Reprint, New York: Arno Press, 1973), pp. 374–375.

7. Eliza Leslie, *Miss Leslie's New Cookery Book* (Philadelphia: T. B. Peterson, 1857), p. 401.

8. Beverley, p. 178.

9. Elizabeth Ellicott Lea, *Domestic Cookery . . . ,* 3rd ed. (Baltimore: Cushings & Bailey, 1851), p. 61.

Beverages

1. "A Lady's Adieu to her Tea Table." Poem from the *Virginia Gazette,* January 20, 1774. In *Virginia Historical Register and Literary Companion* 6 (October, 1853), p. 214.

2. Marietta Minnegerode Andrews, *Memoirs of a Poor Relation* (New York: E. P. Dutton, 1927), pp. 124–125.

Soups

1. Glasse, pp. 176–177.

2. Maria Parloa, *Miss Parloa's New Cook Book* (Boston: Estes & Lauriat, 1880), p. 82.

3. William Byrd, *History of the Dividing Line . . . , 1728.* In *The Prose Works of William Byrd,* edited by Louis B. Wright (Cambridge: Belknap Press, 1966), pp. 279–280.

Entrées

1. Robert Beverley, *The History and Present State of Virginia* (London: 1705. Reprint, edited by Louis B. Wright, Chapel Hill: University of North Carolina Press, 1947), p. 146.

2. John Smith, p. 51.

3. Byrd, *Natural History,* pp. 82–83.

4. Nicholas Cresswell, *The Journal of Nicholas Cresswell, 1774–1777* (New York: Dial Press, 1924), Jan. 1, 1775, p. 52.

5. Byrd, *Natural History,* p. 59.

6. Cresswell, April 13, 1777, p. 199.

7. Evelyn Douglas Ward [1853–1941], "Reminiscences of Bladensfield." Unpublished manuscript. ("Bladensfield," Richmond County, Va. Privately owned, no date).

8. Ward, no date.

9. Leslie, *New Cookery Book,* p. 140; Randolph, p. 23.

10. Leslie, *New Cookery Book,* p. 140.

11. Leslie, *New Cookery Book,* p. 140.

12. Leslie, *New Cookery Book,* p. 141.

13. Elizabeth Nicholson, *Cooking as It Should Be . . . ,* 4th ed., revised and enlarged (Philadelphia: Willis P. Hazard, 1856), p. 41.

14. Conversation with Karen Hess, March 7, 1986.

15. Randolph, p. 25.

16. Mary S. Smith, p. 83.

Vegetables

1. Glasse, p. 29.

2. Randolph, p. 122.

3. Leslie, *New Cookery Book,* p. 344.

4. Robert Carter (of Nomini Hall), "Journal," August 1784–March 1789 (Robert Carter III Papers, Manuscript Division, Library of Congress, Washington, D.C.), April 25, 1788.

5. Elizabeth Osborne Carter, "Diary" (unpublished manuscript compiled at "Oatlands," Loudoun County, Va. privately owned), May 13, 1861.

6. Dumas Malone, *Jefferson The Virginian* (Boston: Little, Brown, 1948), p. 384.

7. Leslie, *New Cookery Book,* p. 340.

Cakes and Little Cakes

1. Randolph, p. 140.

2. Leslie, *Directions for Cookery* . . . , p. 337.

3. Leslie, *Seventy-Five Receipts* . . . , p. 46.

4. Leslie, *Directions for Cookery* . . . , p. 336.

5. Leslie, *Directions for Cookery* . . . , p. 337.

6. Leslie, *Directions for Cookery* . . . , p. 337.

Sweet Pies, Puddings, and Cheesecakes

1. Wilson, p. 321.

2. Wilson, p. 321.

3. Wilson, p. 318.

4. Glasse, p. 242.

5. Wilson, p. 321.

6. Wilson, p. 173.

Custards, Creams, Ices, and Fruit

1. Leslie, *New Cookery Book,* pp. 463–464.

2. Blair, letter to Eliza Whiting, March 20, 1799.

3. Blair, letter to Eliza Whiting, August 16, 1799.

Salad Dressings

1. Evelyn, pp. 137–138.

2. Evelyn, pp. 30–35.

3. Evelyn, p. 98.

4. Evelyn, p. 106.

5. Evelyn, p. 88.

6. Jane Grigson, *Food With the Famous* (Harmondsworth, Middlesex, England: Penguin Books Ltd., 1981), p. 125.

Catchups and Condiments

1. *Martha Washington's Book of Cookery* . . . , transcribed and edited by Karen Hess (New York: Columbia University Press, 1981), p. 174.

Sources for Supplies

Listed here are some sources of antique and reproduction cooking utensils and tools, old-fashioned and hard-to-find foodstuffs, and other hard-to-find items. All the companies listed below will ship anywhere, but write or call them for detailed information and current prices.

Equipment
Early American Life
P.O. Box 1831
Harrisburg, Pa. 17105
Plans for a reflector oven (tin kitchen) may be ordered for $2 and a business-size self-addressed, stamped envelope.

Pat Guthman Antiques
342 Pequot Avenue
Southport, Conn. 06490
Tel. (203) 259-5743
Specializes in 18th- and 19th-century kitchen and hearth items. The owner has done extensive research in the field and has written many articles on the subject.

Richmondtown Restoration
Staten Island Historical Society
441 Clarke Avenue
Staten Island, N.Y. 10306
Tel. (718) 351-1611
Reproduction tinware, redware, and other products.

Peter Ross
3111 Forge Road
Toano, Va. 23168
Tel: (804) 566-0261
Blacksmith: iron cooking and fireplace equipment made to order.

The Taproot
157 Second Street
Williamsburg, Va. 23185
Tel: (804) 229-3722
Cast-iron pots, cranes, utensils. Blacksmith will recreate Colonial utensils and repair equipment. (Contact: David Coppinger)

Flours and Grains, Herbs, Seasonings, Seeds, and Hard-to-find Foods

Evelynton Plantation and Nursery
Route 2, Box 21
Charles City, Va. 23031
Tel: (804) 829-5068/829-5075
Specializes in a number of unusual culinary and medicinal herbs. (Contact: Lisa Ruffin, director)

Johnson & Elder, Inc.
Box 65
Sedley, Va. 23878
Tel: (804) 562-5236
Specializes in stone-ground white cornmeal; family operation since 1853. (Contact: Ed Johnson)

Muskettoe Pointe Herb Farm
White Stone, Va. 22578
Tel.: (804) 435-6359
Carries a variety of culinary and medicinal herb plants. (Contact: Emily Carter)

Old Mill of Guilford
1340 North Carolina 68 North
Oak Ridge, N.C. 27310
Tel: (919) 643-4783
Established in 1753, the Old Mill offers a wide variety of old-fashioned flours and grains as well as honey, molasses, dried herbs, fresh eggs, country ham, and other products brought in by area residents. (Contact: Charles & Heidi Parnell, owners)

Shepherd's Garden Seeds
7389 W. Zayante Road
Felton, Calif. 95018
Tel: (408) 335-5400
Offers seeds for edible flowers, lettuces, European salads, and baby vegetables. Send $1 for catalog, or call to order. (Contact: Renee Shepherd)

Smithfield Packing Co., Inc.
P.O. Box 447
Smithfield, Va. 23430
Tel: (804) 357-4321
Virginia hams of all sorts. Catalog available.

Wade's Mill
Route 1, Box 475
Raphine, Va. 24472
Tel: (703) 348-5420
Excellent assortment of stone-ground flours and grains. (Contact: David C. Beebe)

Williamsburg Pottery Wine & Cheese Shop
Village Shops
Kings Mill
Williamsburg, Va. 23185
Tel: (804) 229-6754
Gourmet and hard-to-locate food items, such as salsify, rose water, dried corn, etc. (Contact: Beverly Ashnault, manager)

Bibliography

Reference Works

The American Heritage Dictionary of the English Language. Edited by William Morris. Boston & New York: American Heritage Publishing Co. and Houghton Mifflin Co., 1971.

Brown, Eleanor, and Bob Brown. *Culinary Americana.* New York: Roving Eye Press, 1961.

Gray, Sarah Virginia. "A History of the Publication of Cook-Books in the United States, 1796–1896." Master's thesis. University of North Carolina at Chapel Hill, 1964.

Kane, Joseph Nation. *Famous First Facts.* 4th ed. New York: W. W. Wilson Co., 1981.

Lowenstein, Eleanor. *Bibliography of American Cookery Books 1742–1860.* Worcester, Massachusetts: American Antiquarian Society; New York: Corner Book Shop, 1972.

Oxford English Dictionary. Compact ed. London: Oxford University Press, 1971.

Manuscripts

Banister, Mary Burton Augusta Bolling. "Cookbook." 1818–1821. Unpublished manuscript compiled in Petersburg, Va. Manuscript Division, Virginia Historical Society, Richmond, Va.

Barraud, Mira Rosanna. Letter to Mrs. Ann Barraud. December 22, 1832. Barraud Family Papers, Earl Gregg Swem Library, College of William and Mary, Williamsburg, Va.

Blackford, L. M. "Recipes in the Culinary Art, Together with Hints on Housewifery, &c." 1852. Lynchburg, Va. Blackford Family Papers, Southern Historical Collection, Library, University of North Carolina at Chapel Hill, Chapel Hill, N.C.

Blair, Anne. Letter to "Dicky," June 14, 1769. Blair, Banister, Braxton, Horner, Whiting Papers, Earl Gregg Swem Library, College of William and Mary, Williamsburg, Va.

———. Letter to Eliza Whiting, March 20, 1799.

———. Letter to Eliza Whiting, August 16, 1799.

Cabell, Jane Charity Alston. "Cookbook," circa 1880. Unpublished manuscript. Richmond, Va. Manuscript Division, Virginia Historical Society, Richmond, Va.

Carter, Elizabeth Osborn. "Diary," 1860–1872. Unpublished manuscript. "Oatlands," Loudoun County, Va. Privately owned.

Carter, Kate Powell. "Cookbook," 1865. Unpublished manuscript compiled at "Oatlands," Loudoun County, Va. Privately owned.

Carter, Robert "King." "Robert Carter Diary," (Acc. No. 3807), Manuscripts Department, Alderman Library, University of Virginia, Charlottesville, Virginia.

———. "Robert Carter Diary," transcript by Francis L. Berkeley, Jr. Manuscripts Department, Alderman Library, University of Virginia, Charlottesville, Va.

Carter, Robert, of Nomini Hall. "Journal," August 1784–March 1789. Robert Carter III Papers, Manuscript Division, Library of Congress, Washington, D.C.

Carter-Walker Family Papers. Lancaster County, Va. Privately owned.

Eppes, Elizabeth. "Cookbook," late 19th century. Unpublished manuscript. Appomattox Manor, Hopewell, Va. Manuscript Division, Virginia Historical Society, Richmond, Va.

Feilds, Rachael. Letter to Nancy Carter Crump, November 23, 1985. Privately owned.

Gray, Virginia Gearhart. "Cookery Collection." Earl Gregg Swem Library, College of William and Mary, Williamsburg, Va.

Gray, Sarah Virginia. Family Papers. Pennsylvania, Maryland, Virginia, North Carolina. Privately owned.

(Hopkins?) "Cookbook," circa 1843. Unpublished manuscript. Hopkins Family Papers, Manuscript Division, Virginia Historical Society, Richmond, Va.

Lee, Mary Ann Randolph Custis. "Cookbook," circa 1860–1865. Unpublished manuscript. Manuscript Division, Virginia Historical Society, Richmond, Va.

"Mason Family Recipes," n.d. Unpublished manuscript. Northumberland County, Va. Privately owned.

Page, John. Letter to St. George Tucker. February 28, 1777. Tucker-Coleman Papers, Earl Gregg Swem Library, College of William and Mary, Williamsburg, Va.

Paul, Araminta G. "Scrapbook of Araminta G. Paul," circa 1850. Samuel Paul Papers, Earl Gregg Swem Library, College of William and Mary, Williamsburg, Va.

Peck, Anna R. "Memorandum Book," 1814. Unpublished manuscript. "Bladensfield," Richmond County, Va. Privately owned.

Peck Family Wills and Estate Inventories, 1793–1829. Manuscripts in Clerk's Office, Richmond County Courthouse, Richmond County, Va.

Poindexter Family. "Cookbook," circa 1852. Unpublished manuscript. Norfolk, Va. Privately owned.

Shirley Plantation Collection, compiled in the late 19th century at Shirley Plantation, Charles City County, Va. Privately owned.

Skipwith Family Papers, Earl Gregg Swem Library, College of William and Mary, Williamsburg, Va.

Southall Papers, Earl Gregg Swem Library, College of William and Mary, Williamsburg, Va.

"Tabb Family Recipe Book," n.d. Unpublished manuscript. Gloucester County, Va. Privately owned.

Tebbs, M. H. D. "Receipt Book," circa 1790–1820. Unpublished manuscript. The Loudoun Museum, Inc., Leesburg, Va.

Townsend, Mary. "Mary Townsend's Recipe Book," 1864. Taliaferro-Saunders Papers, Earl Gregg Swem Library, College of William and Mary, Williamsburg, Va.

"Tucker Family Cookbook," circa 1800. Tucker-Coleman Papers, Earl Gregg Swem Library, College of William and Mary, Williamsburg, Va.

Ward, Evelyn Douglas. "Reminiscences of Bladensfield." Unpublished manuscript. "Bladensfield," Richmond County, Va. Privately owned.

Ward Family "Cookbook," compiled at "Bladensfield." Unpublished manuscript. Richmond County, Va. Privately owned.

Books and Articles

Andrews, Marietta Minnegerode. *Memoirs of a Poor Relation.* New York: E. P. Dutton & Co., 1927.

Bagby, George W. *The Old Virginia Gentleman and Other Sketches.* 5th ed., edited by Allen M. Bagby. Richmond: Dietz Press, 1948.

Belden, Louise Conway. *The Festive Tradition.* New York: W. W. Norton & Co., 1983.

Beverley, Robert. *The History and Present State of Virginia, In Four Parts.* London: printed for R. Parker, 1705.

————. *The History and Present State of Virginia*. London: 1705. Reprint, edited by Louis B. Wright. Chapel Hill: University of North Carolina Press, 1947.

Booth, Sally Smith. *Hung, Strung & Potted*. New York: Clarkson N. Potter, 1971.

Bouvier, Hannah Moore. *The National Cook Book*. 8th ed. Philadelphia: Childs & Peterson, 1857.

Boxer, Arabella, Lady, and Philippa Back. *The Herb Book*. London: Octopus Books, 1980.

Bradley, Martha. *The British Housewife* . . . London: S. Crower & H. Wardgate, 1770.

Brooks, Joshua. "Journal" (unpublished), as cited in *Mount Vernon Ladies' Association of Union. Annual Report*, 1947, pp. 19–25.

Brown, Dale. *American Cooking*. New York: Time-Life Books, 1968.

Bruce, Philip Alexander. *Social Life of Virginia in the Seventeenth Century.* Richmond: 1907. Reprint. Williamstown, Mass.: Corner House Publishers, 1968.

Burnaby, Andrew. "Burnaby's Travels in Virginia in 1759." Extracts from *Travels Through the Middle Settlements in North America in the Years 1759 and 1760*. London: 1775. In *Virginia Historical Register, and Literary Companion* 5 (January, 1852): 27–38.

Byrd, William. *History of the Dividing Line . . . , 1728*. In *The Prose Works of William Byrd*. Edited by Louis B. Wright. Cambridge, Mass.: Belknap Press, 1966.

————. *The Secret Diary of William Byrd of Westover, 1709–1712*. Edited by Louis B. Wright and Marion Tinling. Richmond: Dietz Press, 1941.

————. *William Byrd's Natural History of Virginia, The Newly Discovered Eden.* Bern: 1737. Reprint, edited, and translated from a German version by Richard Croom Beatty and William J. Malloy. Richmond: Dietz Press, 1940.

Carlo, Joyce W. *Trammels, Trenchers & Tartlets*. Old Saybrook, Conn.: Peregrine Press, 1982.

Carson, Jane. *Colonial Virginia Cookery.* Williamsburg, Va.: Colonial Williamsburg, 1968.

Carter, Charles. *The Complete Practical Cook* . . . London: 1730. Facsimile. London: Prospect Books,. 1984.

Conway, Moncure Daniel. "Footprints in Washingtonland." *Harper's New Monthly Magazine* 78 (April, 1889): 738–744.

Cresswell, Nicholas. *The Journal of Nicolas Cresswell, 1774–1777*. New York: Dial Press, 1924.

Cringan, Mrs. John W. *Instructions in Cooking.* Richmond: J. L. Hill Printing Co., 1895.

Crump, Nancy Carter. "History and Cooking: A Natural Combination." *The Business of Herbs* 3 (May/June 1985): 11.

Dabney, Virginius. *Virginia, the New Dominion.* Garden City, N.Y.: Doubleday & Co. 1971.

Daniele, Joseph. "Roast Your Bird in Our Tin Kitchen." *Early American Life* 7 (October, 1976): 26–29.

David, Elizabeth. *English Bread and Yeast Cookery,* American ed. with notes by Karen Hess. New York: Viking Press, 1980.

Donnan, Mrs. William S. *A Collection of Virginia Recipes.* Richmond: Whittet & Shepperson, 1891.

Dunlap, William. *History of the Rise and Progress of the Arts of Design in the United States.* New York: 1834. Reprint. New York: Dover Publications, 1969.

Evelyn, John. *Acetaria, A Discourse of Sallets.* London: 1699. Facsimile, London: Prospect Books, 1982.

Fairfax, Sally Cary. "Diary," *Virginia Magazine of History and Biography.* 11 (June, 1904): 212–214

Feild, Rachael. *Irons in the Fire.* Ramsbury, Marlborough, Great Britain: Crowood Press, 1984.

Fithian, Philip Vickers. *The Journal and Letters of Philip Vickers Fithian, 1773–1774.* Edited by Hunter Dickinson Farish. Williamsburg, Va.: Colonial Williamsburg, 1957.

Glasse, Hannah. *The Art of Cookery Made Plain and Easy* . . . 7th ed. London: for the author, 1760.

———. *The Art of Cookery Made Plain and Easy* . . . New ed. London: 1796. Facsimile, with introduction by Fanny Cradock. Hamden, Conn.: Archon Books, 1971.

———. *The Compleat Confectioner* . . . London: printed by I. Pottinger & J. Williams, 1770.

Glover, E. T. *The Warm Springs Receipt Book.* Compiled between 1881 and 1894. Richmond: B. F. Johnson Publishing Co., 1897.

Gray, Lewis Cecil. *History of Agriculture in the Southern United States to 1860.* Vol. 1. Washington: 1933. Reprint. New York: Peter Smith, 1941.

Gray, Virginia Gearhart. "An American Colonial Cookery, 1607–1800." Typescript of speech presented before the General Davie Chapter, Daughters of the American Revolution, Durham, N.C. 1944. Privately owned.

Greene, Bert. "Jefferson, the Great Gastronome." *Cuisine* 13 (March, 1984): 36–41, 64–72.

Grigson, Jane. *Food With the Famous.* Harmondsworth, Middlesex, England: Penguin Books, Ltd., 1981.

Hakluyt, Richard. *Divers Voyages Touching the Discoverie of America.* London: 1582. Facsimile. Reprinted 19–?.

————. *The Principall Navigations, Voiages and Discoveries of the English Nation.* London: 1589. Facsimile. 2 vols. Cambridge: Cambridge University Press, 1965.

Hamor, Ralph. *A True Discovrse of the Present Estate of Virginia . . .* London: 1615. Reprint. Albany: J. Munsell 1860.

Hariot, Thomas. *A Briefe and True Report of the New found Land in Virginia.* London: Theodore de Bry, 1590. Text accompanying plates translated by Richard Hakluyt. Facsimile. Ann Arbor, Mich.: University Microfilms, 1966.

Harland, Marion. *Common Sense in the Household.* Revised ed. New York: Charles Scribner's Sons, 1888.

Harrower, John. *The Journal of John Harrower . . . , 1773–1776.* Edited by Edward Miles Riley. Williamsburg, Va.: Colonial Williamsburg, 1963.

Hess, John L., and Karen Hess. *The Taste of America.* New York: Grossman Publishers, 1977

Husted, Margaret, "Mary Randolph's *The Virginia Housewife,* America's First Regional Cookbook." *Virginia Cavalcade* 30 (Autumn, 1980): 76–87.

Isaac, Rhys. *The Transformation of Virginia, 1740–1790.* Chapel Hill: University of North Carolina Press, for the Institute of Early American History and Culture, 1982.

Jefferson, Thomas. *Thomas Jefferson's Garden Book.* 1766–1824. Edited by Edwin Morris Betts. Philadelphia: American Philosophical Society, 1944.

————. *Notes on the State of Virginia.* In *Writings.* Edited by Merrill D. Person. New York: Literary Classics, 1984.

Jones, Evan. *American Food.* New York: E. P. Dutton & Co., 1975.

Jones, Hugh. *The Present State of Virginia.* London: 1724. Facsimile. New York: for Joseph Sabin, 1865.

Kimball, Marie. *Thomas Jefferson's Cook Book.* Charlottesville: University of Virginia Press, 1976.

Klapthor, Margaret Brown. *The First Ladies Cook Book.* New York: Parents' Magazine Press, 1977.

Ladd, Paul R. *Early American Fireplaces.* New York: Hastings House, 1977.

Lady, A. *Modern Domestic Cookery: Based on the Well-Known Work of Mrs. Rundell . . .* New and revised ed. London: John Murray, 1855.

"A Lady's Adieu to her Tea Table." Poem from the *Virginia Gazette,* January 20, 1774. In *Virginia Historical Register and Literary Companion.* 6 (October 1853): 214.

Lea, Elizabeth Ellicott. *Domestic Cookery, Useful Receipts, and Hints to Young Housekeepers.* 3rd ed. Baltimore; Cushings & Bailey, 1851.

———. *A Quaker Woman's Cookbook. The 'Domestic Cookery' of Elizabeth Ellicott Lea.* Reprint, edited by William Woys Weaver. Philadelphia: University of Pennsylvania Press, 1982.

Lee, Agnes. *Growing Up In the 1850's.* Edited by Mary Custis Lee DeButts. Chapel Hill: University of North Carolina Press, for the Robert E. Lee Memorial Association, 1984.

Lee, Lucinda. *Journal of a Young Lady of Virginia, 1787.* Stratford, Va. Robert E. Lee Memorial Association, 1976.

Leslie, Eliza. *Directions for Cookery . . .* 31st ed. Philadelphia, 1848. Reprint. New York: Arno Press, 1973.

———. *Miss Leslie's New Cookery Book.* Philadelphia: T. B. Peterson & Brothers, 1857.

———. *Seventy-five Receipts for Pastry, Cakes, and Sweet-meats.* 3rd ed., with appendix. Boston: Munroe & Francis, 1830.

Lewis, Nelly Custis. *Nelly Custis Lewis's Housekeeping Book.* Edited by Patricia Brady Schmit. New Orleans: The Historic New Orleans Collection, 1982.

"Lucifer Matches." *Virginia Historical Register, and Literary Note Book* 3 (July, 1850): 171–172

Malone, Dumas. *Jefferson and the Rights of Man.* Vol. 2 of *Jefferson and His Time.* Boston: Little, Brown & Co., 1951.

———. *Jefferson the Virginian.* Vol. 1 of *Jefferson and His Time.* Boston: Little, Brown & Co., 1948.

Martha Washington's Booke of Cookery . . . Transcribed and edited by Karen Hess. New York: Columbia University Press, 1981.

Mazzei, Philip. "Memoirs of the Life and Voyages of Doctor Philip Mazzei." Translated by E. C. Branchi. *William and Mary College Quarterly Magazine.* Series 2: 9 (July, 1929): 160–174.

McConnaughey, Gibson Jefferson. *Two Centuries of Virginia Cooking.* Amelia, Va.: Mid-South Publishing Company, 1977.

McGee, Harold. *On Food and Cooking.* New York: Charles Scribner's & Sons, 1984.

Mendes, Helen. *The African Heritage Cookbook.* New York: Macmillan Company, 1971.

Miller, Elizabeth Smith, comp., *In the Kitchen.* New York: Henry Holt & Company, 1883.

Moncure, Mrs. M. B. *The Art of Good Living*. Baltimore: William K. Boyle's Steam Press, 1870.

Moore, Carrie Pickett. *The Way to the Heart*. Richmond: Whittet & Shepperson, 1905.

Morgan, Edmund Sears. *American Slavery, American Freedom*. New York: W. W. Norton & Company, 1975.

———. *Virginians at Home*. Williamsburg, Va.: Colonial Williamsburg, 1952

Morton, Richard Lee. *Colonial Virginia*. Vol. 1. Chapel Hill: University of North Carolina Press, for the Virginia Historical Society, 1960.

Nicholson, Elizabeth. *Cookery as It Should Be . . .* 4th ed., revised and enlarged. Philadelphia: Willis P. Hazard, 1856.

Noel Hume, Audrey. *Food*. Williamsburg, Va.: Colonial Williamsburg Foundation, 1978.

Parloa, Maria. *Miss Parloa's New Cook Book*. Boston: Estes & Lauriat, 1880.

Phipps, Frances. *Colonial Kitchens, Their Furnishings, and Their Gardens*. New York: Hawthorn Books, 1972.

Pleasures of Colonial Cooking. Newark, N.J.: New Jersey Historical Society, 1982.

Porter, Mrs. M. E. *Mrs. Porter's New Southern Cookery Book . . .* Philadelphia: 1871. Facsimile. New York: Arno Press, 1973.

Raffald, Elizabeth. *The Experienced English House-Keeper . . .* London: R. Baldwin, 1775.

Randolph, John, Jr. *A Treatise on Gardening*. Reprinted from *American Gardener* by John Gardiner & David Hepburn, 3rd ed., 1826. Reprint edited by Marjorie F. Warner. Richmond: Appeals Press, 1924.

Randolph, Mary. *The Virginia House-Wife*. Washington: Printed by Davis & Force, 1824.

———. *The Virginia House-Wife*. Washington: 1824. Facsimile with excerpts from the 1825 and 1828 editions, edited by Karen Hess. Columbia, S.C.: University of South Carolina Press, 1984.

Rolfe, John. "Virginia in 1616." Reprint of "John Rolf's Relation of the State of Virginia, 17th Century." From *Southern Literary Messenger* 5 (June, 1839): 401. In *Virginia Historical Register, and Literary Advertiser* 1 (July, 1848): 101–113.

Root, Waverly. "Early American Cooking." *Gourmet*. 36 (February, 1976): 18–21, 59–63.

Root, Waverly, and Richard de Rochement. *Eating in America*. New York: William Morrow & Company, 1976.

Rorer, Sarah Tyson. *Philadelphia Cook Book*. Philadelphia: Arnold & Company, 1886.

Simmons, Amelia. *American Cookery*. Hartford: 1796. Reprint, edited by Iris Ihde Frey. Green Farms, Conn.: Silverleaf Press, 1983.

Smith, Elizabeth. *The Compleat Housewife: or Accomplish'd Gentlewoman's Companion* . . . Williamsburg: printed and sold by William Parks, 1742.

Smith, John. *Captain John Smith's History of Virginia, a Selection*. Edited by David Frieman Hawke. Indianapolis: Bobbs-Merrill Co., Inc., 1978.

Smith, Mary Stuart. *Virginia Cookery-Book*. New York: Harper & Brothers, 1885.

Smyth, J. F. D. "Smyth's Travels in Virginia, in 1773." Extracts from *A Tour in the United States of America, & Company*. 2 vols. London: 1784. In *Virginia Historical Register, and Literary Companion* 6 (1853): 11–20, 77–90, 131–143.

Sparks, Elizabeth Hedgecock. *North Carolina and Old Salem Cookery*. Kernersville, N.C.: n.p., 1955.

Spruill, Julia Cherry. *Women's Life and Work in the Southern Colonies*. Chapel Hill: 1938. Reprint. New York: W. W. Norton & Company, 1972.

Stick, David. *Roanoke Island, the Beginnings of English America*. Chapel Hill: University of North Carolina Press, 1983.

Tate, Thad W., and David L. Ammerman, eds. *The Chesapeake in the Seventeenth Century*. Chapel Hill: University of North Carolina Press, for the Institute of Early American History and Culture, 1979.

Trollope, Frances. *Domestic Manners of the Americans*. London: 1832. Reprint, edited by Donald Smalley. Gloucester, Mass.: Peter Smith, 1974.

Tyree, Marion Cabel, ed. *Housekeeping in Old Virginia*. New York: G. W. Carleton & Co., Publishers, 1877.

"Virginia in 1648." Reprint of *A Perfect Description of Virginia*. London: 1649. In *Virginia Historical Register, and Literary Advertiser* 2

Wason, Betty. *Cooks, Gluttons & Gourmets*. Garden City, New York: Doubleday & Company, 1962.

Williams, Susan. *Savory Suppers & Fashionable Feasts*. New York: Pantheon Books, 1985.

Wilson, C. Anne. *Food & Drink in Britain*. New York: Barnes & Noble, 1974.

Wolfe, Linda. *The Cooking of the Caribbean Islands*. New York: Time-Life Books, 1970.

Wurst, Klaus. *The Virginia Germans*. Charlottesville: University of Virginia Press, 1969.

Young, Joanne. *Shirley Plantation*. Charles City, Va.: Shirley Plantation, 1981.

Acknowledgments

I wish to thank the Colonial Williamsburg Foundation for permission to quote certain passages from the 1957 edition of *The Journal and Letters of Philip Vickers Fithian*.

I wish also to thank the following institutions for granting permission to publish material from their collections: The Historical Society of Pennsylvania, Francis Parke Custis Cook Book; The Loudoun County Museum, Incorporated, M.H.D. Tebbs Receipt Book; The Library of Congress, Robert Carter III *Journal*, August 1784–March 1789; Oatlands, Incorporated, Kate Powell Carter Cookbook; Southern Historical Society, Library of the University of North Carolina at Chapel Hill, Blackford Family Papers. Also, Swem Library, College of William and Mary: Virginia Gearhart Gray Cookery Collection; Scrapbook of Araminta G. Paul, Samuel Paul Papers; Southall Papers; Mary Townsend's recipe book, Taliaferro-Saunders Papers; Tucker Family cookbook, Tucker-Coleman Papers; M. R. Barraud to Mrs. Ann Barraud, December 22, 1822, Barraud Family Papers; Anne Blair to "Dicky," June 14, 1769, Blair, Banister, Braxton, Horner, Whiting Papers; Anne Blair to Eliza Whiting, March 20, 1799, Blair, Banister, Braxton, Horner, Whiting Papers; Anne Blair to Eliza Whiting, August 16, 1799, Blair, Banister, Braxton, Horner, Whiting Papers; John Page to St. George Tucker, February 28, 1777, Tucker-Coleman Papers.

Also, the University of Virginia Library (Manuscripts Department), Robert Carter Diary (Acc. #3807), transcript prepared by Francis L. Berkeley; Virginia Historical Society for the Mary Burton Augusta Bolling Banister Cookbook, Jane Charity Alston Cookbook, Elizabeth Eppes Cookbook, Hopkins [?] Family Cookbook, and Mary Ann Randolph Custis Lee Cookbook.

In addition, I thank the following individuals for permission to quote from their private collections: Mr. and Mrs. C. Hill Carter, Jr., Charles City, Va., Shirley Plantation Collection; Mr. and Mrs. David M. French, Alexandria, Va., Jean Brent French Recipe Book; Ms. Sarah Virginia Gray, Williamsburg, Va., "An American Colonial Cookery, 1600–1800" authored by her mother, Virginia Gearhart Gray, Gray Family Papers and "A History of the Publication of Cookbooks in the United States, 1796–1896"; Mrs. Frederick Lyman, *Goshen,* Gloucester, Va., Tabb Family Recipe Book; Mrs. W. R. Ward, Bladensfield, Richmond County, Va., Anna R. Peck Memorandum Book, Evelyn Douglas Ward "Reminiscences of Bladensfield," and Ward Family Cookbook.

Several friends and colleagues must be singled out for aid that goes far beyond the call of duty. They are:

Sarah Virginia Gray ("Sally"), an indefatigable resource person and recipe taster, has provided untold help during the last year. I thank her.

Alice Ross, co-founder of the Culinary Historians of New York, for her perceptive comments, technical advice, and encouragement throughout the writing of this book.

Audrey Stehle, food consultant with *Southern Living* magazine, who has been a font of knowledge on various aspects of American foodways and recipe presentation.

Silvio Bedini at the Smithsonian Institution for his patience in answering my many questions on Thomas Jefferson.

Mr. and Mrs. C. Hill Carter, Jr., at Shirley Plantation, whose excitement about this book has all but equaled my own. In their 18th-century kitchen I have created some memorable meals, and I especially thank them for their help.

Dr. Elizabeth R. Reynolds is deeply thanked for handing me the keys to her Rappahannock River farm where I could write amidst the country surroundings I love.

I thank also the following for rendering assistance in everything from information to recipe testing to handholding: Mrs. W. R. Ward, my dear friend and role model, who provided me with family records and memoirs in addition to hospitality at Bladensfield, a magic spot. Mrs. Edgar D. Flynn of Mobile, Ala., for the photograph of her ancestor, Mary Burton Augusta Bolling Banister. Mr. and Mrs. "Tad" Thompson, Tuckahoe, Goochland County, for permission to photograph at Tuckahoe, the birthplace of Mary Randolph and the boyhood home of Thomas Jefferson.

At the Colonial Williamsburg Foundation: Linda Baumgarten, Susan Berg, John Davis, Leslie Grigsby, John Ingram, Betty Leviner, Eileen Parris, Peter Ross, Donna Sheppard, Jane Strauss, and Mary Wiseman. Historic Christ Church Foundation, Irvington, Va.: Henrietta Goodwin and Jane Shearin. The Loudoun County Museum, Leesburg, Va.: Laura Dutton. Oatlands, Leesburg, Va.: Barbara Dombrowski, acting director, and members of the Oatlands staff, whose hospitality will long be remembered, and former director Nicole Sours for her interest and help. Swem Library, College of William and Mary: Margaret Cook and staff. Virginia Historical Society: Howson Cole and staff. Williamsburg Public Library: Allen Chamberlain. B. C. Salyer, Ann Rideout, and Nancy Alcorn for their perseverance in helping me meet my deadlines.

I am grateful to Emory Waldrop for his fine photography, his patience and constant good humor, to Emily Whaley for her delightful illustrations, and to the *Richmond Times-Dispatch* for permission to use their excellent photographs which appear on the cover of this book. Thanks also to my publisher, Evelyn P. Metzger, for her encouragement and support, and thanks to Joan Cone who started it all.

Others who deserve thanks include Karen Hess, Rachael Feild, Jean Jones, John R. Barden, Richard Hughes Carter, my daughter Jacqueline Hayward, Helen Rountree, Sam Snyder, Mike Gooding, Janet & Phil Schwarz, Virginia Nance, Dan Williams, Carolyn Beckhoff, Jean Louk, and Holly Emory, who was my boon companion throughout the writing process.

N.C.C.

Index

About the Author

Nancy Carter Crump was born in Newport News, Virginia, a descendant of families who settled in Virginia in the mid-17th century. She spent summers as a child on farms in Virginia's Northern Neck where she was first exposed to the old ways of preparing and presenting plantation cooking.

She studied speech and theater at the University of Florida and also soloed in choral groups there. After having three daughters and a son, she completed her BA in history at Virginia Commonwealth University. To help pay for her return to school, Nancy Carter Crump opened a catering business. She specialized in the design of historical parties re-creating with authentic food, costumes, decor and entertainment such scenes as Chaucer's Tabard Inn. Later, as an educational programmer at The Colonial Williamsburg Foundation, she planned study visits for school children and had her first experiences with fireside cooking.

On her own professionally since 1981, the author now gives cooking demonstrations and classes, trains museum interpreters, develops programs for historic sites and researches culinary history. She also finds time for collecting antique kitchen equipment, children's books and old cookbooks; for water sports; and for singing with the Richmond Symphony chorus.

She and her second husband, Jim Emory, a retired foreign service officer, live in Williamsburg where they are often visited by their seven children.